Floyd M. Martinson

Growing Up in Norway, 800 to 1990

With a Foreword by Per Egil Mjaavatn

Southern Illinois University Press
Carbondale and Edwardsville

Copyright © 1992 by Floyd M. Martinson
All rights reserved
Printed in the United States of America
Designed by Duane E. Perkins
Production supervised by Natalia Nadraga

Library of Congress Cataloging-in-Publication Data

Martinson, Floyd Mansfield, 1916–
    Growing up in Norway, 800 to 1990/Floyd M. Martinson : with a
foreword by Per Egil Mjaavatn.
        p. cm.
    Includes bibliographical references (p.) and index.
    1. Children—Norway. 2. Children's rights—Norway. I. Title.
HQ792.N7M37   1992
035.23'09481—dc20   91-20167
        ISBN 0-8093-1778-8   CIP

    The paper used in this publication meets the minimum require-
ments of American National Standard for Information Sciences—
Permanence of Paper for Printed Library Materials, ANSI
Z39.48-1984. ⊗

To the memory of my mother
Otelia Mathilda

Contents

Foreword

THE READERS OF THIS book probably know that Norway is a long and narrow country in northern Europe, famous for its fjords and mountains, its fish and oil production. Some readers will also know that this large area of land is home to 4 million inhabitants. Yet one-quarter of the Norwegian population, the children, are often forgotten in descriptions of the country and its citizens. There are many reasons for this omission, the primary one being that childhood is, to many adults, terra incognita.

The Norwegian government has made children and youth a main area of focus in the 1990s. Respect for children and concern for their welfare is definitely increasing: Child welfare policy and children's basic rights are discussed throughout the country. Indeed, Norway was the first country in the world to establish a public commissioner for children (the Children's Ombudsman). The Norwegian government has its own minister for children and has established the Norwegian Center for Child Research. After many years in the background, children finally occupy center-stage.

Much research on childhood in Norway has been conducted within the last decade, but published only in Norwegian. Floyd M. Martinson, old enough to remember his own childhood and cognizant of the rich multiplicity in child development, has synthesized the most significant literature and combined it with his own knowledge and expertise. His book provides a firm foundation in Norwegian child policy and presents some basic attitudes toward children that characterize research in childhood. It is my hope that *Growing Up in Norway, 800 to 1990* will complete the picture of childhood in general and of Norway in particular.

Per Egil Mjaavatn, Director
The Norwegian Center for Child Research

Preface

CHILDREN RECEIVE A GREAT deal of attention in Norway today. People are aware of how difficult it is for children to live in an increasingly industrialized, urbanized, mechanized, and impersonal society as Norway has become in recent decades. Ongoing public discussion and research have resulted in some initiatives on behalf of children. A number of Norwegian anthropologists, ethnologists, historians, and social scientists have begun to focus their attention on the everyday life of children as it was lived in earlier times and as it is being lived today.

An abundance of literature has been produced in the Western world on the psychology of the child and on child development, that is, on the child in the process of becoming an adult. But there is a dearth of literature on childhood as a stage of life, on children as they live their daily lives, or on the child as being. Studies by Norwegian child researchers in the last ten to twenty years have done much to help us understand the daily life of children. They have made a significant contribution to the literature on the sociology of childhood. Most of the studies are published only in Norwegian; this book is an attempt to bring that body of literature to a larger audience.

Down through history life has, in many ways, been a struggle for Norwegian children, for most Norwegian children have lived in poverty. Norway's emergence out of a life of poverty is so recent that Norwegians alive today can say that poverty characterized life for almost all Norwegians in all generations before them! The physical terrain of Norway is spectacularly beautiful but difficult for human survival, dominated as it is by mountainous rock, forests, fjords, and a rugged coastline. Only 3 percent of the land is arable, and much of it is in small, separated parcels. The North Sea offered an abundance of fish, but fishing is a treacherous occupation and many children have lost their fathers at sea.

Through most of their history Norwegians were fishermen or peasant farmers living a life of hard labor, poverty, and isolation. Even today, with an average of only thirty-two persons per square mile in a country that is over one thousand miles long and on an average only about sixty miles wide, Norway is the most sparsely populated country in Europe.

In contrast to its earlier poverty, Norway today is one of the richest countries in the Organization for Economic Cooperation and Development (OECD)—partly because of the discovery of oil in the North Sea—with a good quality of life and hardly any children living in poverty.

Norway, and Scandinavia in general, gives a great deal of concentrated and purposeful public attention to child care and the concerns of children. Nowhere is public attention given to child care more pervasive. During the 1980s Norway established two social agencies for children that are unique in the Western world, namely, a national office of Commissioner of Children, that is, an ombud whose sole responsibility is to attend to the needs and concerns of children, and the National Center for Child Research, the duty of which is to stimulate research on child life and to disseminate information to child-serving organizations and to the general public. It was my interest in those developments that first piqued my interest in studying childhood in Norway. The number of recent studies on child life carried out by scholars in Norway led me to take a closer look. This book is largely the result of my reading that literature and interpreting it through the eyes of an American sociologist of Norwegian descent.

Preface

It was my good fortune to be invited to spend the 1984–85 academic year as guest researcher at the new Center for Child Research, a strategic location for me, since the Center conducts, supports, and keeps abreast of most of the child research going on in Norway. I am especially indebted to the director of the Center, Per Egil Mjaavatn, to researchers at the Center and at the Universities of Bergen, Oslo, and Trondheim, and to a number of other child researchers and child advocates (very especially the then child ombud, Målfrid Grude Flekkøy) to whom I was introduced through the Center and through the several conferences sponsored by the Center during the year. I also returned to Norway to participate in an international interdisciplinary conference on the life and development of children in modern society sponsored by the Center in June 1987.

I have had other opportunities to observe and study aspects of life in Scandinavia as well. I spent the 1975–76 academic year on a peace research leave of absence in Oslo, Norway, focusing on the topic of children and peace. I especially appreciate the intellectual stimulation and friendship of Professor Erik Grønseth on that occasion and on many others. I also spent two years at Uppsala University in Sweden, one in 1968–69 as visiting researcher and lecturer in the Department of Sociology, the other in 1980–81 as a Fulbright Research Scholar. Professor Jan Trost continues to be my invaluable contact and friend in Sweden. There are others, too numerous to mention, who are remembered and deserve to be recognized, but one who holds a special place is my wife, Beatrice, who has at all times encouraged and supported me in my research and on four separate occasions was willing to disrupt our household for a move overseas.

Growing Up in Norway,
800 to 1990

1

What Is Childhood?

BEFORE DISCUSSING CHILDHOOD in Norway during the various epochs of its history, it is imperative that we define what is meant by childhood. In Norway, as in all Western countries today, there is a category of the population that is referred to as *children* in a period of life referred to as *childhood*—a period during which those in the age group between infancy and adulthood are placed outside the public systems of decision making and production and are treated in ways considered to be appropriate especially to their age and condition.

But not all societies in all times have designated persons in that age category as in need of special treatment, nor has special treatment meant the same thing in all epochs of history in Norway or any other Western nation. In other words, *children* is not an invariant biological category of the population but a social construct or a social category defined by the culture of the society in which the children live. *Infancy,* on the other hand, is a biological category that all societies recognize and must recognize, for human offspring are born so helpless and immobile that adults must provide some form of protection, supervision, and training (Mead and Wolfenstein 1955).

Whether or not a society designates a period of life as *childhood* depends more on the nature of the society than it does on the biological and psychological characteristics of children. In societies where family has been the dominant unit for economic, social, and political life, where formal schooling has not yet been introduced, and where survival is based on hunting, gathering, tilling the soil, and caring for domesticated animals, a special period of life known as childhood has less often been deemed as necessary. So it is that such societies have come to be recognized as societies without childhood (Ariès 1962). There were in such societies supposedly only two periods in life, namely, infancy and adulthood. That does not mean, however, that there was no recognition of the smaller size, lesser strength, and inexperience of younger persons when compared with older persons.

As time passed and as societies became more complex and more demanding, greater reasons emerged for treating the young as a special category of human beings needing a period of protection and instruction.

Over the course of history, we can distinguish a number of different normative perspectives, legitimating ideologies or models concerning children and their treatment. I have collapsed the ideas about children and their status in society into five categories or models. Since the models are constructed out of ideas about children, ideas that appear to logically coalesce, we refer to them as ideal constructs. The five models of childhood are not mutually exclusive. All five models have made their appearance at one time or another in the West, and at most times in Western history several of the models have been extant—sometimes in opposition to one another. The five models follow:

Model I: Children as Private Property

Historically, this is a model that precedes any notion of children as a special category or as a group entitled to special protection and instruction. In Norway the model dates back to pre-Viking times and continues into Viking times and early Norwegian peasant times. It refers to a time when the family was the dominant, sometimes the only, social institution—an institution wherein the head of the family had power of both life and death over members of the family, especially over newborns and slaves. The father's status was similar to that of paterfamilias in Roman law, wherein the head of the household was empowered as one who, in family matters, was his own master, master of his household, and answerable to no higher authority. Under that model children were supposedly cared for because they were potentially capable of serving the needs of the family as interpreted by the head of the household. It is in keeping with a general historical tradition in which only adults have rights and children are treated paternally. That model of parent-child relations was being articulated as late as the seventeenth century in the writings of Hobbes (1651). According to Hobbes, the relationship between parent (father or mother) and child must be based on fear, fear that would make the child totally dependent and compliant, recognizing the parent as a sovereign with power to save or destroy. The relevance of the model in relation to survival and well-being of Norwegian children in Viking and peasant times is discussed in chapter 2.

In Norway the model of children as someone's property was also strongly supported in the perspective on the family that resulted from the Protestant Reformation in the sixteenth century. Lutheran doctrine on the family recognized a hierarchy with all family members belonging to and being responsible to God but with fathers as God's representatives having full authority over members of the family but short of the authority to destroy them. It was a father's authority to shape and control his children's values and behavior in accordance with an absolute standard of conduct believed to be in accordance with the "will of God." Religious reformers of the sixteenth century were interested in character formation at the earliest stage of life as well as in the spiritual well-being of the young. The tradition of authority embodied in Martin Luther's Small Catechism provided a basic pattern for the socialization of children. Elements of this model remain strong in Norwegian culture even today. The Church of Norway is a Lutheran state church, and a model that protects the authority of the family has been influential in restricting legislation legitimizing the authority of the state over the family in regard to support and control of children.

Model II: Children as Participants in Socioeconomic Life

In earliest times in Norway this model was extant at the same time that Model I asserted the absolute authority of the head of the family over children. It is a model commonly found in peasant societies, societies in which children are incorporated directly into the economic and social life of the family and community without benefit of a preparatory period in what is now known as childhood. In rural, preindustrial societies, children by the age of five to seven were considered to have attained common sense or rationality and were broadly categorized in a different way than they were before that age. They were expected to assume serious obligations and responsibilities in the family and in the community. According to one study of fifty preliterate cultures, children at such young ages were expected to be responsible for the care of younger children, for tending animals, for carrying out household chores, and for gathering materials needed in the home (Rogoff et al. 1976). Children partook not only in the work life of the family and community but also in the social life. After the age of about three or four children began to play the same games as adults did, either with other children or with adults (Ariès 1962). In other words, there was little attempt to separate children or to shield them from adult pastimes as was more and more the case in subsequent generations. Children played cards, dice, and backgammon. Story telling and dancing also occupied important places in the everyday lives of both children and adults.

Children took part in the seasonal festivals that regularly brought the whole community together. There were also festivities intended primarily for children and youth with adults only as bystanders or observers.

It was not until approximately 1600 that toys intended exclusively for children made their appearance.

Model III: Children as Evil

From this perspective children were seen as weak, even as imbecilic; as impulsive and wanting instant gratification; as incapable of fully rational decision making; as gullible, malleable, and impressionable. For those who saw children in that way from a religious perspective, children were unreliable not so much because of their innocence but because of their depraved nature. They were seen as born in sin and hence in need of salvation. Children as evil was never a dominant perspective on childhood in Norwegian history, but elements of it are to be found in the teachings of some of the religious reformers.

Model IV: Children Becoming Adults

This model places a heavy burden especially on parents but also on other adults — nannies, nurseries, kindergartens, schools, churches, and governmental agencies — to protect and guide children successfully through a process of becoming adults. From that perspective parents are regarded as having an adequate conception of a child's interests and needs and as willing to act in the child's best interests. Children, in the process of becoming, need to be guided and molded according to adult preconceptions of what the outcome of the process ought to be. In other words, children do not simply *grow* to be adults: they have to *learn* to be adults. Protection and guidance go hand in hand in this model. First, protection. Childhood is seen as a vulnerable period of life, and not all influences in society are seen as good for children. Parents must discern the better influence. Second, children lack competence and reason; hence, even their own actions might be detrimental to them. They need to be protected both from external injury and from their own actions. Thus, they need to be segregated, encapsulated in a protective environment where they will, insofar as possible, see none of the evil in society, hear no evil, and do no evil. In a real sense, they must be excluded from much of life as it is lived by adults. They need a world designed especially for them—a safe and healthy environment where they can play and learn. Health, nutrition, play, education, loving parents, and a "strong and joyous life" are the goals (Rauschenbusch 1915). Nothing is to be expected of children now; responsible behavior will come later when they are ready to take their places in adult society.

A strong utilitarian aspect informs the model, focusing as it does not on the needs of children but on the needs of society as adults interpret them. In other words, it can be seen as an economic model of childhood. Expressions used in this perspective are: "Children are our most precious natural resource" (Cahill 1986); children are "human capital to be invested" in such a way as to "maximize the overall good of society" and thereby bring about "the greatest happiness of the greatest number" (Worsfold 1974). Such statements express concern for the future needs of society, not for the present needs of children. The economic elements in the model raise a question as to whether children, and indeed adult men and women, are to be valued per se or whether present concerns and needs are to be sacrificed for future societal outcomes (Cahill 1986).

As society and culture became more complex, more impersonal, and more dangerous for children, a need was felt to artificially prolong childhood into adolescence and even into young adulthood. Because of that extension, Model IV is a very expensive model for society since it lengthens childhood and makes more specialized the care and training that the young must receive. Able-bodied persons are kept out of the labor force for an extended period of their lives. The middle class were the first to see the need for such a model, for they were engaged in occupations that required specialized training and education, and they were best able to afford a prolonged childhood for their children. The idea of protection and guidance for children gradually trickled down to the lower classes largely because of legislative support for such a perspective.

An even more expensive and demanding refinement of Model IV calls for treating each child as unique, each as having qualities that must be recognized (or discovered) and provided for through an enriched environment in order that each child may reach its own unique, full potential—a child who will enjoy life, will enjoy school, and will be prepared later in life to make a unique and creative contribution to society. That individualized perspective calls for sensitive, perceptive parents, teachers, and other caretakers and hence requires an enormous amount of adult attention to each child.

Model IV has been the dominant model influencing the treatment of children through much of recent history in Norway and the other Western nations.

A more idealistic or romantic form of the model sees the process of becoming as more or less automatic. That is, children need no help with the process. All the child needs to develop its full potential—besides basic care and protection—is freedom, freedom for self-realization through self-discovery and self-motivated activity. Children, therefore, should not be restrained by any kind of repressive socialization. Child care should be permissive. Socialization or formal education of any sort raises the specter of brainwashing (Rousseau 1979; Worsfold 1974). In that pessimistic view of society, adults have very little to offer but much to learn from children because children are spontaneous and open, having not yet been molded and repressed by an inadequate adult culture. Some idealistic social reformers have suggested that children should be shielded from corrupt Western society in order that they might fashion anew a culture more consistent with their childlike, pristine nature. Elements of that perspective are to be found in the writings of both Friedrich Froebel, originator of the kindergarten, and Maria Montessori, who established the Montessori school. Many of those elements are to be found in the free education *(fri oppdragelse)* movement that was quite influential in Norway during the first half of the twentieth century (Nordland et al. 1960).

Model V: Children as Citizens

Children are not seen as private property or as depraved or incompetent; they are seen as *becoming* but also as *being*, recognized by custom and by law as the subjects, rather than the objects, of rights and duties. Historically, it is a relatively new legitimizing ideology or model of children, which has been publicly supported in Norway during the 1980s. It is a model that responds to the negative effects that many feel resulted from the segregating/encapsulating requirements of Model IV. In protecting, segregating, encapsulating children, advocates of Model V claim that we have, in fact, "infantilized" children. Rather than becoming adults, they remain in a prolonged state of infancy that pays little attention to their interests and rights and that does not prepare them for adulthood (Berggreen 1988).

Model V is an idealistic model; it is also an action model. The goal is, as it was in peasant society, to integrate children into society—albeit into a society much more complex and much more averse to having children enter in than was peasant society, for it is an adult-centered, technical, industrial, computerized, motorized, and in many ways highly impersonal and dangerous society for children.

Can children be integrated into such a society? Can changes be made in society in order that children might be accommodated? Is it likely that such changes will be made at any time in the foreseeable future? Those are questions that adult supporters of Model V are asking and attempting to answer in a positive way. A country foremost in asking those questions in the 1980s has been Norway.

There are two basic ways of treating children, either integrating them into the social and economic world of adults or protecting them from certain types of activities and topics of conversation by means of physical barriers and silence (Berggreen 1988). Barring children from parts of the adult world keeps them outside the adult culture. That in effect keeps them ignorant of many things and contributes to their appearance of innocence and incompetence. Exponents of Model V hold that children should be presumed to be rational and adequate to engage in the life of society. It is extremely difficult to ascertain what is meant by rationality and whether it can be operationalized precisely enough to determine whether an individual at a particular age and condition possesses the capacity of rationality (Worsfold 1974). We cannot contest Berggreen's (1988) assertion that all evidence shows that children have an ability to observe and interpret society that is beyond the imagination of adults, for adults in modern times have not expected very much of them—the so-called underestimation fallacy (Kurth-Schai 1988). In comparing contemporary Norwegian and Southeast Asian six- to eight-year-olds, Hundeide (1988a) found that the socially integrated Asian children developed a special social sensitivity and intelligence that Norwegian children did not have. Interacting with persons of various ages as participants in the struggle for survival was reflected in the structure of the Asian children's cognitive competency.

According to Model V, even if there are areas where children must be denied the exercise of freedom, they should at least be consulted about their aims and preferences. The society should also be called on to acknowledge the just claims of children, even if it is not advantageous for adults to do so. That perspective makes adults more accountable to children than did earlier models of childhood. The model puts children's rights as society's citizens on a par with those of adults, even with those of their parents, though the interests of children and parents are not synonymous. Needless to say, that perspective requires that more be learned about how to allow for the varying levels of judgment and responsibility demonstrated by each individual child at each developmental stage. It calls also for balancing the needs of children, the state's interest in insuring that those needs be met, and the prerequisites of parental authority with children's rights as citizens (Ross 1982).

The Norwegian ethicist, Dagny Kaul (1984) has spelled out in some detail how adults, and adult culture and society, can benefit through observing children and interacting with them—children taken seriously as persons of equal worth with adults. Kaul sees children as possessing unique traits that can serve as correctives for some major ills in contemporary society, primarily the current weak point in the adult-centric perspective on mankind that sees adults as individualists with free will pursuing their own interests with little regard to the social fabric. From Kaul's perspective, humanity is a life story, and each epoch in that life story, including childhood, has something to contribute to the whole. Children represent the first epoch—human life's beginning, a period characterized by germination, newness, and development. A special characteristic of children is the great importance that they place on the body and communication through the body as a part of the wholeness of personality, in contrast to adult concern with the mind, with reason. From that perspective Kaul sees adults as one-sided as they live out their technical-rational life-style. Children can teach adults about the importance of communication where body and mind enter in as a unity and of the unity with things around them—with animals and with nature. A special characteristic of children is their dependence on others in order to survive. If children in all their dependency are recognized as of equal worth with adults, it means that dependency can no longer be seen as something negative but must be taken into the model of what it means to be human. In an adult-centered model of life, children are a nuisance, albeit a sometimes enjoyable nuisance. According to Kaul, if they are taken seriously, they contribute to a more humane, social model of human existence.

A fourth trait actualizes the child's acceptance and its integration into the human model and society (Kaul 1984). To the extent that the adults recognize the child as a "you" in a personal meeting, the adult relates positively to human life's possibilities for renewal and growth. If adults are to live in relationship to children as fellow beings, it means that adults in their culture-creating activity must prioritize children's needs as highly as they do their own, which they do not now do.

In claiming their rights, the powerless assert limits to others' power (O'Neill 1988). Hence, if Model V were taken seriously, it could result in violent upheavals and call forth drastic modifications in the social fabric. Acceptance of human worth regardless of age would have deep social and political consequences for society since it would inevitably shift emphasis from a power principle to one of human rights (Kaul 1983). Adult society as structured has made it impossible to accommodate many of children's interests and needs. It is a society that has taken children's subordination as a given and has been tailor-made to children's subordinate position and adults' continual dominance.

From a legal point of view, Model V makes children subjects of the law, not objects of the law (Smith 1984): it calls for the entitlement of so-called minors to standard political and civil rights. That is, when judicial decisions are made, the subjects of those decisions, in this case children, have the opportunity, through counsel, to be heard. Under traditional legal doctrine, the parents have virtually unlimited authority over their children, or in instances of egregious action by the parents, the state, under the doctrine of *parens patriae,* assumes comparable parental authority (Knitzer 1982).

What has come to be called the Children's Rights Movement has generated a new threshold of awareness. The term *children's rights* has taken on a symbolic, also a pejorative, life of its own in the public debate, not least in Norway and in the other Scandinavian countries. Even the right to vote at early ages is entertained as a topic for discussion in Scandinavia today.

How powerful are these five models, or any legitimating ideologies, in effecting change in the treatment of children? They are important, but we must not overemphasize their power. It must be remembered that they are legitimating; they are not categorical imperatives. They lend approval to certain behavior; they do not absolutize it. There is little empirical evidence to confirm the power of the various models or legitimating idealogies. In part, the power that they do have is limited because they never occur in a vacuum. They are dependent on major ways in which social life is organized, and when those aspects of social life change, corresponding shifts occur in the ideological realm also where childen are concerned (Cohen 1969).

In reviewing the history of various models and their effectiveness, Pollock (1983) concludes that the history of childhood in the Western world is a subject dominated by myth. The sources are overwhelmingly secondary, and the studies "bear the hallmark of sloppiness." Nor is there reliable evidence from earlier historical epochs as to how parents actually reared their children. Using a total of 537 American and British sources, mostly middle-class adults' diaries, children's diaries, autobiographies, and manuscripts covering the period from 1500 to 1900, Pollock concluded that the link between behavior and values is more complex than historians have realized. In every century studied, parents accommodated to the needs of their offspring. There are limits on variation because of the dependency of the child and the acceptance of responsibility for the protection and socialization of that child by the parents. One could argue that the limits of variation, especially in the latter, are greater if one begins at an earlier epoch of human history, as we can with the Norwegian data. Pollock found that data from the 1500s to the present showed that almost all parents were "extremely concerned" whenever any of their offspring were ill, irrespective of the century they lived in. Overall, she found "surprisingly little" change from 1500 to 1900. The diaries suggested that there was a large section of the population whose methods of child-rearing appeared to be no harsher in the earlier generations than they are today. The method of discipline used by parents varied according to the parent and the child rather than by the historical period, with the possible exception of the early nineteenth century when parents did appear to be stricter. Pollock concludes that, in general, life for infants from the sixteenth century on was relatively pleasant; children formed an integral part of the family unit and the parent-child relationship was not formal as some historians have claimed—all of this despite the fact that there had been some changes in attitudes toward children.

There appears to have been a growing unsureness in parents as to their ability to rear their children properly in modern times in Norway as elsewhere, but Pollock found that parental ambivalence in American and British families with regard to how children should be raised was reported by parents in each of the centuries studied. Once again, Pollock was struck with the lack of change over the centuries.

But others question Pollock's conclusions regarding change (Sather 1989). The extent of change over the centuries in patterns of parental care of children is a difficult question to research and one that cannot be definitively answered with the evidence at hand to date (Beales 1975).

What kinds of physical and social environments are best for children, and what perspectives on childhood are best for them? This is a moot question, and we appear less sure of the answer now than we were several generations ago. There may be no easy answer (Boocock 1981). It is widely held today that children's lives are shaped by their surroundings. Children display initiative, imagination, and often great ingenuity in coping with their surroundings, even in places that are re-garded as anything but ideal for children to live in (Werner 1989).

Diverse neighborhoods and communities do provide sub-stantially different opportunities for children's interactions and development. We could say that in some ways Model II (Children as Participants in Socioeconomic Life) provides the richest and most realistic setting in which children can live. Hundeide (1988a) found that though children in such settings may grow up in poverty and have limited opportunities for formal education, they usually have caring duties in the family and develop empathy, concern for others, and responsible attitudes. They also develop attitudes toward work as a natural obligation and regard school as a privilege. Because of their fuller participation in all kinds of social relations, they develop skills in such relations. On the other hand, growing up in an affluent modern suburb can mean limited social contacts with other than one's family and a few age peers, little opportunity to engage fully in the work and social life of the community, but with all the advantages that Model IV (Children Becoming Adults) protection and guidance can provide.

In pondering the question as to the best environment for small children, Boocock (1981) concluded that the best community type for children would be one that is a good place for persons of all ages to live. Such a community would include jobs that are nearby and have flexible working hours, shopping facilities located in such a way as to reduce the dependence on the automobile, and a variety of child-care possibilities. Child-care systems today lack the flexibility and diversity that the great majority of parents in all industrialized countries say they want. A Model V community would no doubt include all of those elements coupled with a focus on children as persons with full citizen rights. Whether that is realistic and obtainable is debatable.

In the chapters to follow we trace the daily lives of children during various epochs of Norwegian history, under varying social and economic conditions, and in a changing culture that over time has articulated different perspectives on children: (1) as property; (2) as participants in the socioeconomic life of family and community; (3) as innocent and impulsive, yes even evil; (4) as incomplete adults in the process of becoming adults; and (5) as citizens with freedoms and rights of their own.

2

Birth and Survival

THROUGHOUT MUCH OF HUMAN history birth gave no assurance that one would survive childhood and grow to be an adult: Norway was no exception. With long seasons of cold and murky weather, a baby might be born into a dark and dank house with an earthen floor and heated only by an open hearth, for in early times most Norwegians lived in poverty (Benedictow 1985). The poverty of the family and the lack of protection from cold, wet, disease, and illness meant that survival through infancy was doubtful. Even as late as the 1800s it could be expected that around 20 percent of all babies would die in infancy.

Norwegian folk tradition suggests that from early times infants were looked on as vulnerable and essentially defenseless and in need of constant attention from adults. Many life-threatening powers were thought to exist—illness, evil people, and the invisible subterranean folk called *huldrer.* The huldrer, feared as wicked, alluring sirens, beautiful in appearance but with long, cowlike tails, were constantly trying to exchange one of their dull or deformed offspring for a human baby. Belief that children with defects were changlings helped account for common diseases and deformities that afflicted children, such as Down's syndrome, athrepsia, or rickets, profound disabilities due to lack of food, inadequate nutrition, vitamin deficiency, and unhygienic surroundings (Kvidelund and Sehmsdorf 1988).

Numerous measures were taken to ensure newborns' survival in the face of many threats, measures some of which would today be regarded as useless or even counterproductive.

It is difficult to separate the rational from the irrational and magical in ancient folk wisdom. The most common means of protecting a child in olden days was to place something made of iron in the crib of the newborn—a knife, an ax, or other object. Something made of silver or a piece of flatbread placed in the baby's crib might also suffice. Fire was powerful, too, and could be used to consecrate the crib and the baby. An ember or live coal on the baby's breast was also thought to cure it of illness.

Even after the introduction of Christianity, which came to Norway around A.D. 1000, newborns were thought to be in danger from life-threatening powers at least until they were baptized, that is, as long as they were "heathen" (Hodne, Ø. 1984). Christianity brought additional mystical means of protection. Protective measures combined aspects of Christian and pagan ideology. One could place a portion of the Word of God or a page from the Bible or the hymnbook in the baby's swaddling clothes. The sign of the cross could be used in several ways: one could cross the baby's arms, make the sign of the cross over the baby, or mark the cradle with the sign of the cross. It was important that an unbaptized baby never come under the open sky after it was dark outside because of fear of the evil powers and that a baby never to be left alone at night. In many places in Norway parents did not allow a baby to be alone in the crib until after it had been baptized because of fear of the netherworld. A light kept burning at night was an added precaution. The baby slept in bed with the mother or with both parents. As added protection, the mother was instructed to lie next to the wall and the father to lie on the outside. In that way the huldrer could less easily accomplish their task. Strangers were never to come into a baby's presence, for they could do damage with "the evil eye."

It is not difficult to see why there was urgency to have a baby baptized as soon as possible. Christian IV's proclamation of 1636 stated that a baby should be baptized within four days after birth. Distance, difficult terrain, and cold and snowy winter weather meant that many families did not get to church often during the winter. But a baby needing to be baptized could call forth superhuman effort to get the baby to the church on time.

In the early folk literature there are many other bits of advice regarding provision of magical protection for infants. The first one to dress a baby was to take the right arm first. If one took the left arm, the child would be left-handed. If the father dropped the offering money on the floor at the time of baptism, the child could grow up to be careless in some manner or other. If the pastor made a mistake in reading the baptismal service, the child would be a poor reader. If one desired a wise or intelligent child, a hymnbook or a page from Luther's catechism in the baptismal clothing would help (Hodne, Ø. 1984).

Protective care was manifest in customs and rituals surrounding infants before, during, and after the trip to church on the day of baptism. Before leaving the house it was important to bless the baby with the sign of the cross or the Lord's Prayer and to fire, that is, to drive out evil spirits, with a torch or glowing piece of bread over the baby and the one who carried it. Over the whole land it was common that the baby, after coming home, should sleep awhile in the baptismal dress (which may well have had protective items sewn into it, such as a silver button, a rusty knife, a piece of bread, and the stump of a Christmas candle) in order to ensure that the baby would grow to be a good and tranquil child (Hodne, Ø. 1984).

It is apparent that throughout infancy the child's conscientious parents worried over its well-being and were present and attentive. It wasn't exclusively love of the infant that motivated adults to take solicitous, protective measures. There was a strong element of fear and guilt in the solicitude, for the baby was thought to be supernatural and its proper care was a heavy responsibility. The word *angel* was used in talking about babies since they had come from God and were thought to be bearers of the light. Since they had traveled such a long way, babies were to be fed a good deal right after birth. Even in those times of poverty parents were obsessed with the importance of preventing a newborn from experiencing material want. That was symbolized by placing bread or a sweet on the baby or offering a little of all manner of food after the baptismal trip.

All newborns were thought to be clairvoyant. It was only Christian baptism that protected them against the difficult and oppressive fate of permanent clairvoyance. Parents were concerned about interpreting correctly the message that a clairvoyant baby might express through its actions. Most of the actions were interpreted as warning from the newborn that either it or another was soon to die — another reason for preserving the custom of a church baptism as quickly as possible.

That parents were loving toward and solicitous of their children as well as mystical and superstitious we learn from the so-called miracle stories recorded by the clergy during the Middle Ages. The clergy were in the practice of recording accounts of illnesses and injuries sustained by both adults and children, and especially in those cases where the victim experienced a partial or full recovery. The accounts were referred to as miracle stories, but on the average no more than 10–20 percent of the accounts contain evidence of the supernatural. Eighty to ninety percent of the Nordic miracles studied to date contain no evidence of anything that could not be explained rationally (Krötzl 1989). Because of the late arrival of Christianity in Scandinavia, most of the miracle stories can be dated in the main as coming from the thirteenth to the fifteenth century, a period during which such collections of miracles were produced in accordance with the canonical requirements of the papal investigation commission. Many of the stories deal with children's illnesses and accidents and how their parents and the community dealt with them. The children in the stories come mostly from peasant families. Numerous stories relate to delivery and childbirth and clearly indicate that children were wanted, loved, and mourned in death (Krötzl 1989). If a baby was stillborn or if it died immediately after delivery, often hope was expressed that it could be brought back to life once more, and a long wait ensued—several hours or even a day—to see if there was any sign of life before the fact of death was finally accepted. Another reason for wanting the baby to live was the hope that it would be baptized.

The attitude toward breast-feeding was a positive one in medieval times, and even mothers belonging to the higher social classes breast-fed their children. However, a health hazard that Norwegian babies had to tolerate in the later Middle Ages and until the 1600s was a custom of postponing onset of suckling at the mother's breast for a number of days or weeks after birth while the baby was fed other foods. The prohibition of immediate breast-feeding was the result of a generally held view among medieval physicians that the first milk, the colostrum, was injurious to newborns. One authority recommended that mother's milk should not be used for the first twenty days after birth (as reported by Tønnessen 1982). Newborns were given sour-cream porridge, butter, and other unhealthful foodstuffs. Thereby babies were denied proper nourishment, the immunity to infection that colostrum provides, as well as the early bonding between baby and mother that attends early suckling. Delay in breast-feeding appears to have played a significant part in increasing infant mortality toward the end of the High Middle Ages, thereby insuring a relatively stable population size in medieval Norway.

Between 1680 and the breakthrough of modern medicine, a concomitant decline in infant mortality is probably attributable to a change back to the custom of immediate breast-feeding. With the decrease in infant mortality and the limited methods of birth control available at the time, it was not unusual that the last baby born into a family would find that ten or eleven siblings were already present in the family. On the average, a family of five children was more common, however.

There was a comprehensive process at work in medieval times in Norway, a process that incorporated the newborn into family and community and also gave it status as an independent being (as participant in the economic and social life—Model II). That process started soon after birth, and parents, relatives, neighbors, and other members of the parish took part in it (Hodne, Ø. 1984). There were several elements in the process. First of all, a baby was given a place of honor by being recognized as human, that is, as a creature of inestimably greater value than an offspring of one of the *huldrefolk*. To proudly "show the baby" or to "go and see the baby" was a widespread custom. It was common that a neighbor woman or a relative would take with her a young child, preferably a daughter, when she visited the confined mother and the baby. They would bring a small gift, probably hold the baby, and say some words about it, such as who it looked like, that it was cute, that having a baby was a special kind of riches. A second occasion of recognition came with baptism when the newborn was accepted by God, by its baptismal sponsors, by the Christian Church at large, and into a congregational fellowship. Third, in the public and ritualistic setting of baptism, the newborn was given a name that recognized its independent status. Naming was very important, for the name was to be one that would be advantageous for the child. It was a prevailing folk belief that the child would come to resemble the one after whom it was named. A common custom was to choose the name of a respected ancestor. The eldest son was commonly named after the paternal grandfather and the second son after the maternal grandfather. Eldest and second eldest daughters similarly were named after paternal and maternal grandmothers. After those names were used, great-grandparents' names could be used. Special circumstances could interfere with the order. The name of a deceased spouse was commonly used first, for instance. Through the practice of naming, the memory of a respected ancestor was also restored to ongoing status in the life of the family circle.

According to the accounts in the miracle stories, children who fell ill or were injured were not passively left to their fate. Parents, fathers as well as mothers, were often mentioned as nursing them and very actively trying cures — medicine, ointment, incantations by healers, and various methods of resuscitating a child who had passed into unconsciousness or had drowned. For example, a father rolled his eight-year-old daughter over and over for several hours in the hope of emptying water from her stomach. In cases of accident, signs of neighborly support and help are also particularly apparent, such as when a father was joined by twenty or thirty neighbors as he went in search of his seven-year-old son who had vanished in the forest. If all else failed, supernatural help was sought. A saint might be appealed to by taking an ill or injured child to a shrine in search of a cure or by promising a pilgrimage or a votive offering. Parents were known to take lengthy and laborious pilgrimages with their children in the hope of finding cures. Nor were parents left alone to sorrow or to mourn the loss of a child: neighbors and friends shared in their grief.

Parents as a Threat to Infant Birth and Survival

We have been talking about the treatment of babies who were normal, wanted, or at least accepted. But parents in early times, as now, were confused and ambivalent about how to deal with more offspring than they wanted or could care for or those who were severely handicapped or deformed. Today it is common to rely on contraceptives or abortion to prevent the birth of unwanted children. And institutions are available for the care of severely handicapped children who will not or cannot be cared for at home.

But what of early times when reliable knowledge of contraception and abortion was limited or unavailable and when society was not prepared to care for the handicapped? An excess of births was viewed as a burden in Norway in times of population growth, crop failure, and other stress on resources. In medieval times only the few who were literate were aware that classical and medieval medical books described methods of contraception and abortion; the rest depended on folk knowledge (Benedictow 1985). Abstaining from sexual intercourse, an effective though not entirely agreeable way to space babies, was in use early on. The husband was expected to keep himself from his wife as long as she was nursing a baby, and some women nursed their babies for extended periods of time. Dissatisfaction with this method might be what led to a statement in the Borgarthing law of the 1000s proscribing the suckling of a baby for more than two fasts or up until a third— that is, for more than two or three years! However, no part of the Christian law, the only part of the Borgarthing law to be preserved, obligated the Norse people to observe sexual abstinence during the period of breast-feeding for any period of time or spelled out any fines to be paid for infringement. All penitentials containing a judgment censuring postpartum sexual intercourse refer only to the period after confinement and until the woman in confinement is churched (Benedictow 1988). The ritual of "churching" a woman who had given birth continued for many centuries as witness the experience of Elias Aas, pastor of a Norwegian-American congregation in Minnesota in the late 1880s:

I was ready to begin the worship service, after having written down the names of several children to be baptized, when one reminded me that there was to be a "churching." I then remembered that it was customary in Norway, when a woman had given birth, that the pastor delivered a talk to her in the church entrance and thereafter conducted her into the church. This custom I had not seen or heard about before in America (since my arrival from Norway in 1883). I was then shown a woman sitting in a corner in the log house. There I performed my first and last "churching" service. It was characteristic of these people from Sætersdalen in Norway to be deeply attached to old church customs.[°]

A later marriage age was also recommended as a way of preventing excess births (Tønnessen 1982). Apparently, the recommendation was taken seriously, for by the 1880s women, on the average, were having first births as late as twenty-eight years of age and last births at age forty.

Lack of knowledge about what constitutes healthful infant care was a major reason for infant deaths in early times. For example, even after the general reintroduction of undelayed breast-feeding, some infants were exclusively breast-fed and consequently suffered "breast starvation" (Benedictow 1985). Other infants were at risk because of the practice of periodic fasting, introduced into Norway by the early Christian Church. During a period of fasting, a new pregnancy could present the suckling infant, the exhausted mother, as well as a new fetus, with a nutritional crisis. According to Benedictow, that was one of the major reasons for a high level of miscarriages and infant mortality and a lower life expectancy for women than for men. It was upon a population already living in poverty that the church imposed far-reaching demands for fasting. One-third of

---

[°]   From unpublished autobiography of Elias Aas (1855–1941) describing experiences as a pioneer pastor in Polk and Marshall counties, Minnesota (1885–89). Later translated by his son, Leif H. Awes, with the title, *The Pioneer Pastor*.

the days of the year were covered—one-half of the days if the recommended voluntary fast days were included. Beyond this, the church also imposed fasting as a penance on individuals. Eventually, there was public reaction against excessive fasting that was threatening the health of womenfolk and children; according to the Borgarthing law, exemption from certain periods of fasting was obtained for nursing and pregnant mothers. The Christian practice of fasting, when used along with the early widespread distrust of the first milk of the mother, put the newborn in double milk-loss jeopardy. The practice was less serious in prosperous families where wet nurses were commonly employed.

Despite such health hazards in child care, the greatest number of infant and child deaths were the result of epidemics and periods of hunger due to crop failure. A series of plagues struck Norway, starting with the Black Death in 1349. The pestilence probably resulted in the death of more than half of the population, contributing to impoverishment of the country for centuries. Much of the farmland went out of cultivation. And the literate classes as well, the clergy in particular, were decimated by the plagues (Skard 1980).

Not only were the antidotes to such diseases as smallpox unknown, but epidemics were even welcomed at times as a way of ridding a community of more mouths than it could feed (Tønnessen 1982). Such hazards of the time were not always adequate to keep in balance the number of mouths to be fed and the available food supply. It was especially under such circumstances that the desperate measures of neonaticide and infanticide were employed.

From Gulathing and Frostathing law, which probably prevailed throughout a number of centuries prior to the law being written down in the 1100s, we learn that human life was not as rigorously protected as was personal property in Viking times (Jonassen 1983). There were a number of situations in which a man was allowed to kill without his being in danger of a death penalty. The lightest sentence appeared to apply if one killed a slave. Slaves existed in large numbers in Viking times, and even if one intentionally killed a slave, one was only required to make good the loss to the slave's owner. Viking society was patriarchal, and males possessed the power of life and death over others. A husband could kill an adulterous wife and her lover, whereas he himself was not penalized if he kept a concubine or had children outside marriage (Foote and Wilson 1970).

An effective means of controlling population increase was neonaticide, exposing unwanted newborns to die or actively bringing about their demise. The practice of neonaticide, infanticide, and the killing of adult members of the household is consistent with a Model I perspective on family members as private property. Theoretically at least, the decision to keep or to destroy was a decision that was made every time a baby was born. Technically, if a baby had received nourishment, it was considered murder to desert it. If it had not received nourishment, it might be carried out beyond the bounds of the manor and left to its own fate (Undset 1968). A baby would likely be allowed to live if it was legitimate and if pressure on family resources did not dictate otherwise.

Fathers had the right to determine whether or not a newborn should live, but there were cases in which an undernourished and exhausted mother wished to have her newborn disposed of. She could be overruled by her husband, however.

According to Foote and Wilson (1970), unwanted infants (including neonates) were chiefly the offspring of slaves and those born out of wedlock. But during periods of famine other infants presumably stood a chance of being eliminated. Whether such decisions were made by community leaders rather than by heads of families is an open question (Clover 1988). Healthy male infants appear to have been unlikely candidates for exposure, whereas female infanticide was a fairly widespread societal practice in Viking times (Clover 1988).

The Christian Church opposed the killings and had been effective in bringing about its criminalization in Europe as early as A.D. 374, long before Scandinavia was Christianized. With the coming of Christianity to Scandinavia, the practice of neonaticide and infanticide was generally prohibited. The law spoke quite explicitly against exposure, infant strangulation, and the suffocating of children in bed, called "overlying" (*ihjelligging*). But it took some time before the population accepted the proscription, and even early Christian law, as a compromise with earlier pagan practices, permitted the elimination of "defective" infants.

Sections of early Christian law referred to women as potential killers of newborns and required that at least two other women be present during childbirth to prevent such an occurrence. And stillborn neonates were to be inspected to determine whether or not they had been strangled. Given Norway's sparse population, it could be difficult to comply with the requirement that two other women be present when a baby was born.

According to a popular belief still current in the fifteenth century, bears were a threat to pregnant women especially if a woman was carrying a male fetus. Ingrid from Hamar was brought before the court, charged with having concealed a birth, which was also illegal, and of having murdered the baby. Ingrid claimed that labor had come on unexpectedly while she was out in the forest and that a bear had taken the baby. With that defense Ingrid of Hamar's punishment only required that she take a pilgrimage (Benedictow 1985).

Did infanticide come to an end or merely go underground after it was prohibited? The evidence suggests that it was not universally taboo among Norwegian peasants for decades to come. As already mentioned, the church did allow the exposure of deformed infants for a time. Another sanctioned practice had to do with babies of freed serfs or slaves. According to Gulathing law, if such parents were destitute in time of great need, grave diggers could be directed to dig a grave in the church cemetery, place the excess babies in it, and let them die in the open grave. Perhaps in part to assuage his guilt, the former master of the freed slaves was instructed to take up from the grave and to support the baby that lived the longest. This practice was an ingenious, albeit grim, compromise between what abject poverty of the time demanded and the church's requirement that all healthy newborns be cared for. At least the hardiest baby was saved while the others died and were buried in consecrated ground (Tønnessen 1982)!

Survival was especially in jeopardy for handicapped or sick infants. In early times they were called changlings, huldrer offspring who had been left by their parents in exchange for a human baby. These poor creatures were exposed, and if not, they could be subjected to isolation, flogging, other mistreatment, and challenged as changlings to reveal their troll identity. It was not uncommon to regard the life in a changling as the reincarnation of something untoward in the extended family, a prolonged curse that people sought to defend themselves against by all possible means (Hodne, Ø. 1984).

The imbalance between resources and population lasted a very long time in Norway. Infanticide continued during early Christian times but not as openly as in Viking times. We should not assume any marked difference in attitude toward infanticide between Vikings and the early Christians, however. That neither Vikings nor early Christians took the practice of infanticide lightly is witnessed by the fact that death was a dominant subject in Viking folklore, and they were haunted by the ghosts of dead children. Child ghosts were a constant reminder to the survivors that an infant or a child had been murdered. The ghosts of young children were variously pictured as naked and crippled, cold and abandoned, going around calling for their mothers, or begging for clothing, baptism, or to be buried in consecrated ground. Their shrieks frightened people particularly when they were alone in isolated places. The ghost tradition suggests collective anguish and guilt feelings: the death of infants and children was not taken lightly.

Unwanted babies were not only exposed, but some died because of malign neglect, such as drowning, falling in the fire, and scalding with boiling water. There is almost complete silence about such cases in early Norwegian law, indicating that, as in England, such calamities were not investigated or reported to legal authorities, though they might be brought to the attention of the parish priest.

The alleged accidental death of an infant due to overlying, that is, being suffocated by an adult in the same bed falling asleep and rolling onto the infant was frequently mentioned. In his multi-volume work on daily life in the North in the 1500s, Troels-Lund (1880-1901) reports that it was a common cause of death. Given small, cold houses, large families, and not enough beds, it was necessary to have several in each bed and for the youngest to sleep with one or both parents.

Suffocation by overlying had too large an incidence, however, to be blamed only on accidents. Such deaths appear to have been treated as unavoidable, the way high fatality rates resulting from automobile accidents are often reported in industrialized countries (Fingerhut et al. 1988). There is no way to ascertain whether these fatalities were due to accident, intentional suffocation, or what is referred to today as sudden infant death syndrome. The Norwegian historian Ståle Dyrvik reports that he found what appears to be extensive use of infanticide in a Norwegian farming community even toward the end of the eighteenth century. The deaths were attributed to other causes, however (Dyrvik 1980).

Wealthy families sometimes kept alive the memory of a child who had died by having a family portrait painted. There is, for instance, a painting in Vats Church, Rogaland, from around the year 1600, which pictures a father and mother and their twenty-seven children, nineteen dead and eight living. It was not uncommon to include both living and dead children in a portrait. The dead family members were customarily painted wearing white clothing or carrying palms in their hands (Tønnessen 1982).

When the first institutions for parentless children were opened in the 1830s, an alternative to infanticide became available. Many daughters of extremely poor peasants were forced by necessity to leave home to find work at ten or twelve years of age. That often placed them at the mercy of unscrupulous males in the master's household, and many girls became pregnant only to be abandoned by those who fathered the children. The first several centuries after the Reformation was a period of singularly arduous attempts to eliminate illegitimate births by controlling fornication and adultery. Christian V's Norwegian Law (1687) made a clear distinction between children born in and outside marriage. But church records also show that of young women who married, as many as one-half were pregnant at the time of marriage (Tønnessen 1982).

"Having an accident" was a euphemistic way of referring to a pregnancy out of wedlock. To hide one's "sin" became an important goal for the unlucky woman. The young women, rejected and despised, sometime abandoned their babies on the church steps or some other place where they would be found and placed in a home or in one of the early child-care institutions, called asylums. But, purely quantitatively speaking, those institutions met very little of the need.

A number of old church books have been examined with the aim of seeing what happened to the children of unwed mothers. The evidence is striking. No other group showed greater attrition through abandonment or death than did those infants. Neonaticide and infanticide were not unique to unwed mothers in Norway, of course (Higginbotham 1989); infanticide and especially neonaticide have been practiced throughout the history of Western societies. Of 617 executions in Sweden between 1759 and 1778, 217 were for killing a child (Boli 1989). In America, the killing of illegitimate newborns was thought to be so common in the 1600s that a law was enacted making the concealment of a murdered illegitimate child a capital offense. The law was modeled after an English statute (Saunders 1989).

The prohibition of infanticide was one of the factors stimulating attempts to find other ways of controlling family size. Norwegian medical books of the late Middle Ages contain advice on how to induce abortion, referring to abortive potions that were made from rusty iron or from the parboiling of a mixture of willow twigs and flowers (Benedictow 1985). However, the church very early took note of abortion as a threat, and the archbishop issued an order against inducing abortion as early as around 1340.

In Norway, almost all babies were delivered at home up through the 1800s; only in the first half of the 1900s did hospital deliveries dominate (Blom, I. 1987). With great improvement in child health care from near the end of the 1800s, infant mortality rates in Norway began to decline and have continued to do so until the present time. In 1920, forty of a thousand children who were alive at birth and born of married parents died; for unmarried mothers the number was almost twice as high. Norway now has one of the lower infant mortality rates in Western societies, about eight per thousand for married persons and ten per thousand for the unmarried. In the Scandinavian countries in general, there is no connection between infant death and parent's social background, indicating that equal health care is available to all (Frønes 1989).

Nineteen seventy-four was the last year in Norway that the number of births exceeded the replacement level. Families in the upper social classes were first to lower the number of births. Earlier it had been precisely the families who were better off who had the largest number of children. The last to significantly limit their birth rate were families in primary industries: farming, lumbering, and fishing. The average family size has decreased from five to the presently desired level of two children per family. Few Norwegian children today have more than one sibling, especially in urban areas.

The practice of having two children within a short time span and a decrease in the average number of offspring from five in 1875 to two today are recent demographic changes in Norway. It was not until modern times, through the use of effective contraceptive methods, infrequent coitus, and in some cases abortion, that married couples held the number of offspring within the desired family size (Hollos 1974).

While half of all children as recently as in 1970 were born to women under twenty-five years, by 1984 the number was only one-third (Kristiansen 1986). Today, on the average, Norwegian women have a first baby at age twenty-five and a last at age twenty-eight. Though there are fewer children born than earlier, more women are having babies. Of women born before 1930, almost 20 percent were childless; today 90 percent of women have children.

Hence, it can be said that on average Norwegian couples have solved the problem of surplus offspring. Whether the society will remain sanguine about the long-range effects of a current birth rate below replacement levels remains to be seen. There are indications that it may not.

The law in force in the 1950s laid down penalties for anyone who destroyed a fetus, though abortion was permitted as an emergency measure, that is, to save the mother's life or if her health was endangered. The law of 1964 extended the legitimate reasons for abortion, and legalized abortion increased from 4.67 abortions per one thousand women to 14.3 in just six years (Ramsøy and Vaa 1975). A new, more liberal abortion law passed in 1975, and further liberalized in 1978, gives women themselves the right to decide if an abortion should be performed. Strenuous opposition from the church has accompanied each liberalization of the abortion law, but the majority of people respect the woman's right to abortion today. Bishops of the State Church have made explicit their support of the use of contraceptives in marriage, as well as the provision of contraceptive education within the framework of ethical education in the public schools, as a measure in their fight against the "abortion evil."

The issue of abortion is still hotly debated, and the debate is not likely to subside. A recent advertisement sponsored by the Norwegian pro-life organization pictured an eight-week-old fetus bearing the text "I am a person—restore my legal protection"; it was carried in all but one of the Norwegian newspapers, and that one accepted the text but not the picture. It is not only so-called pro-life groups who object to abortion in Norway. Many pro-choice citizens are not sanguine about abortion used as a backup method for the neglect or the failure of contraceptives.

Accidents

While Norway has made remarkable strides in reducing infant and child mortality, Norwegians express great concern over the high rate of infant and child accidents and accidental deaths. Infant and child deaths due to accidents are not a problem unique to Norway, but Norway's conspicuous public concern about it is unique. Child accident statistics are regularly reported, and corrective measures are proposed. It is more dangerous to be a child in Norway than it is in any other

Scandinavian country, and child advocates in Norway are painfully aware of it.

Approximately 14 percent of all Norwegian children each year are exposed to accidents that require treatment by a doctor (Lund 1985). In 1984 it was reported that 150–170 children were killed annually because of accidents during the previous seven to eight years (Lereim and Sahlim 1984). Traffic accidents made up 40–50 percent. Children bear a larger measure of the harm resulting from traffic accidents.

Traffic is recognized as the bane of children's existence, particularly in heavily populated areas in Norway. Over half of the restrictions parents placed on their children in one older city area were restrictions due to the assumed danger from automobiles. Strand (1979) asserts categorically that the developmental possibilities of children are reduced as a consequence of living with the automobile.

Compared with the other Scandinavian countries, not as much attention has been paid to the safety of children in previous decades in the design of family dwellings, in the planning of streets and highways, or in the planning of play areas. As child advocates in Norway point out, children and adults are essentially different as travelers; children travel mainly on foot or bicycle on the way to school, to a friend's home, or to a playground, and it is five times more dangerous to be a cyclist and three times more dangerous to be a pedestrian than to be a driver or passenger in an automobile. Seventy percent of children injured or killed are pedestrians. Most of the children who lose their lives in traffic are under the school age of seven years (*Oslo Aftenposten,* 3 January 1985). The remainder of accidental deaths are due to drowning, poisoning, electrical shock, many different kinds of falls, and burning. In one recent year, 30 percent of burn injuries were suffered by children from birth to four years of age, an age group with only 7 percent of the total of Norway's slightly more than four million people (Berge 1983).

Every year sixty thousand children are injured within or in the immediate vicinity of their homes, constituting about 45 percent of all child accidents. Between ten and twenty children die each year as a result of such injuries. Those statistics are regularly highlighted in Norway.

Studies of activities in housing areas show that most children are out in the afternoon from 1:00 to 5:00 P.M., a time when automobile traffic is most intense. No place and no time of day are completely spared of children's accidents in Norway, but the vast majority of accidents, 85 percent, take place during leisure time, at home, at school (particularly during recess), and during play time and sports activity (Lereim and Sahlim 1984). Outdoor play and leisure activities present the most hazards. Safer play places than the out-of-doors for young Norwegian children are child-care centers, day-time institutions, and schools. It has been asserted that many of the children's amusement parks in Norway would have to be closed if appropriate safety standards were enforced (Hansen 1987).

In other words, Norwegian children live dangerously. It is a theme that one hears repeatedly in Norway. In part, the danger is due to a traditional way of rearing children in Norway. The argument for that method of child care runs as follows: Children should grow up as free from restraint as possible; fresh air and exercise are good for them, and they should spend as much time outdoors as possible; children enjoy life and learn life through adventurous, creative play, particularly with their peers; children seek out interesting things to do and places to play and not necessarily with their own safety in mind; it is impossible—in fact, undesirable—to have a supervising adult with them at all times in order to prevent injury (Lund 1985). Being out in nature and taking part in outdoor activities are given high value in all of the Scandinavian countries and highest value in Norway (Naroll 1983).

Part of the child-care tradition in Norway involves the practice of putting young children out to play. It has become a controversial practice in recent decades, and there is some class difference in the use of the practice. More working-class than business and professional people continue the practice. Gullestad (1984) found in a working-class section of Bergen that babies were kept inside most of the day, but when a child was about two years old, irrespective of sex, it was allowed to go out to play without organized supervision. The mothers thought that the give-and-take of unsupervised play provided experience and challenges that taught children what life was really all about. It was, however, a sign of good parenting that one brought the children in relatively early in the evening.

Norway's distinctiveness in regard to child rearing can be seen by comparing child-care attitudes and practices and the accident rate in Norway with those of neighboring Sweden. Norway consistently shows higher injury and death rates for infants and children than does Sweden. A striking statistic from a 1973 World Health Organization report will illustrate. The deaths due to drowning, traffic, and other kinds of accidents per one hundred thousand infants and children aged one to four in Norway was 30.7 and in Sweden 10.8 (Berge 1983). Norway has the highest and Sweden the lowest death rate due to accidents among children in the Nordic countries. Norwegian researchers point to the cultural differences, asserting that people in Sweden are more safety conscious resulting in fewer child accidents. For instance, in Stockholm little girls wear protective helmets when figure skating, as do Swedish children when sliding on sleds and riding bicycles. That is not commonly seen in Norway. Sweden also has made greater efforts to minimize the hazards from automobile traffic and enforces more stringent building codes for dwellings, with accident prevention in view. Swedes are seen by some Norwegians as providing a safer, albeit a more boring, milieu for children.

Birth and Survival

A member of the child ombud's office in Oslo, in pondering the question of the accident differential for the two countries, referred to these cultural differences. Culturally, Norwegians tend to be explorers and adventurers, she said, while Swedes are more accepting of restrictions on their movement and are more regulated. The deeply ingrained traditional child-care attitudes and practices extant in Norway make safety measures more difficult to legislate and to enforce.

According to a Swedish study, children's accidents can be reduced up to 80 percent in housing areas if dwellings and the area are planned according to modern safe-planning principles (Strand 1979). Methods of reducing the hazards of traffic are well known, though they are not employed as much in Norway as in Sweden. According to Strand, the initiatives are:

1. Separate the different types of travelers. For example, build walks and bicycle paths.
2. Blend the different types of travelers but with the advantage given to the weaker by giving more consideration to safety than to speed and convenience for the automotive traffic.
3. Regulate speed.
4. Reorganize traffic. For example, eliminate auto traffic on certain streets.
5. Install traffic lights, guardrails, fences.
6. Build roads for automobiles around the most heavily populated areas.
7. Change to safer methods of travel than the personal automobile.
8. Teach safety measures to children.

The primary attention in Norway has been directed toward the last initiative, that is, improving individual behavior rather than toward changing modes and patterns of traffic. Children are given traffic education in school and as members of children's traffic clubs. On radio's "Traffic and Music" program, which reaches most Norwegians, there is a constant main suggestion that parents must look after their children so they do not play in the streets and on the roads. Contests sponsored by automobile associations and other organizations are securely anchored in that safety education tradition. On the whole, there is relatively little effort made to make the traffic milieu safer for children. Scandinavian safety experts claim that the problem with a safety education approach is that children are not always rational in their behavior. Young children lack the capacity to behave rationally in traffic, and the environment must give room for irrational behavior that could cause accidents. Traffic education can make children more cautious, but it is not the answer to the problem.

It is asserted that child safety does not carry a high priority when decisions about traffic are made in Norway. Children and their parents have little clout in contrast to members of production and service organizations, automobile associations, legislators, and motorists. For the situation to change, the rights and needs of pedestrians and cyclists would have to become more apparent and urgent than they are today. Given Norway's mountainous terrain, the building of walks and cycling paths, as well as streets and highways for automobiles, is enormously expensive. Even in highly congested areas in Norway one often finds that passageway is provided only for automotive traffic, and pedestrians and cyclists are left to fend for themselves, often at great personal risk.

In sum, over time the birth of a surfeit of children has been brought under control and survival throughout childhood has been made much less problematic, yet no one is more aware than are Norwegian child advocates that there is still room for improvement.

3

Children at Home

NORWEGIAN CHILD RESEARCHERS have been in the forefront in developing a theoretical perspective that focuses on
the social life of children rather than on the developmental
stages of children in their growth to maturity. In other words,
there is a great deal of emphasis on children interacting in
community. In the community, the home is a child's primary
social setting.

Bringing up children is far more than passing on a culture
from active and knowledgeable adults to passive, innocent, and
impressionable youngsters. Children are not merely passive
receivers of an already existing culture. Socialization is instead
a two-way process that takes place through interaction between the child and the persons in his or her network of
associations. From that perspective, emphasis focuses on the
social network as a context wherein the child's life and development takes place—the network consisting of a dynamic set of
relationships between persons. There are many such relationships in family and neighborhood; *active personal network* is a
term used to include all the persons whom the anchor person,
in our case the child, recognizes as those with whom active
communication and interaction take place.

The kind of community in which a child lives and grows is
crucial for the extent to which a child experiences and enjoys
life. Children's behavior is in large part a result of their own
experiences in the environment in which they live and only
indirectly a result of adults' interpretations of those experiences. It is what children see, hear, and sense, taken as a whole,

that not only shapes their experiences but also helps to form their personalities. Hence, the human networks in which children are enmeshed and the quality of life children experience within them are a field of study in their own right. That humanistic, Model V perspective on children and on child research guides much of child research and policy in Norway today. It also informs all of the discussion of Norwegian children in this book, both because it is the focus of the Norwegian research on which the book is based and because I am convinced of its fruitfulness.

In doing research on children, their environment, and their culture, the technique of interviewing children—rather than interviewing only parents and teachers—has been employed in Norway, but primarily only in the last several decades. Thus, we do not have comparable data from children who grew up in Norway in earlier times. Nevertheless, awareness of the importance of the social interaction of children within an environment of people, places, animals, and objects during their growing-up period so permeates child research and public policy in Norway today that it markedly affects the focus of historical research on childhood as well, the bulk of which has been carried on within the last two decades and has really only begun (Dyrvik 1979; Sætersdal and Ørjasæter 1981; Tønnessen 1982; Hodne and Sogner 1984).

Since the contacts that children have during their early years are so important to their development and to the quality of their lives, where they live and what the family and neighbors do and say are crucial. Children are more dependent on and affected by local environment than are persons of any other age. They are often more familiar with intimate and minute details of that environment than are older persons,since children are less mobile and they interact in smaller physical space than do adults. Regardless of which environment we are speaking about, adult comprehension and experience is more extensive than is that of young children, but that of children may be more intensive.

In Viking times (eighth–tenth century), the extended family was the dominant social unit in Norway.* A single individual or a single nuclear family, and certainly a single child, had almost no independent social existence; the extended family was everything (Tønnessen 1982). It was a society that, though possessing organs for legal process and judgment, required the execution of law by the adult individual himself. The lowest status of all was that of slaves, a very well populated class of people in Viking times. Slaves could have wives and children, but they could own nothing and inherit nothing, although it was possible that their own freedom could be purchased (Foote and Wilson 1970).

We get a hint, and only a hint, of what life was like for slaves and their children from the poem "Rigspula" in the *Elder Edda,* which is thought to have been written in the period 890–920. The poet tells of a girl named Thir (which means bond-maid), with her scarred feet, sunburned arms, and hooked nose, who meets Thrall (bondsman). They marry without much ceremony and have children. Their status in society and the status of their children are represented by the contemptuous names that the poet gives them, presumably because of their appearance, their habits, and the work they do. The numerous sons bore names such as Stable Boy, Clumsy One, Brawler, Coarse, Slave, Fowl, Lump, Laggard; and the daughters were She-lump, Clump, Thicklegs, Beaked Nose, Noise, Torrent-talker, Tatter-coat, and Crane-shank (Gjerset 1915; Foote and Wilson 1970).

---

*   It was during the Viking Age (c. 800–1050) that provincial chieftainships began to develop into a kind of state, but with weak central government. Battles among the various chieftains in Norway resulted in the victory of Harald the Fairhaired (Hårfager) in 872. As he consolidated his power, chieftains dissatisfied with the outcome emigrated, many to the Faroe Islands and especially to Iceland.

Viking raiders captured slaves all over Europe. Many of them, perhaps most, were female (Karras 1990). Those who owned slaves had sexual access to slave women as in other slaveholding societies. Slaves who became concubines were not counted as plural wives, but their children could apparently inherit from their father but solely at his discretion. Otherwise, slaves were at the bottom of the social order. Little is known about the poor, though free, Vikings. At the top of the social order were wealthy Viking farmers and traders. Wealthy leaders in the Viking Age and early medieval period had a following of able-bodied men in their service. Some of them might live in the locality and turn out only in case of need or for a summer expedition, but others formed a permanent retinue (Foote and Wilson 1970). The many wares brought in by enterprising Viking traders added comfort to the homes of the wealthy and created a taste for fine clothing, ornamentation, and luxury in various forms. Their wealth was no doubt reflected in the lives of their children as well. The writer of "Rigspula" gives an account of a male baby who at its birth was swaddled in silk, sprinkled with water, and called jarl, or earl, reflecting a life of some honor and indulgence. A wealthy Viking might have concubines as well as wives. The child of a wealthy man and his servant concubine took the rank not of its father but of its mother. The father could liberate his unfree child if he chose, but he was not obligated to do so.

Settlement patterns are a major factor affecting structure and activity in a child's social network, but little is known about the settlement patterns in Viking times. For many centuries after the end of the Viking Age, Norway continued to have a predominately rural population. Some large farms were close to self-sufficient, especially in sparsely populated areas. It could happen that children who lived on such farms—before the development of the elementary school—had almost no contact with persons other than household members. But the members of such a household could provide them with numerous experiences, for it might contain the farmer, his wife, their children, older family members, adult unwed siblings, and more distant relatives, in addition to servant folk. All activity—work, social, and leisure—took place within the family setting. This has been referred to as the amorphous family because of its open, unstructured form and lack of privacy for individuals or for members of the nuclear unit of husband, wife, and children. On the other hand, many of the farm units were so small and the produce so meager that they could support only a nuclear family unit of husband, wife, and children. One early rural settlement pattern that gave children of nuclear family units a larger social network was the so-called multiuse farmyard where separate houses were clustered so closely that everyday contact was possible and hardly anything went on in any of the households without all knowing about it. In such settlements both comradeship and strife with others were important parts of the social milieu that children experienced (Tønnessen 1982).

One could say that traditionally almost all Norwegian children grew up in essentially the same social environment since the population was a homogeneous racial and ethnic group with the same language and almost all were rural and lived in poverty. While that is true, there were great differences in the physical settings in which children grew and experienced life, and those various physical settings dictated different activities not only for adults but also for children. Through most of Norway's long history, most children grew up in peasant families—on the plains, on the mountains, in the forests, or by the fjords or ocean. The children were on intimate terms with the environment where they grew up—the soil, the elements, the changing seasons, and the animals, both domesticated and wild. They lived out their childhood in close proximity to their parents who wrestled with a sometimes intractable terrain to provide sustenance and shelter. All engaged in the struggle to survive. The farm and its importance was the foundation of peasant society, and it, rather than the nuclear family or the individuals in it, received first consideration.

It was not an environment peopled only by human beings and animals, for a whole body of magic and witchcraft was very much a reality in the peasant worldview, even until the end of the nineteenth century (Frykman and Löfgren 1987). People believed they were a part of nature and lived close to it. Norse religion, prior to the coming of Christianity in about A.D. 1000, was made up of sky gods and earthbound creatures who were in and of nature. The god Odin, for example, was preternatural and adept at manipulating the forces of nature. Beliefs taught by the Christian Church merged with those from Viking times and both survived in folk tradition.

The peasants perceived their environment in mystical but at the same time very practical terms. They responded to nature as though it were animate, possessed of will and thus capable of aiding or harming them. One needed to cooperate with the spirit world. The farm spirit (*nisse*), for instance, could ensure the prosperity of farm and home, but if crossed he could deprive the peasant of his very crops or livestock. The precarious life of the peasant family depended on mutuality and respect between humans and those in the spirit world (Kvidelund and Sehmsdorf 1988). It was an important lesson that the children of peasants learned as they absorbed the rich, mystical, and practical subsistence culture into which they were born.

Peasant children's contact with spirits and animals was not restricted to the forest and the farmyard, for spirits, poultry, and young domestic animals also shared the family dwelling. Keeping small animals in the living quarters on the farm was still common in some areas until the end of the nineteenth century. Landless farm laborers and cotters cohabited with their small animals as late as the turn of the century. The animals were not kept in the house in order to entertain little children; the reasons were much more pragmatic. Animals' heat helped warm the interior of the house, and animals were known to thrive better with housebound care. Hens were said to lay more eggs and young calves to grow stronger faster.

Peasant children did not grow up with a heavy layer of material culture shielding them from nature and its functions as is true today. As we have said, the dwellings that they lived in were apt to be dark, dank, and inadequately heated. Water was carried into the house from outside and was carefully rationed. By current standards both the house and the inhabitants would be judged to be physically dirty. Houses were not cleaned and dusted as is done today. Hands and faces might be washed occasionally, but the body was rarely if ever washed. Bodywashing, if it did occur, was done less for cleanliness or hygienic purposes than as a ritual, such as a bath before Christmas, or, in later times, a Saturday bath in preparation for church attendance on Sunday. When a bath was taken, it was not uncommon for all members of the family to use the same water.

One can hardly imagine the stench that family members lived with in a peasant house—sweat; the odor from unwashed bodies; the smell of domesticated animals; the smoky downdraft of the chimney; the stench from the slop bucket in the kitchen and the pots under or by the beds; as well as the odors from meals being cooked (Frykman and Löfgren 1987). Even after the Saturday bath became somewhat common, the week constituted a single work shift, and during that shift the same work clothes were worn for an entire week, were perhaps replaced by Sunday clothing, but were not necessarily washed before being worn again for another week (Sundt 1975).

There were neither toilets nor bathrooms in early peasant houses. Body waste could be disposed of in pots, on the manure pile, in the cow barn, or while sitting on a board protruding from the wall of the house or suspended between two buildings. Cleaning after defecating was equally primitive. Grass, moss, or snow might be used for wiping. Frykman and Löfgren (1987) tell of a woman who reported never having used anything other than her index finger throughout her long life.

Urine was thought to have medicinal value because it was sterile. Gloves were not worn when people worked outside, and often the hands became rough and sore. In the absence of hand lotion, one's own urine was often used in treating sore hands.

Around 1800 there were still only a little under one million people living in all of Norway. A small upper class, or the cultured people (*de kondisjonerte*), consisted of the great merchants, operators of mines and mills, and wealthy landowners and made up about 2 percent of the population. Another 50 percent or so were farmers, craftsmen, and petty bourgeois of various kinds. The remainder consisted of cotters, day laborers, servants, and a large number of paupers. More than 90 percent of the population lived in rural areas. Small farms predominated—small cultivated farms, mountain farms, farms along the coast that combined fishing and farming. All farm families, as a rule, carried on a barter economy.

Beneath the small farmers in social rank were the cotters, tenants with life tenure on a small plot of land, a group that increased markedly in the 1800s. In the middle of the century, approximately every fifth Norwegian belonged to a cotter's family. The cotter commonly had heavy work responsibility on the owner's farm along with work on the small patch of land he was permitted to till. Often great need prevailed in the homes. Exhaustion both for adults and children was common because of overwork and lack of sustenance. There were shortages of almost everything important to a young child: food, clothing, playthings, time for play, and sometimes affection (Tønnessen 1982).

Socioeconomic status of the family does affect the structure and activity in a child's social networks. The life of most peasant children was markedly different from the life of the few children whose parents were of the gentry. We must add, however, that Norway has not been a society with marked class differences: in fact, it is a society with few class differences whether one looks at early times when the majority lived in a state of poverty or today when Norwegians are relatively affluent (Naroll 1983).

It is evident that children were cared for in many ways in peasant families, but the modern sentimental praxis cannot be demonstrated to have been one of them (Thorsen 1987). Children were very seldom hugged or kissed, for instance. Wrapping babies in swaddling clothes was a common practice from earliest known times and up until the present century, in some places until the 1950s or later (Tønnessen 1982). A painting from 1561 that graces the front of the altar of Norslunde Church in Sjælland depicts a baby being baptized. The baby is swaddled from head to toe; other members of the baptismal party are well dressed, indicating a family of some means. Apparently, swaddling clothes were proper attire for babies even on such an auspicious occasion. The painting has additional historical significance in that it is the first known depiction of a Lutheran church service wherein water at baptism is applied only to the head of the baby. Earlier it was customary to undress the baby who was to be baptized and to immerse it several times in the baptismal font (Heffermehl 1990).

Swaddling restricted arm and leg movement and made it easier to supervise infants while at the same time providing protection from dangers that might befall them. The practice varied somewhat with the baby's age, temperament, quality of infant care available, and the style of dress in vogue. When infants were provided with shirts and jackets, for instance, the arms at least were free.

The ever-present and affectionate mother as an ideal was not unknown, but she appeared relatively seldom in peasant society even as late as the 1950s. Proof of affection toward children who had passed infancy is hard to find. That is not to imply that children were not loved and as well cared for as was possible, but the demanding work on the farm plus the mentality of work—the overriding belief in the primary importance of work—slowed down the internalization of the ever-present, affectionate mother as a pattern of life. Only gradually the elaboration of intimacy moved "from silence to outspokenness, from concealment to openness and from distance to closeness" (Thorsen 1987:108).

Peasantry as a way of life is not such a distant past but that most Norwegians even today have a heritage of peasant life not far back in their ancestry, and they are affected by it. The effects that peasant life had on the values and perspectives of those who experienced it did not die with the passage of the peasantry.

Modernization (*hamskiftet*) came relatively late to Norway, but it did bring advantages to the homes of people of all classes—new farming methods and equipment, stores, dairies, more consumer goods, post, telegraph, and railroads (Tønnessen 1982). There was a steady decline in the number of persons living in isolated and sparsely settled regions of northern Norway. However, Hollos (1974) tells of an isolated community in eastern Norway where even as late as the middle of the present century, formal visits of one family to another were so rare that preschool children, unaccustomed as they were to strangers, often threw up and had crying fits as the time for such visits approached.

Modernization happened mainly in the last century and a half, and the changes must not be allowed to hide the fact that throughout most of Norway's history rural families and poor families were the predominant types. Into the 1800s many

Children at Home

Norwegian children grew up in physical want and with the demeaning status that so often characterized a life of limited means. Their relatively low estate became more apparent to them as their contacts were broadened through the introduction of the elementary school and later through migration to urban centers.

Children in Workers' Families

Between 1840 and 1940 industrialization and urbanization brought to Norway a new family type, the family of the poorly paid, salaried industrial worker. Sometimes both father and mother worked outside the home, father in a factory and mother in a factory or in a private home as a maid. But the majority of Norwegian women did not work outside the home. The workday in the factory could be from six in the morning until nine at night, and with only one income to depend on, and that a modest one, small children had their mother's care but often in poor quality, overcrowded housing. By 1930 there was throughout the country an average in homes of 1.1 persons per room, including the kitchen. Almost 19 percent of the population lived two persons per room. Twelve percent of city dwellings and 6 percent of country dwellings had bathrooms (Frønes 1989). The lack of indoor plumbing meant that many activities that are considered private today might take place outside the family dwelling, such as washing and drying clothes outdoors or going to the toilet in a nearby outhouse. As with the rural peasants, many workers' families existed in dire need. Twenty percent of a sample of persons born in 1920 reported periodically having difficulty getting enough food.

The ever-present threat of industrial workers being laid off and the lack of labor unions or governmental agencies to protect workers were further threats to the economic stability of the workers' families. Their working conditions left them little leisure or energy for relaxed and affectionate parenting, and most of the descriptions of life in the workers' families speak of quite authoritarian and at times brutal fathers. It is not uncommon that parents who are themselves closely supervised or controlled by superiors and by the consequences of their work life employ physical or coercive forms of punishment with their children. From an economic point of view, workers' children were first and foremost a burden since every small child was another mouth to feed; many workers' children were unwanted children (Tønnessen 1982).

Weekends were not spent at a cabin, a common practice in Norway today. Much of social and leisure time was spent either in the crowded flat or in the street, the common public place for children to play and for youth and adults to meet. Children did not pedal off to playgrounds or other places of interest. People lived, worked, and played close to each other less because of choice than because of their common poverty (Frønes 1989). The years following World War II signaled the beginning of a new era marking the end of economic poverty. Of those who were born in the 1950s, next to no one reported having experienced difficulty in getting enough to eat.

The Bourgeois Family

The bourgeois family developed at roughly the same time as the industrial working-class family, for that family type, too, was largely a product of industrialization. Fathers in those families worked outside the home in commerce and industry. Mothers stayed at home and had the main responsibility for running the household and caring for the children. The households of middle-class families might include (besides the nuclear family of father, mother, and children) single aunts, a grandparent, and even servants if the family budget would allow for their hiring (Tønnessen 1982). It was possible for children of the bourgeoisie to receive not only life's necessities but also some of the luxuries of living in families where children's feelings and needs could be more fully attended to. It was among mothers of the bourgeoisie that the model of an ever-present, affectionate mother replaced the peasant work mentality. The children were more likely to go to school and did not need to seek work outside the home in order to supplement the family income.

Child and Family Today

Throughout Norway's history from Viking times to the present, young children have been and are seen primarily and unequivocally as the "property" of their parents (Andenæs 1984; Haavind 1979). Information from Viking times (Foote and Wilson 1970; Tønnessen 1982), as well as studies and surveys made from the 1940s to the 1980s, supports that conclusion (Grønseth 1975; Rodnick 1955; Andenæs 1984; Dahl 1984; Gulbrandsen and Miljeteig-Olssen 1979; Haavind 1979; Wærness 1984; Hollekim 1986). However, there has been a marked ideological change in what children as property means over the decades. What is emphasized today is not the *authority* of the parents to rule over their children but their *responsibility* to meet the needs of their children (Andenæs and Haavind 1987).

Families form the overwhelmingly predominant pattern for interpersonal proximate life throughout Norway today as they have throughout most of Norwegian history. Generally speaking, couples valued children in the past and they do today, but in smaller numbers (Haavind 1979). Urban couples today have one child, often two children, but seldom three. The proportion of families that have four children or more varies from a little more than 1 percent in Oslo to over 10 percent in the northern district of Finnmark. It is taken for granted that it is best for a child to have at least one sibling; however, at least every tenth child grows up without a sibling. Though many mothers are now employed outside the home, married women continue to regard consideration for the needs of spouse and children as primary over their desire for income and a career (Andenæs 1984).

Within the family, children have been seen as belonging especially to their mothers. Even today there is a tendency for mothers to view a child not so much as belonging to both parents as belonging to its mother (Haavind 1979). Rodnick (1955) described Norwegian mothers of thirty years ago as persons with great responsibility and psychologically good to their children, but as overworked, tired, and getting no help from their husbands in shopping, cleaning, mending, doing the laundry, taking care of the house, or cooking.

Even today most families think that it is practical for the mother to have the responsibility on the home front. Norwegians, both men and women and younger and older adults, report that they think that women ought to be at home while their children are small (Hollekim 1986). Hence, parenting is gender-specific, and having children has great consequences in the lives of mothers. Failure in parenting is seen largely as the mother's fault. For infants and small children it means that concerned, sometimes anxious, mothers are a dominant presence in their lives. Even with a marked increase in mothers employed outside the home and an increase in child-care facilities, it is generally understood that parents cannot turn to anyone outside the family for the primary care of their children. Norway is among the Western European countries with the lowest public support for families. Working mothers return to the home whenever a child shows any signs of not thriving (Andenæs 1984).

Today seven of ten Norwegian women are in salaried work, full or part-time; more of them are in part-time work than in the other Nordic countries. But mothers see their desire for a career and income to be secondary considerations. Whether or not employed, most women continue to do much of the necessary work in the home (Dahl 1984; Haavind 1979). They are ambivalent about salaried work outside the home. Haavind found that almost all mothers would like paid work:

- if they could find part-time work;
- if the work place did not lie too far from home;
- if the family did not need to move to advance her husband's work or for better housing conditions;
- if proper child care could be arranged;
- if their children thrived;
- if they had permission to work at irregular hours;
- if they could take work home;
- if they could be free during school vacations;
- if they could find work befitting their qualifications and salary expectations.

Child care was never a primary priority for working fathers in Norway. That is not to say that the father was not regarded as being in charge of the family, for Norway was a patriarchal society from Viking times and throughout the time that Lutheran perspectives dominated; but he was in charge from a distance.

Many factors are playing a part in a gradual redefinition of the father role in Norway, for the traditional Norwegian value system with its emphasis on individual freedom and equality for all makes the elite and privileged position of men difficult to justify (Jonassen 1983). The change has been gradual. Historically, Norwegian fathers were generally humane, kind, and indulgent to their children, but they assumed no responsibility in disciplining, educating, or playing with them. All the various studies of child care done in the 1950s and 1960s show fathers to be primarily socially and emotionally distant.

Fathers still remain basically passive in the child-care sphere. They are doing more, but their interaction with children can in large part be characterized as play, while mothers set the standard for care and oversight (Haavind 1979). Professionals today point to the importance of children's interacting with their fathers. That creates what some Scandinavian researchers refer to as a new burden for women, that is, the burden of urging and arranging occasions for father and child to be together. The modern Norwegian mother thinks it more important for the child and father to spend some time together than for the father to take part in housework (Andenæs 1984).

In families where both parents work outside the home one would expect that young children spend much less time with a parent than when mother does not work outside the home. But that is not true. According to time-allocation studies, mothers who are employed part-time spend on the average 8.8 hours together with their preschool children, and mothers who work full-time spend as much as 7.8 hours. That does not include time when the children are sleeping. There is ground for believing that families with small children have never spent so much time together as they do now—and especially time together that centers on the needs and interests of the child (Andenæs and Haavind 1987).

Because of the general affluence in Norway since World War II, few children live in substandard housing. Also in the last years there has been a change in attitude toward children's use of the home. Steadily more homes have become child-friendly. Modern mothers of small children distance themselves from mothers of the 1950s who had "dust on the brain," that is, mothers who lived to keep a highly polished house with children expected to play outside or to play in their own room. When mother is in the kitchen, the young ones often play there; when social life moves to the living room, they are there (Andenæs and Haavind 1987; Frønes 1989). The emphasis today is on a house or apartment (72 percent of dwellings are one- or two-family dwellings in Norway, the highest in any of the Nordic countries) that will accommodate an active family life. Children have their own rooms, but today's parents do not feel that play should only take place there. The living room may be equipped primarily for use by adults, and mothers may not feel that the children should play there when no one else is in the living room, but in homes where there are small children, living rooms are not show places. They are equipped with furniture that can be used by children without hard use causing constant annoyance to parents. That does not mean, however, that the living room is devoid of decoration, for the women take pride in their homes. The home is a center of family life; mothers like to get everything cleaned up and ready for afternoon and early evening family life together.

Norwegian school-age children have relatively short school days, and half-grown children are apt to spend some of their time at home without either parent being there. Hence, in many areas the latchkey child is no longer a distinct type as the unattended home has become part of the child's environment. And children bring their friends along; Frønes (1989) reports nine-year-olds meeting at each other's homes during the day before mother or father arrive from work.

The difference in attitudes toward child-care roles of parents becomes clear in cases where the parents are divorced. Among working-class wives in Bergen, for instance, Gullestad (1984) found that it was out of the question for a father to have custody of the children after divorce. The husband has to leave home: the mother "throws him out" and retains custody of the children. Norwegian society has been so arranged that for mothers children *must* come first; it is rather the parent's love relationship that is at risk (Andenæs and Haavind 1987).

Today, everyday life in Norwegian families is pretty much alike from one family to another (Andenæs 1984). Yet each family is isolated in the sense that life in Norway is home-centered, and each nuclear family tends to be closed to non-family persons and to turn inward on itself. Parents build protective rings around their families. Norwegians generally appear reluctant to create secondary "play worlds" outside the home (Gullestad 1984). There is much interaction and activity within the family and less interaction across families. Networks that are formed tend to follow generational lines in one's own family. The network can be used to provide help and support when it is needed, but it is contact with close relatives and being together socially that is prized most highly. Contact between children and their grandparents continues to be common. In families with two parents and two sets of grandparents, daily or weekly contact with grandparents is common. Sixty percent see their grandparents that often; only 13 percent see grandparents less often than once a month. Young children often stay overnight in the home of grandparents. Nearly 40 percent of four-to-five-year-olds did so at least three nights during the year. Most grandparents lived in the country into the 1950s and 1960s. Visits to them helped to continue elements of the outdoor life of older Norwegians in children's culture (Frønes 1989). Contacts with uncles, aunts, and cousins are not nearly as frequent, but over half also see some of those relatives daily or weekly (Andenæs and Haavind 1987). Gullestad's observation that "social and geographic mobility represent the Norwegian nightmare, rather than the Norwegian dream" is evidence of a situation in which relatives continue to live so near each other that daily and weekly visits are possible ("Typisk Norsk—the Norwegian way of being," in News of Norway, November 1990, p. 67).

With no siblings or a small number of siblings, and living in closed nuclear families, young children today have intimate interaction with a limited number of persons and are more directly under the purview of their parents when parents are at home than was true in earlier times (Dyrvik 1979). Children who do have siblings appreciate them and often choose them as models for their own behavior.

Not as many children live in intact nuclear families today as did in earlier times. An increased acceptance of unwed parenthood and a rise in the incidence of divorce has meant that at present 10–11 percent of all children under seven are living with only one of their parents. At the present rate of divorce, it can be expected that before they are seventeen years of age 20 percent of all children will experience having their parents part company. On the other hand, the increased number of divorced adults who subsequently live in cohabiting relationship or remarry means that more children live in some form of reconstituted family unit (Andenæs and Haavind 1987).

Living with Father and Mother

It is the out-of-home, public arena that has been the man's world throughout most of Norwegian history. A masculine perspective on life valued the traits of physical prowess, endurance, tenacity, strength, bravery, aggressiveness, and adventurous activity—traits that served a people who survived in a land of rugged terrain, nearly untillable land, and inclement weather, and a dangerous life at sea.

Norwegian women have been known to consider themselves stronger than their husbands, having grown up accepting the belief that their mothers dominated their fathers but that men ought to be allowed to think that they are the stronger sex (Grønseth 1975). While men ruled the public domain, the home was almost exclusively the domain of women. Living in a patriarchal society, women nevertheless affirmed a belief in equality and their own personal freedom of thought and action. Norwegian husbands often complained that their wives were domineering and critical and subordinated everything to the children. Historically, the idea of love between a husband and a wife received little emphasis and was treated rather matter-of-factly (Hendin 1964). It is still the case in some Norwegian families that home and child care are so much the domain of women that men appear somehow not to feel completely at ease in their own homes (Gullestad 1984). Tiller (1960) sees the role of the father as partly that of "buffer" over against the mother's authority and especially over against her tendency to overprotect the children and her demand for their nearness to her. Her relationship to the child can be loving but also aggressive (Haavind 1979).

Work roles of both men and women in Norwegian society have changed over time; there is less in the world outside the home to accommodate the masculine perspective, and women's activity is less confined to home and child care than formerly. The majority of both husbands and wives have paid work, divide tasks in the home with some reference to the idea of sharing, and have more free time for each other. Gullestad finds today that women are committed to searching for the one particular man that is "right" for them and to having a relationship that works out best. Love and attraction have become central values in their lives. Feelings of closeness and intimacy, including sexual intimacy, have become central parts of the marital relationship.

In general, children born into a Norwegian family today can expect to experience fewer manifestations of machismo in fathers, less domesticity in mothers, some sharing of responsibility and some expression of intimacy and affection between their parents. But we speak in general terms, of course. Old patterns of life have a tenacity and often a rationale that causes them to persist beyond the time when they are functional or even faddish. As long as children are not grown and are at home, their relationships to their mothers continue to be extremely close and, for various reasons, fathers are reluctant to invade those relationships. There are still mothers who undervalue the father's role in the lives of their children even when their children do not. Norwegian children value care given them by their fathers more than mothers realize they do (Tiller 1984).

Perspectives and Goals of Child Care in Norway

Perspectives on children and the goals to be achieved in the raising of children have changed in Norway over its long history. In a sense, several perspectives have followed each other over time, yet it is difficult to say when and to what extent older perspectives are replaced by newer ones. Like older gender role patterns, older perspectives on children and child care persist and are employed even after they have passed out of vogue and general favor.

Little evidence exists as to what perspective on child care guided parents in early times. There was not a great deal of theorizing about the nature of childhood and how children should be reared. In his attempt to trace the development of the conception of childhood as a special phase in life, Ariès (1962) argues that it was in the family that infants and young children first were singled out for special treatment, treatment characterized by coddling of them "as charming toys," while a second conception of childhood sprang out of sources outside the family, such as church and state, sources that saw children not as charming toys but as fragile creatures of God who were to be safeguarded or reformed. That conception of childhood later found its way into family life.

Ariès's formulation has some utility in tracing the history of conceptions of childhood in Norway. Though there is evidence that children were sometimes treated harshly in early times, yet mild and indulgent child care was widespread in Norway and persisted even after a systematized, disciplined perspective was brought into Norway with the coming of Catholicism, was further elaborated in the Protestant Reformation, and was made legal with the Christianizing of the Norwegian state. The custom called household flogging empowered the master of the house to flog his children, wife, servants, and farmhands. The prescription of household flogging was reaffirmed in Sweden at least until 1833, but by then flogging was to be employed only as a last resort, and it should not lead to serious bodily injury (Boli 1989).

There are humanizing traits of personality and character that make the demands of strict, unemotional, rule-bound child rearing difficult to sustain. Bjarne Hodne (1984) reports that beginning early in the twentieth century love between parents and between parents and children became a part of the new family ideal, but there are many examples of loving and caring relations between parents and children prior to that time. From his travels in Norway in the middle of the last century, Sundt (as reported in Tønnessen 1982) pictures a not very demanding type of child rearing. He tells of families where life was probably strenuous for children, but he also tells of parents watching over their children with care and warmest love.

A fascinating study of gentle and indulgent child care in this century is that by Hollos (1974) who studied families in one dispersed rural community in eastern Norway, which she calls Flathill. Infants were much indulged and were not swaddled. They were thought to be physically frail and in need of protection. In fact, physical overprotection was manifested in delayed independency training in such areas as dressing, feeding themselves, and toilet training, resulting in sustained physical and emotional dependence on the mother. Even children up to three years of age could not necessarily feed themselves without assistance. Throughout the first two years the child was considered to be especially weak and tender and thought to require constant care and attention, reminiscent of the accounts of overprotection of infants in early Norse literature. During the night the baby slept in a crib next to the mother, and during the day the baby carriage was placed in the kitchen. The baby's crib, and later the bed, remained in the parent's bedroom until the child was about ten years of age.

Night crying of a baby was immediately responded to. Many babies ended up sleeping in their mothers' beds, a practice generally difficult to discontinue once it has begun. Initially, infants in Flathill were breast fed. The stated ideal was scheduled feeding; however, all five mothers with young babies during the period of Hollos's fieldwork fed their babies on demand.

Nevertheless, the relationship between mother and child was not particularly emotional or characterized by close bodily contact. Mothers almost never caressed or kissed their children. Instead, they showed their love and concern and provided warmth and security by their constant presence and their particular form of detached attention.

Children over the age of two or three were free to roam and spend their time with whatever they pleased. Most preschool children were thoroughly familiar with the kinds of plants, berries, birds, and trees in the region. When outside they played in the dirt or water; picked assorted flowers and berries; watched hay being brought in and made their own haystacks; watched cows being milked and milk being poured into containers; and the like.

When child and mother were together, the days were filled with short episodes of nonverbal, nondirective, occasionally cooperative activity, but most frequently parallel and independent action in the vicinity of each other. Children were rarely alone, but that meant in the vicinity or immediate region of other persons, not necessarily in interaction with them. When old enough to crawl and walk, a child was neither confined nor encouraged. The children were free to explore and investigate while the mother somewhat anxiously watched and only stopped them from hurting themselves. Once they could walk, they stayed inside relatively briefly.

There was little pressure on children in terms of either time or achievement. Adults did not stimulate or consciously teach. Learning was initiated by the child. Such child care gave children a great deal of opportunity for self-directed, relatively solitary observation and play. Children received little reaction from adults. They were neither quieted if they played noisily and disturbed adults nor engaged in conversation, told stories, or played with. Mothers and children never had extended conversations or question-and-answer periods. For children up to age seven (when they began school in Norway), little was expected in the area of responsibility, obedience, or achievement.

Even the idea of using reward and punishment in disciplining children, when suggested, was received with surprise by the mothers. When children were finished eating they were permitted to leave the table. After the evening meal the entire family watched television until the mother put them to bed around nine or ten o'clock. Very frequently children, having been put to bed, would return to the living room and sit in their pajamas and continue to watch TV. When they finally tired and fell asleep, the mother carried them back to bed. During the family TV watching time, children generally made a nuisance of themselves. No adult tried to stop them. The children generally reacted to indirect attempts at control rather negatively or not at all.

That indulgent pattern of child care cannot be judged to be representative of parental neglect, for Hollos found parents to be conscious of a perspective on children and child care that they could articulate. The child was thought of as an individual with its own potential that could not be much influenced by adults. People felt that direct orders and commands would only hamper a child's development and would not be in keeping with the idea of equality. No adult should try to impose his will on a child. Mothers felt that children should be kept away from people and influences that would curb or hamper them. For that reason, even grandmothers had very little to do with their grandchildren, for parents felt that older people have less patience and are inclined to quiet noisy children or to bribe them with gifts. They believed that the child will inevitably progress unaided through a procession of developmental stages. Minding one's own business appeared to have been an accepted behavior pattern both for children and adults in Flathill. As we have already indicated, keeping children and their grandparents apart is not the usual pattern of behavior in Norway (Frønes 1989).

In doing fieldwork in a mountain community in central Norway in 1951, Barth (1960) found a similarly relaxed pattern of child care. No strict feeding schedule was kept. Breastfeeding continued throughout the first year. Training was highly individualized and not strict, and the child was toilet trained around the age of two or frequently later. Little punishment was used in disciplining children; control in this community was by explanation and admonition. Early childhood appeared to be a very happy time. Children were active and smiling though shy toward strangers. Farm mothers were always present, and attention centered on the parents as a source of love and encouragement. A Norwegian agronomist also observed that farmers were very indulgent toward their children and that children grew up with few inhibitions.

About the same time that Barth was doing his fieldwork in central Norway, Stephenson (1960) was observing family life in an industrial community in southeastern Norway. He also found fairly relaxed and indulgent child care. Toilet training varied depending on the time available and the attention given to it by the mother. The age of training varied from the first to the third year. People appeared to be child-oriented and considerate of children. The young child was usually in the company of its mother but was later left to its own devices in choosing playmates and outside activity. There appeared to be an air of confidence and understanding between children and parents. Rodnick (1955) has also reported Norwegian mothers as patient with young children and fathers as humane, kind, and indulgent. However, he did find that in Oslo neither working-class nor middle-class mothers took a relaxed attitude toward beginning the toilet training of their children. They began to train their children very early, sometimes at three months for working-class mothers and six months for middle-class. The goal was to complete training by the first birthday despite the fact that pediatricians were urging mothers to begin training much later.

Hendin (1964) found that Norwegian children were not expected to be as emotionally controlled, as well behaved, or as neat, clean, and well dressed as children in Sweden and Denmark. Norwegian mothers did not emphasize competition and success for their children. They were very involved emotionally with their children and were ambivalent about their becoming independent. At the same time, they allowed their children physical freedom (Hendin 1964; Block and Christiansen 1966).

Examples of child-parent relations such as the observations of researchers we have reported may account for the "notable ease, freedom, and relaxed independence shown by Norwegian children as they grow up" (Nordland et al. 1960).

Three pervasive traits in Norwegian culture are important in understanding the treatment that children received: a predominant and conspicuous masculine perspective on life, a strong but less conspicuous egalitarian ethos calling for equality of the sexes, and a high regard for individualism—individualism seen as personal independence in thought and action.

The masculine perspective that celebrates traits of courage, bravery, aggression, and vitality has prevailed in Norway from Viking times. Boys especially were encouraged to be active, brave, take initiative, and use good sense (Jonassen 1983). Norwegian boys learned early on that males were supposed to join and support other males in order to conquer the world. Intellectualism was also considered to be a masculine trait. Girls were encouraged to emulate boys in order to show that they were potentially able to do whatever boys could do. Still at mid-century equality had not been achieved; boys were twice as likely as girls to receive a high school diploma or more education (Svalastoga 1954).

We turn now to the perspective on children and childhood that was introduced by the Christian Church and that became infused into prevailing child-care practices (Ariès 1962). For Norway the Protestant (in this case Lutheran) Reformation coincided in time with the country's being declared a province of Denmark in 1536. Hence, the country came under foreign political domination and under a foreign religious movement, Lutheranism, sponsored and supported by the Dano-Norwegian monarchy.

The theorizing about children and child care that came with the Protestant Reformation in the sixteenth century was in the nature of a religious sociology of the child and the family. What was introduced was a hierarchy of God-ordained statuses for family members with father at the top and other family members subservient to him as God's representative. Husband and wife were expected to maintain an orderly household, to be models of self-control, to instruct and admonish their children, and to discipline them, using corporal punishment if necessary. Children, for their part, were expected to be respectful, subservient, and self-controlled, that is, obedient, industrious, responsible, and honest, and to experience guilt and shame if they did not live up to the high expectations of their God and their parents. There was nothing uniquely Lutheran about utilizing guilt and shame in the rearing of children. The early American cleric, Cotton Mather, in *Magnala Christi Americana,* wrote "Whatever you do, be sure to maintain shame in them; for if that be once gone, there is no hope that they'll ever come to good" (see Demos 1971:327).

Children were disciplined both before and after the formation of an absolute monarchy in Norway, but Christian V in 1687 was the first king to formulate laws specifically on child discipline (Sandvik 1979). According to the Norwegian Law of 1687, children could be punished, and punished severely but not so severely as to maim them; impudent children could be imprisoned for life at hard labor; children who struck their parents could receive the death penalty; disobedient children could lose their inheritance. What it meant was that parents who could not control their own children could, if they chose, appeal to the authority of the state. In order that parents and children might be kept reminded of the law, it was specified that pastors read aloud after the sermon this royal law on child discipline. That harsh law remained on the statute books until the 1800s and was utilized on occasion (Sandvik 1979).

The state also had something to say about the religious upbringing of children. Up until passage of a dissenter's law in 1842, it was next to illegal to cultivate any other religion in Norway than Evangelical Lutheranism. The law specified that a child should be baptized before the eighth day after birth. That prescription regarding baptism has never been formally annulled. Confirmation, which the godly King Christian VI instituted in 1736, was obligatory until 1912. Communion was a condition for marriage, and no one could go to Communion without having been confirmed.

In the early 1800s the influence of Rousseau inspired a number of books emphasizing guidance rather than discipline.

But the influence of Rousseau's ideas was short-lived, and books that came out later in the 1800s again emphasized the sinful nature of children and the need to bend their wills to the supreme authority of parents as God's representatives. Guilt, shame, and discipline, including punishment, were the means to that end. The goal was absolute obedience (Tønnessen 1982).

How effective the prescriptions and proscriptions of Lutheran practices were in competition with traditionally more relaxed child-rearing patterns of a peasant society is impossible to determine. Rodnick (1955) reports finding that in children under fourteen guilt had been securely implanted. Almost none said that they would always do the right thing if left alone. Most thought they were not kind, diligent, or disciplined enough and that they needed more discipline and guidance. The fear of not living up to parental expectations had a tendency to make children cautious in expressing themselves and reluctant to reveal their inner thoughts. Most mothers also felt that they perhaps were not as good parents as they ought to be (Rodnick 1955).

There is some evidence supporting the point of view that after many generations of stress on the religious ideal of the perfectly conforming child, the pendulum swung to the other extreme. There is no question but that child-rearing policy and practice have changed in this century from the traditional Lutheran ideal of complete child submission in a hierarchy of God-ordained statuses and rules to a perspective on childhood that recognizes the special needs of children and is aware of consequences that might follow if those needs are not met.

During the free education movement of the 1930s and 1940s, the chief, or even the only, goal in bringing up children was to make them free (Nordlund et al. 1960). But change was not immediate. In 1953 Waal found in a small, nonrandom sample of fifty-four children in Oslo that twelve reported having had a "free" upbringing and thirty-eight, having been brought up with the main emphasis on obedience. For the remaining fourteen there was no information. Some advocates of freedom saw early on the danger in complete freedom. In the 1930s Schjelderup (1937) made a distinction between healthy and unhealthy freedom. He argued that there are some things that children must learn: there are times when they must keep to a schedule, adjust to rules of cleanliness, and have consideration for others. The point for Schjelderup was how that should be done. Whereas the authoritarian posture was to force the child to behave through awakening feelings of guilt and shame, free education aimed at building up healthy habits from the beginning by an adult's being a good example to the child and by showing approval of every good tendency in the child.

The idea of free education caught on and among Norwegian writings in the 1940s and 1950s great stress was placed on helping children grow into healthy human beings. It became widespread throughout Scandinavia, at least by the 1950s, for parents to take as their principal child-rearing ideal the development of the physical and intellectual resourcefulness of the child (Svalastoga 1954).

Writing in the 1950s, Nordlund sensed a growing uncertainty among parents. First there were the Lutherans who claimed to know how children should be raised, now the free educationists. Parents became self-conscious about child rearing. Fathers and mothers were no longer sure that they knew what was the right way to treat their sons and daughters. Parental child care was becoming professionalized, but the divergent teachings of the various experts were confusing to parents who were familiar with the several points of view. The ideas of the professionals and others who gave the impression that they knew how children should be reared were available through many channels, not the least through books on child care. And they were being read. By 1950 one of the most popular of these, *Mor og Barn* (Mother and child) by Alfred Sundal (1950), was in its fourteenth edition. Sundal's advice was in opposition to the autocratic method of ordering, forbidding, and punishing. He recommended a more relaxed and sympathetic approach—let the child feel the security of affection; find outlets for the child's energy in things that will capture a child's interest; let a child discover or run its own projects, but be willing to help; teach by good example in a peaceful home; don't force a child, but enlist its interest as your coworker; show courtesy and respect as to an adult; and encourage contacts with other children to avoid shyness and to produce considerateness.

The child was less to be made to adjust to the adult world than child and parent were to adjust to each other. But that is not easy, and there has yet been no resolution of the problem for the conscientious parent. The discrepancy between what the child wants, what is good for the child, and what is necessary for the child is the reality that the modern parent must try to resolve. According to Haavind (1979), it is unthinkable not to satisfy the demands of the child, but it doesn't help to ask parents to satisfy those demands if they do not involve a wider social responsibility.

In studying urban families with small children, Haavind (1979) found that the "enlightened and idealistic" middle-class mother places great demands on herself. She sets aside considerations of her own activities and necessary duties in order to attend to what seems to be good for and likable to the child and what is necessary for the child to learn or to get used to. In other words, she is dominated by what is thought to be good for the child. Life in such families has taken on an almost therapeutic quality dominated by personal and emotional relationships. The objective of preparing children for the future as a part of child care has in a sense been shoved into the background. The focus is more on feelings than on duties in child-parent time together.

Andenæs (1984) asked a group of mothers what they did together with their five-year-olds. All appeared to have guilty consciences because they weren't doing as much as they thought they should. In fact, especially arranged activities were very uncommon, and mothers felt guilty about it. Especially among intellectuals, it is felt that children should be encouraged to be active and to participate in association with adults and to be free to interrupt them. That is less true among the working class.

Gullestad (1983) found mothers in working-class families following more traditional patterns. Children seldom play in the living room. When inside they play in the corridors, the kitchen, or in the children's room. Unlike children of the middle class and intellectuals, working-class children are encouraged to be passive in the house with adults and to be active, independent, self-governing, and inquisitive outside. Though the mother puts the child outside, she is still available, however. A balance between closeness and distance is established by the mother's being available but not taking much initiative toward the child (Gullestad 1984). Initiative is expected to come from the child's side. Motherhood means that mother is to be accessible at all times, expecting steady interruptions of her activity by her child (Andenæs 1984). There may be discrepancy between what is good for the child and what is necessary. Modern, approved child care calls for both care and control. It is difficult at times to distinguish what is mostly protective control and what is ruling control; the latter is anathema to most Norwegian parents.

In 1947 Norwegian parents were polled as to whether they had ever spanked their children. Those who had and those who had not were evenly divided. More mothers than fathers had spanked. Of those who had spanked, one-fourth considered it wrong. In a 1948 Gallup poll, 52 percent reported that they felt modern child upbringing lacked discipline. About the same time, Hambro (1951) asked between six and seven hundred adolescents in Oslo about their experience with corporal punishment; over half reported having been so punished. Most of them, and especially the girls, had been spanked before school age and not afterwards. Corporal punishment had been used more by the lower socioeconomic classes than by the higher socioeconomic groups. Discipline for the two sexes was more nearly alike in the upper classes.

In a later Gallup poll (1952), 41 percent of both men and women thought they had been brought up less strictly than their parents had been, and half of them thought that they brought up their children less strictly than they themselves had been brought up. That was especially true for younger parents, parents living in urban areas, and those with higher income.

A random sample of adults in Oslo reacting to a number of statements (Grønseth 1975) showed that the vast majority felt that child care was too indulgent, that children got their own way too much. Two-thirds agreed that it was more important to teach one's child order and cleanliness than it was to give them love; only 29 percent disagreed. On a question about whether children between the ages of ten and fifteen should be asked their opinion when important decisions were being made, a fourth of the respondents answered "now and then," "often," or "all the time," while 65 percent answered "seldom" or "never." When asked whether children should be free to criticize their fathers or mothers, 69 percent answered that they should not be free to criticize either parent.

The answers of children also reflect Norwegian ambivalence in child rearing between indulgence and discipline. In the study of adolescents in Oslo, Hambro (1951) found that fewer girls than boys felt they had received severe upbringing.

About one-third of both sexes felt that they had received a mild upbringing. When inhabitants of a small rural community in southeastern Norway were asked in 1963 to react to the statement, "Obedience and respect for authority are the most important verities children should learn," 83 percent agreed and only 2 percent disagreed. Reaction of University of Oslo students to the same statement was much more permissive: 31percent agree, 55 percent disagreed, and 14 percent were uncertain.

Reflecting on the ambivalence over the punishment of children, Gallup asked in a 1970 poll whether parents should continue to have the right to physically punish their children, either through spanking or slapping. Nearly three-fourths thought that parents should have that right; one-fourth thought they should not. In particular, persons with conservative Christian views thought parents should have that right (82 percent). Parents' right to use moderate physical punishment in disciplining their children had been publicly affirmed in a statute of 1891; it was repealed in 1972. Yet at regular intervals over the years thereafter there were adherents of conservative Christian morality who strongly advocated the use of spanking as a part of the legitimate regimen in the upbringing of children. Finally in 1986 an amendment was made to the law on children and parents (*Lov om barn og foreldre,* or *barnelova*) expressly forbidding violence against children. According to the law, a child must not be exposed to violence or be treated in any way so as to cause bodily injury or to expose a child to danger to its physical health (Andenæs and Haavind 1987). No specific punishment is connected to the law, but provisions in the criminal law dealing with assault and battery are to apply. Provisions of the new law are less intended to punish guilty parties than to be supportive of humane methods of child discipline. Sweden has a law similar to the one in Norway. It is widely believed that no such law would receive general approval in the United States.

And Norwegian children are aware of their rights under the law as indicated in the following account concerning a Norwegian second grader and his parents ("Editorial," in *Norway Times,* 4 October 1990, p. 2):

> Several years ago, when my son was attending second grade at his Norwegian school, he and I had a little quarrel, resulting in him being sent to his room to stay there for the rest of the evening with no supper before going to bed. After an hour or so, he returned to the living room, with a book in his hand, saying it was against the law to make children unhappy. And then he started reading aloud from his Norwegian schoolbook—some paragraph from *The Rights of the Child.*
>
> Of course his parents' hearts softened, and the act of sending the children to bed as punishment for bad behavior has never been reintroduced in our home.
>
> On the other hand, we of course had to make our children understand that parents also have rights—and duties, for example teaching children how to behave, teaching them the necessity to work hard to reach one's goals, etc.

Ten years after the repeal of the law permitting physical punishment of children, Gallup again polled Norwegians as to their views on corporal punishment, both slapping and spanking. At the later date, the majority of the respondents felt that it was acceptable to slap a child on the hand now and then if he did something wrong, but less than one-third thought it was acceptable to spank a child of five to six years of age, even if the child had done something "really" wrong. Two-thirds said it was never acceptable. In addition, they were asked whether they had ever slapped or spanked a child of theirs, a child in the three- to six-year-old age range. Forty-four percent said they had slapped on the hand, 1 percent said that they had spanked, and 25 percent said that they had done both. A fourth of all respondents had done neither, and of those adults under thirty years of age, 45 percent answered that they had done neither, indicating a marked decline in the use of corporal punishment. Gullestad (1984) found that physical punishment was used relatively little among working-class mothers in Bergen. It was most common to vigorously shake the arm of a disobedient child or to give the child an occasional spank on the bottom. Gulbrandsen and Miljeteig-Olssen (1979) found no systematic difference between Norwegian mothers and fathers in carrying out the control function.

It is probably impossible to determine with any accuracy what proportion of Norwegian children are subjected to authoritarian or permissive parenting. Jonassen (1983), an American sociologist, concludes that the available evidence suggests that the most pervasive influence in Norwegian families and schools in the past two centuries has been the traditional Lutheran conception of authority, order, discipline, and repression rather than liberalism and permissiveness and that it has been "tremendously effective." He asserts that, even today, from their earliest years children are imbued with a strong sense of responsibility to parents, family, community, and God.

Not all agree, however. According to Berggreen (1987), a Norwegian ethnologist, consciousness of the child per se, its needs and its best interest, is now the predominant concern of Norwegian parents. Parents with small children look to professionals for guidance. Few speak out against the experts, publicly at least. It is accepted that parents have much to learn and that there are those who have answers (Andenæs and Haavind 1987). Obedience is a word that has almost disappeared from the modern child-rearing vocabulary. Even *upbringing* is more and more set aside for the weaker term *socializing*. Parents are afraid to intrude for the purpose of directing a child. There is a presumption that children know better than parents what they need at every stage in life. Never before have Norwegian parents been more alarmed over the possibility that they might be controlling their children rather than allowing them free-dom of choice. Today's parents had their childhood and youth in the 1950s and 1960s, at the time when that perspective established itself. Generally speaking, it is only religious or otherwise strongly ideologically anchored Norwegian parents today who are willing to declare themselves in control over their children. According to Berggreen, what that means, in effect, is that children, in larger measure than ever before, have to guess at what their parents want or do not want for them, but they must be regulated by what their parents want all the same! It indicates a great deal of parental ambivalence over what parenting roles ought to be. Parents do not seem to recognize how decisive a role they play as sanctioning authorities in their children's personal development.

With all the variation in child-rearing patterns and prac-tices over Norway's long history, on balance it appears that the tendency in child discipline has been in the direction of what Norwegians today generally agree is in the right way, that is, in the direction of gentleness and understanding in dealing with young children (Tønnessen 1982). Norwegian mothers appear to outside observers to be very patient with young children. Few attempts are made to inhibit their behavior unless they annoy others, which does not appear to happen very often, at least among fellow Norwegians. Persons from other Western countries, England and the United States, for instance, often report that the relaxed Norwegian way of supervising pre-school and even older children takes some "getting used to."

The intimacy of a small family of parents and children has many things to commend it as a setting in which children can experience and enjoy life in an intimate and secure environ-ment. But this intimate unit, in large part closed to the view or surveillance of the public, holds potential dangers for small children as well, and in Norway as elsewhere. The close proximity of family members to one another, the extensive interaction, as well as the enormous disparity in power between parents and children (physically and psychologically) and the disparity in knowledge and experience, can constitute a threat to the child. Norway has belatedly come to a recognition of family violence and the child as victim of such violence. Authorities are now convinced that violence in the family is contributing to psychic and physical health problems for a large number of children.

It was not until in the 1980s that Norway had its first comprehensive survey of the incidence of child sex abuse (Ingnes 1984). According to results of the survey, every sixth child was exposed to some form of sexual abuse before the age of eighteen. But in the vast majority of cases sexual intercourse or attempted sexual intercourse was not involved; rather, the perpetrator exposed himself, cuddled or fondled the child, made sexual advances or sexual demands. Eighty percent of the victims were abused by men, 10 percent by women, and the remainder by both sexes, or the relationship between perpetrator and victim was not clear. The assailant was usually known to the child but in many cases was not a relative.

Norway is employing, or is considering employing, techniques for dealing with violence and sex abuse problems that have been used in other countries, for example, counseling rather than court action, joint custody rather than placing the child with the non-offending parent, preparatory courses for preschool and elementary school teachers, video films for use on TV and in school, and role playing to learn how to say no to sexual advances. In the spring of 1991, a National Center for the Prevention of Sexual Abuse of Children was opened in Oslo, the first of its kind in Europe (*Aftenposten*, 29 October 1990, p. 48). It will be financed during its first five years by the Save the Children (*Redd Barna*) organization. The goal is public funding thereafter. The Center disseminates information and provides educational materials, first to preschool and school teachers, health personnel, police, and others who work with children and youth. Research into causes, treatment, and prevention of sexual abuse is an important part of the Center's work.

The Child's Community Network

Only small children on very isolated farms do not have contact with persons other than members of their own family. In more heavily populated areas, there are five categories of persons, other than immediate family members, with whom a child interacts without going outside the neighborhood. A sociability network of relatives and others surrounds and interacts with the family on a more or less regular basis. Second, there are coequals or peers, a group made up of siblings, playmates, and schoolmates. Three other categories of persons become especially important in the lives of children as society becomes more complex and social roles are differentiated. First are mediapersons—those who are confronted through nursery rhymes, storybooks, and radio and TV programs. Second are child-care experts—physicians, teachers, social workers, and others who shape and dictate broader processes by which a society deals with its children. Third are public-place others, such as store clerks and customers, persons who deliver mail, and police. The two most important categories are family members and peers. They can be designated as orientationally significant, for they help to shape conceptions of self, provide vocabularies of motive, furnish symbolic environments, and promote a sense of solidarity with others (Denzin 1982).

Recently a small sample of eight-year-old children from three types of community settings in Norway were asked which persons they included in their active personal network (Gulbrandsen and Miljeteig-Olssen 1979). Ten children were from an island off the coast of Norway, ten were from a central area in Oslo, and ten from an Oslo suburb. Their mothers were also asked to indicate the persons they thought were part of their child's personal network. Children's networks included between fifteen and twenty-five persons, many more than the mothers had anticipated would be included. The networks varied with community type. In the rural, isolated setting, children's networks were characterized by the inclusion of persons over a large age span and of both sexes. Relatives constituted a large part of their networks, and contact with them was often on a daily basis. In Oslo there were not many relatives in children's networks, and the members were largely of a similar age and of the same sex as the respondent. Most of the children reported having contact with their playmate's parents as well as with some few other adults. As one would expect, children were most often together with those who lived nearby. That was true in all the community types. Eight of the ten fell in the category of short distances and frequent contacts (Tiller 1983). A large majority of the children said they preferred activity that presupposed several participants. But half of the children said they also liked to be alone, girls more often than boys.

The balance between interacting with family members and interacting with peers and child-care experts shifts markedly at age seven, the age at which Norwegian children begin elementary school. The switch begins earlier for those who are away from home in day care.

Even for children aged ten to eleven, parents are still a more important reference group than are the children's peers (Berggreen 1987), but parents notice a tendency for their ten- and eleven-year-olds to rebel against too much family togetherness and to want to be out of the home doing things with their friends. They may not want to go with the family to the cabin or on a weekend trip unless they can take a friend along. The home continues to be the child's primary social unit, however.

4

Children at Work

EVER SINCE VIKING TIMES, Norway has been an agricultural economy. And agricultural economies — based on the care and utilization of domesticated animals (cattle, sheep, horses, goats, chickens, and pigs), the harvesting of wild and domesticated grasses and cereal crops, and the gathering of fruits and nuts — lend themselves well to the utilization of children as part of the family work force. All family members engage in the enterprise of making a living, even children as young as five or six years of age.

Ariès (1962) asserts that children participated fully in the economic and social life of family and community in European countries until the late sixteenth and early seventeenth centuries when children, especially boys, began to go to school in large numbers. In Norway the change from children as workers to children as an especially protected and educated population did not take place in many peasants' and workers' families until around 1900.

Children were participants in or at least observers of almost every activity on the peasant holding. They were regarded as a resource because of both their present and future labor power. Work was not something that began at a certain age. Most farm children worked, but the hours and the type of work varied with the type of agriculture, the socioeconomic class of the family, and the means of production employed. Farming was combined with fishing in the coastal areas and with forestry in the inland. In this century a new combination has arisen for the farmers, namely, farming and wage labor.

A characteristic feature of Norwegian agriculture was the isolated farm or small hamlets of single farms (*grend*) as opposed to the European village organization (Thorsen 1986c). There were basically two types of farms, the minority of farms that were large enough or had sufficient resources so that children could stay at home and work alongside their parents, and the majority of farms so small or so poor that children were hired out as servants or laborers on larger and more prosperous farms. The hired labor class in early times in rural Norway was nothing else than other people's children who were in service during their childhood and youth. The proportion of cotter families, families that cultivated parts of farms or manors on revocable leases in return for labor, increased markedly in the 1700s and 1800s. It meant that the number of children who had to work away from home increased as well and included children as young as six or eight years of age.

There were also families less well off than the cotters, such as squatters on others' land who had no contractual rights and who depended on casual labor and rootless rural paupers and their families (Barton 1986).

Children from poor families commonly worked away from home for the entire year (Slettan 1984). The work that children did reflected the prevalent gender division of labor. The cowshed, the pigsty, and hen coop belonged to the female's sphere of work. Women's work was regarded as subordinate to men's work. As a rule, female members of the family did not do plowing or sowing, but they did other heavy work like picking stones from the fields and cutting cereal crops. In early peasant times, men never participated in indoor work either in the house or in the barns. The boundary line between the work spheres of the two sexes was less distinct where children were concerned, however. Small boys might assist their mothers in textile work, like carding, and might assist in cleaning and feeding in the cowshed, though children rarely helped in the milking, which was women's work. In households with only girls, a daughter might accompany her father in traditional male fieldwork (Thorsen 1986c).

Gender distinctions were apparent in the custom of apportioning food at mealtime to members of the family, based on how strenuous and how important the work of each was judged to be. The rule was that more food was given to the men and less to the women; some say women got half as much as men, some say two-thirds. Children received the smallest portion, and there was some difference between what boys and girls received. This custom of apportioning food was most characteristic of poor households, but it was not only there that the custom was practiced (Tønnessen 1982).

Herding was a major activity for Norwegian children, for Norwegian agriculture was also characterized by the utilization of vast mountain pasturelands for grazing purposes. Sometimes the mountain pasture was close to where the children lived, but there were remote parts of Norway wherein children from the poorest regions went on several days' migration every spring in order to get herding or other work for the summer. As young as age seven, children were known to be herding goats and cattle from April until the animals were brought back down from the mountain pastures in November.

Herding was lonely, demanding, and often frightening work for children. There was the danger that animals would run away and join other flocks, would be stolen, would get mired down in marshes, or would be attacked by wild animals. It was especially difficult to control goats. Inclement weather also stood central in the herder's thoughts as is reflected in songs that children composed and communicated to each other during the long days and nights in the mountains (Blom, Å. 1984). There were rain and storms to contend with, and it could get very cold for barefooted herders—especially in the early spring and in the fall. One girl recalls that the best she knew was to put her feet down where the critters had urinated and thereby get a little warmth in that manner (Slettan 1984). The warming effect was short-lived, of course, but urine was also recognized as having medicinal properties that could serve as a balm for sore and bruised hands and feet.

Sometimes children would try to influence the weather through magical songs. Children used songs to entice the animals to return to them when they strayed and to calm the animals. There are songs that show that there were good and happy days in the mountains, but the songs more often tell of bad days.

During long, lonely hours of herding, often away from family and friends, relations between herder and the domesticated animals sometimes became intimate in ways not approved of by society, and certainly not by the church. Observing the sexual behavior of the animals, and curiosity, hormonal urges, the lack of consolation and affection, and long periods of isolation from others provided the temptation as well as the solitude for sexual experimentation. But also when with other herding boys, playing and in high spirits, boys inspired and aided each other in such activity (Liliequist 1991). Simply stated, herding settings like those common for boys in isolated rural areas of Scandinavia created temptation and opportunity for bestiality for maturing boys. Alarmed by the number of reports of bestiality, the court in Sweden in 1686 ordered priests to instruct boys in Christianity, while at the same time proposing to the king a prohibition on the use of boys for herding cattle. This resulted in a royal ordinance to that effect, which was repeatedly read in public at meetings of county courts and in church. But the tradition of using young boys as herders was a deeply rooted rural practice.

Farmers who were wealthy enough to have dairy cows also pastured them in the mountains in summer. Normally, an adult woman, older girl, or sometimes the housewife was in charge of the dairy work while children did the herding. The alpine cottage (*setra*) was the center of this dairying activity. The milk had to be processed into butter or cheese, or if the distance was not great, the milk could be carried from the setra morning and evening. Herding was on the way out through the 1870s, although there were large geographic variations. Already in the beginning of the twentieth century mountain dairy farming was largely replaced by more efficient dairy farms. The refining of milk was taken over by dairies (Thorsen 1986c). Herding continued the longest in the north, being widespread even in the period between the two world wars.

The summer mountain milkmaid is not entirely a thing of the past, however. Grete Steiger, a farmer's wife, has gone to the mountains every summer as a milkmaid and has had responsibility for cows, goats, and sheep for forty-six years (*Aftenposten*, 31 August 1989). Nine cows and twenty goats have to be milked twice a day and one hundred sheep and lambs have to be cared for. The milk is now picked up by a dairy truck four times a week. There is no electricity at the mountain cabin; hence, the cans of milk are still kept cool in the old way, that is, by placing them in a brook. "This life is for me," Grete says. "Here at the setra I thrive the best."

For a peasant family with limited resources and many mouths to feed, hiring out the children to other families was profitable in several ways. While in the employ of another, they received their food, and sometimes children came home with good clothes and some money besides (Fløystad 1979). As one shepherd girl reported, the pay was food and some coins that would be kept until confirmation (Slettan 1984).

Children not only worked because it was necessary for them to do so. A "mentality of work" dominated peasant life. Work was seen as the paramount constituent of life; the essential human virtues were industry and enterprise. Work was the basic cultural category of peasant culture (Thorsen

1986c, 1987). Work was seen as good and proper, not only for adults but also for children, an important ingredient in their proper upbringing. The ideal of femininity for peasants was that of laborious girls and women of physical vigor and health. Interviews with peasant women reveal that many of them felt trapped between peasant society's expectations of them to be industrious workers and their own wish to be intimate, tender, care-giving mothers. The daily need for labor and the mentality of work were an efficient hindrance to the emergence on the farm of a bourgeois ideal of femininity involving refinement or fragility.

The experience of Johanne Hansdatter, daughter of a peasant renter, represents a common pattern for girls up until about a hundred years ago. Johanne was seven years old when she was first sent away from home as a herder. Later she was a herder in the summer and a child servant in the winter up until confirmation at age fourteen or fifteen, confirmation being not only a religious rite but a mark of the end of childhood. Thereafter Johanne was hired as an adult servant girl, which she was until she married at age twenty-three.

Nor did life become easier after marriage. It is widely agreed today, by both men and women, that peasant women had longer working days than did men. Since their role was seen as subordinate, their time was commonly characterized as being other people's time. Women and girls were expected to be on the alert at all times, to drop their own work and to take their place alongside husband or father at times and seasons when the man felt that their labor input was necessary for his part of the farming enterprise, such as during harvest season. It was not unusual to find that the periods of illness that struck down the young farm woman corresponded to a phase in the life course when the married woman had to care for the farm household, her small children, fieldwork, the cowshed, and to look after old people in need of nursing (Thorsen 1987). Even today in the Norwegian countryside girls are expected to be especially helpful to others. Many girls look after neighbors' children. Since girls are expected to be helpful, they cannot take for granted that they will be paid. They may get money or fruit for their service, but not always. Caring for others' children and visiting the old and the sick are all consistent with an "ideology of helpfulness," which continues to be a prevalent expectation for females in rural Norway (Gullestad 1988).

The fifty years from around 1860 up until the First World War are usually counted as a critical period that brought major changes in economic techniques and sociocultural character for Norway's agricultural population. The period has been given the designation *hamskiftet*, which literally means "changing of skin" or, figuratively, changing of colors or change of allegiance (Slettan 1984). Hence, it involves not only change in agricultural techniques but also the beginning of changes in values and in perspectives on life in general. It spelled the beginning of the end of peasantry in Norway. From an economic point of view, there are no more peasants in Norway today. When the term *peasant culture* or *peasant society* is used today, it only implies that agrarian culture still contains elements that have their origin in preprofessional agricultural society (Thorsen 1987).

The first major technological breakthrough was the widespread introduction of the use of horsepower in agriculture. After the horse was introduced into farming, it became the one animal that was under the care of males (Thorsen 1986c). There were also new investments in cattle breeding, the use of commercial fertilizers, and the introduction of grass seed. Cultivation of grass, timothy, and clover meant that mechanized haying operations replaced much of the handwork that previously characterized haying operations, handwork that had been fairly well adapted to child labor.

The investment in cattle breeding increased the opportunities for children to participate in the care and feeding of animals. Keeping the barn clean was made easier with the addition of a manure pit underneath the cattle barn.

Within the house there was a gradual increase in attention given to accumulating more furnishings and to household cleaning. With the sharp gender division of labor that prevailed, this meant increased work, especially for girls. Changes in household equipment, such as the addition of the cookstove and kitchen counters, made housework more convenient, but it didn't change children's household tasks very much. A change that meant the most for children was the installation of some method of getting a water supply directly into the house, thus eliminating a major child's activity, namely, carrying water from some distance.

On the whole, children's work on the farm didn't decrease essentially during the early modernization period, perhaps with the exception of work on the few really large farms where dependence on mechanized equipment was greatest. There were changes in the work life of children who had been hired out by their parents, however. The long periods of work away from home required by herding in the mountains were reduced and whole-year child service was on the way out. The introduction of compulsory elementary education was a major reason for the change. Work away from home was changed to shorter harvest season work and other work near home. But there is no clear evidence that children did less work than when they served as herders (Slettan 1984).

A second technological transformation in agriculture that affected gender division of labor on the farm and children's involvement in farm work came in the 1940s with the introduction of the tractor and tractor-drawn and -powered equipment. In many ways it was the major change, but there were also milking machines, drinking vessels in the barn for farm animals, hay slings, silos, and crop spraying. As long as the cutting of hay and cereal grains was done by hand, it remained women's and children's work. With the coming of mechanized cutting machines, it passed into the hands of men. The same was true of milking: the milking machine and the man both entered the cowshed in the 1940s and 1950s.

In many ways it was mechanization in agriculture and not new ideologies of femininity that gradually modified perspectives on females and on what the nature of their work should be, although the bourgeois idea of femininity—that the woman should exclusively manage the home and care for family members—was held up at the time as the ideal. For peasant women the ideal had no breakthrough (Thorsen 1986a, 1986b, 1986c, 1987). As late as the 1960s one could still distinguish separate work worlds for men and women on the farm, and women's and girls' work was still subordinate to men's and boys' work.

The 1950s have been characterized as the transition period before a serious decrease in children's work took place in rural Norway. In the 1960s the change began in earnest. Farming was on the way to becoming a profession among other professions. Mechanization brought larger farm units, technological complexity, and specialization, and farm work became more dangerous for children to participate in. Mechanization in the last twenty-five years has further eliminated some of the tasks formerly performed by children. Sorting, planting, and gathering machines for potatoes and other crops have taken over the manual work, machine sowing of seed and crop spraying have replaced weeding and thinning, and the combine has taken over most operations surrounding grain harvesting and processing. Norwegian agriculture today is characterized by high-technology farming, which is integrated into the market economy. The hired farm worker, adult or child, is almost nonexistent in Norwegian agriculture today (Thorsen 1986c).

House and barn work are least changed, however, and it is in those two areas that children can continue to participate.

Many women claimed that the milking machine was one of the few examples of husbands spending money on something that would reduce the burden of women's work but that it was done for economic reason rather than to reduce the work load for women! A household technological revolution did not take place in Norway until the 1960s.

Farm work at home has become a small part of each day for rural children. Paid work for persons other than one's parents, if there is any, is in the form of school vacation work. There are still farms on which the entire family might work together on tasks related to harvesting and potato picking, however, besides children's being expected to do a few household chores. Hollos (1974) found in the farming area of Flathill that children were not even required to help with household chores until they had completed their nine years of schooling; they were free to roam and spend their time doing whatever they pleased.

Regarding children's work in rural Norway, one can conclude that the goal of socializing children through participation in work was eminently served during the time that Norway was primarily a peasant society, for work, family life, and social life were all e-nmeshed in the daily experience of children. The commercialization and professionalization of agriculture, as it is practiced today, is accompanied by a weakening of the social fabric of farming for all family members. There is a sense in which farm children are being alienated from the rich experiences of farm and rural life. The extent of the alienation is reflected in the comment of one farmer who, in speaking about his own children, said that now when they are thirteen or fourteen years old he consciously takes them with him to the barn so they will learn about farm work. They must begin to accompany him if they are going to learn to handle a tractor and equipment (Slettan 1984). There is still a very small isolated population in modern Norway where the daily work and social life for all family members is intertwined (Thorsen 1986c; Gulbrandsen and Miljeteig-Olssen 1979).

Children at Work

In a sense, there are two ways of socializing children: either through integrating them into the economic and social life of adults, or through isolating them and protecting them from many aspects of adult life. Certainly the socializing of children in Norway in peasant society was of the first order. Only about 2 percent of the Norwegian population belonged to an ideological and social class where children were kept out of the work force and were treated more as children are today. The peasant class made up between 80 and 90 percent of the population.

It would be easy to falsely romanticize the best aspects of "the good old days" of peasant life, but the numerous hardships, the limited perspectives, and the limited opportunities of that life are not something that people want to return to. In modern times the Norwegian 4-H has been introduced by adults in order to familiarize rural youth with positive aspects of farming and rural life in the hope of stemming the tide of out-migration from rural areas—more about that when we discuss organizations for children in a later chapter.

Work in Industry

Work was central to children's upbringing, not only among the cotters and small farmers but also among people of limited means in the towns and cities. Going to school came in second place as a socializing factor for such families (Schrumpf 1988). There was a time during Norway's transition from a peasant-rural to an urban-industrial society when children worked as hired laborers in industry. The two oldest industries, lumbering and mining, were rural industries that got a foothold in Norway as early as the 1500s–1600s. Children worked in lumber mills, mines, and tobacco, match, and textile factories. They were called the "children's industries" (Fløystad 1979). Close to half of all workers in them were children. In glassworks, 20 percent of the workers were children. The tobacco, match, and glass industries employed most of the working children under twelve. Industries employing boys mainly or exclusively were lumbering, tobacco, steel, and mining, with some workers being employed at as young as eight or nine years. Most of the child workers in match factories were girls as were the child workers in textiles.

Although children as herders and children in other types of farm work sometimes had at least as hard lives as did children in industry, in practice industrial work was perhaps harder than other children's work because it was tied to steady work and an unreasonably long workday (Bull 1984). On the average, the workday was ten and one-half hours when children were not in school and five and one-half hours when they were in school. Night work was also common in lumbering and the glassworks.

Factory work could be very risky for children — unguarded machines and locations that were dangerous to health because of poisonous materials and nicotine. Children working in tobacco factories had brown fingers because of the tobacco juice, and they smelled so strongly of tobacco that teachers and other pupils complained (Fløystad 1979). Large industries often had their own schools so that work and school could be integrated. In the glassworks children went to school in the evening after having worked the whole day in the factory.

According to Fløystad (1979), in the 1870s one-fourth of all elementary school-age children in cities had paid work, and Bull (1984) concluded from his study of children in industry that regular and paid work before confirmation age was normal in the Norwegian working-class until the beginning of this century and probably a little longer. Yet factory statistics for 1875 list less than 2 percent between the ages of ten and fourteen as employed in industry. The figures may not be reliable, however, for the census was filled out by the employers themselves and not everyone complied. It is also possible that child labor reached its highest incidence before society began to keep a register. Also, in most cities child care by girls and the running of errands by boys, not factory work, were the predominant kinds of work for children. Running errands was especially prevalent before the introduction and widespread use of the telephone as a means of communication. Girls more often avoided paid work before confirmation than did boys, not because they did not work, but because much of their work was unpaid child care and housework.

The main reason parents permitted their children to work in factories, where the hours were long and the conditions of work often unhealthy and dangerous, was financial need. Parents felt that children's income was needed to maintain the household, and the dedication of parents to their children's education was less important than the family's economy (Hodne, B. 1984). Many children were well aware of their family's financial straits. They knew they belonged to the class that must toil, that working folk they were and working folk they would remain. "I wasn't old before I understood what poverty was," said one (Fløystad 1979). Said another, "The food situation was bad, so we had to leave early. I felt that I had to escape in order that I could get enough to eat." Many children felt shame over the obvious evidence of their poverty. "We who were poor received free books and got to eat our lunch at school. We were ridiculed by the other children because our clothes weren't suitable, they were a little too large, perhaps" (Hodne, B. 1984:57).

Children had mixed reactions to their work experiences; they weren't all negative. Many children thought it was totally in order that they begin work during childhood. Sometimes they found the work to be fun, and it made them feel that they were grown-up. "We felt we had become something then. We felt that it was when we began work that we were manly" (Bull 1984:80). Earning money also was a positive experience for them. And there were children who pressured their parents to allow them to take jobs, especially if their comrades were already working. Many quickly lost their enthusiasm for work, however.

On a few occasions child workers even organized and went on strike. On one such occasion twenty-five boys employed in a steel mill went on strike for better wages. Striking was a dangerous undertaking for them because many of their parents did not approve and pressured them to go back to work. But if they did go back to work, they were beaten by other children who were on strike. In the end they got an increase in wages from about twenty-five to thirty cents per week. It didn't always work so well, however. In a sawmill strike in the 1880s, boys demanded a raise from about seven and one-half to nine cents per day. But when the boys came home and told their parents that they were striking, they were chased back to work. The result was that their wages were cut from seven and one-half to six cents per day (Bull 1984).

There were communities wherein both parent and child, even in poor cotters' families, worked quite contentedly under the supervision of enlightened and sympathetic plant owners. Take, for instance, the case of Anders Isaksen (Schrumpf 1988). Anders was born in 1870 and was one of five children in a cotter's family in a commune where the dominant industry was the Ulefoss sawmill. Ander's father had a contract for a cotter's dwelling on a parcel of land located on the Ulefoss farm, which was also owned by the proprietor of the sawmill. The contract imposed a work duty on the family. Ander's mother and the children who were not at the sawmill were in charge of the farm work. Besides cultivating the small plot, a cotter might also have some animals—a hen, pig, or cow. Anders's father worked as a sawmill smith. Anders began working in the mill when he was ten years old, but he didn't work full time. Boys were a reserve labor force. In fact, the monthly listing from the mill shows that they might work for only one day or up to twenty-six days in the month. Besides, this was typically seasonal work for the boys. They worked in the hectic summer season but not in the winter months. Their work day was as long as that of adults, namely, twelve hours. They began at six in the morning and worked until six in the evening with three rest periods totaling two hours. Nor were the boys exempt from the night shift. One tells about a mother who accompanied one boy to work at midnight and accompanied her other son home again.

When Anders was twenty years old, he became a smith's helper and later he became a machinist. Anders is representative of many of the boys who lived in the sawmill area toward the end of the last century. Boys were recruited into the business at a young age, either through their fathers' help or that of another relative. The fathers of 72 percent of the boys worked in the sawmill as well in the period from 1840 to 1900. They began work when they were ten to thirteen years old, though it was possible to begin at eight or nine. Once they had begun, it was often the beginning of a lifelong work career, unlike herding that was a children's occupation practiced only until confirmation.

Lumbering never employed as many child laborers as did the tobacco and match-making industries. A boy who got to work in the Ulefoss sawmill was counted as lucky. There were more than economic reasons for this, for work in the mill gradually introduced the boys into an adult's work life, which was considered important and placed them in a stronger competitive position when regular work became available in the sawmill. Over half of the boys continued working in sawmills as adults. The working children were considered as privileged, not only because they had gotten admission into an area that was forbidden to other children but also because they experienced a part of the adult reality that was so closely connected to the social and economic life of a lumbering community. By working in the mill they came into a work fellowship quite unlike herding, which gave no comparable preparation for future employment.

Unlike herding, in sawmill society the relationship was close and tight and the families lived in a protected environment. More children worked as herders, however. Even so late as the census of January 1891, 31 percent of all children who had their own "occupation" were registered as herders over against 12 percent in factory work.

When action was finally taken to control child labor, it was not children, parents, or employers who led the fight, but school personnel (Bull 1984). Employers had come to rely on cheap child labor, and poor families welcomed the income children brought in.

It was a school commission in 1871 that gave support to the first studies of factory work, studies that in about twenty years led to the regulation of child labor. The action of the school officials was aided by a general philanthropic tendency sweeping the country at the time that aided in finally getting factory work laws passed. Parliament passed the first law on factory work for children in 1892.

The main provision of the first child labor law provided that factory work be forbidden for children under age fourteen. But the provision was soon modified so that children between the ages of twelve and fourteen could work up to six hours a day at "lighter work, which did not damage their health or hamper their physical development." A provision forbidding night work was also modified to allow exceptions. Nor was compliance with the law rigidly enforced. At first, only two factory inspectors were employed to supervise child labor law compliance in the whole country, and many of the industries employing the most children were located in less accessible parts of the country. In spite of these limitations, it appears that regular factory work for children under age fifteen was in large part done away with shortly after the turn of the century.

Children at Work

There were probably many reasons for effective change other than the passage of the work laws. We have already mentioned a philanthropic tendency in the land. School was taking more time; the number of children in workers' families was decreasing markedly; adults' real income was increasing, making reliance on their children's meager earnings less urgent; and leaders of the developing labor unions felt that child workers were a threat to the adult market (Bull 1984).

It was only regular industrial work that was affected by the first child labor laws. Girls' child care and cleaning along with boys' errand work and farm work continued. Nevertheless, as telephone lines interlaced the streets of cities in the 1900s, the flourishing vocation of errand boys in delivering telegrams and other messages largely disappeared in urban-industrial areas.

With the passage of a second child labor law in 1936, children under age fifteen were generally forbidden to work in large areas of the economy, but again with certain exceptions. Even children under twelve years of age were legally permitted to be errand boys, for instance (Fløystad 1979). The current law in Norway permits any child over thirteen years of age to engage in light work. Some younger children do hold jobs, but not legally. Today, 10 percent of eleven- to twelve-year-olds do work in ordinary business establishments or as babysitters. Of those twelve to fifteen years of age, every tenth one has part-time work and one out of five has occasional jobs. It means that fifty thousand to two hundred and fifty thousand children in that age group have paid work today (*Aftenposten*, 14 February 1987).

Many children help out at home. In one survey, Tiller (1983) found that eight of ten children reported that they helped. Slightly less than half of the children said that they received one or more forms of pay for the work they did. That was more often true for boys than for girls. It is difficult to separate what is pay from what is given to children as an allowance albeit with some understanding that the child is expected to help. Berggreen (1987) reports that today Norwegian children get on the average of one dollar and fifty cents to two dollars and fifty cents per week, which they are free to use as they like and which they spend on small objects—comic books and the like. Money that they get exclusively as wages, as well as sums of money received at Christmas, on birthdays, or on confirmation day, may be saved and used for larger purchases such as cassette players or bicycles.

Previous studies of household work in Norway have focused on the division of labor between husbands and wives with a view to determining whether or not husbands are taking on more of the household tasks now than they did earlier. They are. But in those studies children have been viewed only as part of the work load, particularly of the mother, and not as part of the labor force. They are part of the work load, but as recent studies have shown, they also contribute a not insignificant amount of work to the family enterprise and to others in the community.

In the most recent study of children's work at home and in the community (Solberg and Vestby 1987), children's work appears to be an important part of the division of labor in the home, and work plays an important part in the exchange of services in the community. In a way, Norway, like many other Western countries, is on the way back to a situation that was common among peasants and among city people of modest means in the 1800s. That is, both parents work at providing for the family; therefore, children must be brought up to be independent and to participate in the work of the household. One difference between now and the 1800s is that today males, both fathers and sons, are more consciously pressed into work that goes on in the home.

Solberg and Vestby gathered data from eight hundred pupils from ten to twelve years of age regarding their work activity. They were found to devote as much as nine hours a week to household duties. A large majority cleaned their own rooms, washed dishes, and set and cleared the table. Half of them made their own lunches and about a third cleaned and vacuumed rooms other than their own, prepared food, and baked one or more times a week. It is the more creative tasks, food preparation and baking, that Norwegian children prefer to do within the home rather than cleaning jobs (Berggreen 1987). Many children fetched the mail, carried out the garbage, and went to the store. They also spent as much as one and one-half hours a week on the average playing with, feeding, and caring for younger siblings. More than a third of them worked outside the house on such projects as shoveling snow or lawn work. Around 20 percent were with their parents on the parent's job once a week or oftener. Many of the latter were farm children, especially farm boys.

Tasks for others in the community added another significant block of time to children's work load. Work for others included housework, running errands, shoveling snow, walking dogs, feeding calves, and washing cars, with the most time being devoted to the care of children, which both boys and girls did, and visiting old and sick persons, which is more exclusively girls' work in Norway. Children also delivered papers, gathered and sold empty containers, and sold lottery tickets.

Gullestad (1988) has described the current role of the *passepike*, literally the "girl who looks after" or "the baby walker." The passepike, as Gullestad observed in Bergen, is a girl from nine to fifteen years of age, most typically eleven to twelve, who regularly, and for a fee, looks after and takes care of a small child up to three years old from approximately three to five o'clock in the afternoon. The girl volunteers to take care of the child, and for her to volunteer, it is important that the "kid is cute and easy to look after, the clothes and baby carriage are nice, the pay is good, and the mother is OK." It continues to be important to Norwegian parents that children are out in the fresh air every day, and this is a service that the passepike provides. It is important that the passepike like the child because she is expected not only to push it around in the baby carriage or stroller but also to play with it, something that mothers seldom do. A close and intimate relationship often develops among the passepike, the child, and the child's family.

When the numbers of children and adults who take part in different household tasks on a given day were compared, the percentages were similar.

	Children (%)	Adults (%)
Food preparation	71	63
Washing dishes	38	52
Vacuuming/cleaning house	49	51

(Solberg 1988)

However, adults spent about twice as much time on household tasks as did children. Both boys and girls took part in household tasks more often than did fathers, but less often than did mothers. If the family was larger than the average or if the mother worked full time, children performed more household tasks. Indoor work, in terms of time spent, continues to lie more in the female domain and for both women and girls. Girls on the average worked two and one-half hours more at household tasks than did boys. Whiting and Edwards (1988) found that girls were assigned more work for the family than were boys in eleven of thirteen communities around the world in which they studied the formation of social behavior of children ten years old and under. The two exceptions were in Kenya, where boys herd cattle, and in a community in the United States, where none of the children were expected to be particularly helpful. Solberg (1988) concluded that for Norway we

must abandon the notion of the father as the principal suppor-
ter of the mother when it comes to work in and around the
home.

Over the years the major goal has been to pass and enforce
legislation that would restrict the kinds of work and the hours
of work that children are permitted to engage in. Now the
pendulum appears to be swinging a little in Norway as closer
contact of children and youth with work life is being considered
important, if not essential, to their life and to their growth and
development. Participation in work, to a reasonable degree, is
seen as giving children valuable experience and challenges and
making them feel as if they are contributing members of
society. School, not work, stands central in Norwegian children's lives today, however.

The extent to which children's work experience in the past
was positive or negative is a moot question (Lerstang 1983;
Hundeide 1988a; Schrumpf 1988). The work was often hard
and tiring, and there were long workdays. No one would want
to return to a time of inhuman toil, drudgery, exploitation, or
tyranny in the work life. At the same time, it is clear to many in
Norway today that something important has been lost. When
children were a part of the family's productive work force and
contributed to the family's support through their work, children had an important position within the family and society.
They were useful and essential. They were a resource. The
child and adult worlds were not divided as they are today. Today
children in Norway are thought to experience the fact that they
are superfluous to the productive work force both in the family
and in society. Even though they carry out some work responsibilities, they are today first and foremost valued as a potential
adult work force, aside from the fact that they satisfy certain
emotional needs in the lives of their parents; they may be
economically worthless but emotionally priceless (Zelizer 1985).

The experience of helping others and serving the family may have intangible consequences that mitigate children's egoistic motives. There are Norwegian mothers who value having their three- and four-year-old children lend a hand with housework (Andenæs and Haavind 1987). Taking part is not seen as an obligation; it is the child's interest in helping that is valued.

5

Children in School

WHEN SCHOOLS ARE INTRODUCED into a country for the first time, they bring something very different and artificial into the lives of children. Before formal schooling was introduced in Norway, work, play, and associating with family members taught children what they needed to know to make their way in the nomadic, seafaring, and peasant life.

It is difficult to overemphasize the significance to children when schooling is made a part of their daily lives. Formal schooling ushers in a time when society determines that it is necessary to set children apart for a period of training and preparation. The school brings a new social structure, a new environment that children do not share with their parents. There were now school days and free days, lessons and recess, rules of order and rules of behavior. When school started, children could no longer run free; "our hearts were heavy in us that day," writes Hudson (1918:25), recalling his reaction when he learned that a teacher had been obtained. School brings the greatest restraint during the period when the call of nature, the instincts of play and adventure, are most urgent (Hudson 1918). Schooling more and more replaces socializing in the family setting as part of children's growing-up process (Schrumpf 1988).

Nor was the introduction of schooling in Norway a threat only to children; it was a threat to parents who felt they needed their children's involvement in the family's work life or the income that they could earn from work outside the home. There were also parents who feared that school would be a threat to their own authority and that children would acquire knowledge and values that were suspect.

In and with the school came the teacher, a new authority in children's daily lives, a new voice to listen to in matters of knowledge and in questions of right and wrong. The teacher knew more than parents, on some topics at least, and could teach competencies that the parents did not possess, such as the ability to read and write (Dokka 1979). School also broadened and solidified children's peer groups and children's own culture and authority. School introduced a formalized crossing field between family and peers as socializing agents. School also introduced children to a new and largely artificial way of noting status, namely, through age-graded classes and marks. The marks became a new, visible, and permanent way of recognizing differences between persons, based on their ability in school. A sense of failure in schoolwork threatened to undermine the self-esteem of many children. School changed the social behavior of children as well. Whiting and Edwards (1988) found in their study of children in thirteen communities around the world that in societies with schools where children spend extended periods of time segregated into age groups there is a high proportion of dominance struggles and competitiveness.

In sum, the introduction of formal education cannot be seen as anything other than a dramatic, revolutionary change in children's environment and in the psychological and social structuring of their lives. Its impact on childhood cannot be overemphasized.

Actually, the nations of the North entered late into the kind of culture that introduces formal education for children. Their populations were small in number and scattered, their resources limited, living as they did along the margin of habitable regions. Despite those limitations, some contact with the culture of southern Europe occurred early. As early as the late

Stone Age, in the second millennium B.C., there is evidence of influences from the Mediterranean region. The influences were limited to a small upper class in Norway; they remained decidedly foreign in character, and they did not greatly affect later cultural developments in Norway. Nordic tribes instead developed their own culture, a culture not based upon extensive written literature or formal education. Children learned by observing, imitating, listening, and participating in the daily life experiences of the family.

The great period of expansion of the Nordic tribes occurred in A.D. 800 to 1050 (Skard 1980). In a series of expeditions, made possible by superior naval techniques, the Vikings explored widely, raided, plundered, and eventually established permanent settlements all around the North Sea. Those forays into other lands brought the Vikings into contact with medieval Western civilization, life-styles, and the Christian religion. The Viking exploits were the beginning of continuous and intimate contact between Norway and the outside world. Quite a few sons of the subsequent small, ruling, aristocratic class studied abroad. As a case in point, as early as about A.D. 930 Harald the Fairhaired (Harald Hårfager) sent his son to England to be educated.

The first formal schooling in Norway came with the introduction of the values, belief systems, and social structures characteristic of the Christian culture of the South, a culture that gradually replaced Viking culture and institutions. Sporadic attempts at Christianizing Norway were made earlier, but Christianity was not systematically promoted until the eleventh century when the most tangible institutional innovations were made (Flint 1960). The consolidation of the new culture in Norway took place during what is referred to as the High Middle Ages from the eleventh to the fourteenth century.

It is especially appropriate to mention Norway's religio-cultural history when introducing the subject of children's formal education, for from the beginning in the eleventh century until the present time religion has played a significant role in the education of children in Norway, even in education received in compulsory, public schools.

The first organized schools in Norway were not in any sense public, compulsory schools. That was to come later. They were private schools organized and operated by the Roman Catholic Church, and they were not elementary schools but schools of higher learning (Skard 1980). At that time in Norway, as well as elsewhere in Western Europe, the educated leaders, both in church and state, were well acquainted with Catholic thought with its solid foundation in classical ideas and classical education. As Castberg (1954) expressed it, it was remarkable to read accounts of the life of Norwegian people in the Middle Ages and to see how much the Christianity of Roman Catholicism at that time set its mark on people's daily lives and their entire attitude to life. For the Norwegian essayist and novelist Sigrid Undset (1968), the most significant part of Norway's medieval history was not the Viking pagan period but the Catholic Middle Ages when, she asserts, Norway acquired a Christian civilization that was rapidly assimilated throughout Norway. That is not the conclusion that all scholars reach, however. A traditionally more accepted conclusion has been that the impulses from Christianity, and especially Catholicism, did not go deep in the culture or in the lives of Norwegian people. Winsnes (1953) attributes the latter conclusion in part to Protestant prejudice and ignorance of the culture, doctrines, and essential nature of Catholicism. There is also a romantic tendency that regards the pagan period—and not least the Viking Age—as the time that made the greatest impact on Norwegian personality and saw the most marvelous flowering of the "heroic spirit of the north." It is a moot question.

When Christianity came to Norway, priests became teachers. The priests, in turn, urged parents to learn the credo and

Lord's Prayer and to thereby help in the religious instruction of their own children. A church law worked out by Archbishop Rande in 1272–1277 made it obligatory for anyone who had been sponsor at a baptism to teach the child, or to have it taught, the credo, the Lord's Prayer, and the Ave Maria. Every child seven years of age or older was to know these; if anyone of normal mental ability was found at age fifteen who did not know them, that child was to be levied a substantial fine.

Monasteries were established centers of education by 1130, and the chief step taken toward a hierarchic organization of the church in Norway came when Norway was recognized as a separate province in ecclesiastical affairs with the establishment of the Archdiocese of Nidaros located at Trondheim. It was there that the first of the Catholic schools of higher learning, Schola Nidrosiensis, was in operation at least from the year 1031. Cathedral schools were subsequently organized in several of the larger cities. The cathedral schools mediated the international culture of knowledge, language, and faith. During the twelfth and thirteenth centuries the religious element increasingly made itself felt not only in the spheres of language, literature, morals, and religion but also in the everyday questions of social and political life.

The cathedral schools, also referred to as scholarly or Latin schools, were small in both staff and enrollment and primarily prepared boys only for clerical careers. Most of the Norwegian parish priests received their training in such schools, supplemented by individual study in the libraries connected to the cathedrals. During the Middle Ages these schools provided the highest education that could be gotten in Norway. Those who wished to receive university education had to go abroad, to Paris or later to Copenhagen.

Boys were not accepted into the cathedral or Latin schools until they were ten years old, and before that they had to have come a good way both in reading and arithmetic. To do so, sons—primarily the sons of wealthier families—went to a private elementary school, got their preparatory education at home from a house teacher or governess, or went abroad for an education.

The main stress in the cathedral schools was laid on the study of Latin; Greek was also read, and Hebrew, logic, metaphysics, and rhetoric were studied in the highest class. Much time was devoted to devotional exercises and singing. Such subjects as history and mathematics were neglected. Because of the classical education that the candidates for the ministry and the sons of the aristocracy received, the use of Latin became a matter of course in certain areas of life—in international correspondence, treaties, negotiations of courts and clergy, state documents, as well as at many solemn or special occasions. The last academic commencement speech given in Latin was made in 1845 (Skard 1980).

There were no textbooks in the mother tongue until 1668, though literature in Norse was available. The first historical account written in Norse on Norwegian soil and probably by a Norwegian dates from around 1190. The discipline in the cathedral schools was severe, corporal punishment was inflicted, and fines were imposed for various offenses. Hence, the boys, the few who were in school, under stern discipline "devoted their best energy to the study of a civilization long passed away, and its dead languages, while hardly any attention was paid the past and the present, including the language, of the country in which they were to live their own lives" (Skard 1980:57). There was no age-grading as such and no courses or activities designed to appeal to the normal interests and needs of the boys themselves.

But in the long haul, classical erudition was not destined to play the same part in Norway as it did in nations closer to Mediterranean civilization. The classical tradition was not deeply assimilated. Since the bulk of the population did not receive any formal education, education in Norway during the Middle Ages was sparse at best except for the education of priests and nobility and a small population of leaders in business and government.

In the sixteenth century what some regard as the great age of classical medieval Norway came to an abrupt end. In the words of Winsnes (1953:108), "The Norwegian empire fell in ruins; the Lutheran Church came to replace the Catholic; darkness sank once more over the land." Skard (1980) concurs in believing that this was the nadir in Norwegian cultural history. Norway had come under foreign domination, Danish, and was to remain so for four hundred years. The Protestant Reformation, like Catholicism before it, brought a religious perspective and a cultural emphasis that was foreign to Norway. Resistance to the earlier introduction of Catholicism had been more notable and long lasting, yet state power was also necessary to carry through the Protestant Reformation in Norway. In 1536 Reformation dogma was adopted by the Dano-Norwegian monarchy as the official religion of Norway. It was reaffirmed at the Constitutional Convention in 1814 that Evangelical Lutheranism was to be the official religion of the country.

Catholic archbishops were driven out at the time of the Protestant Reformation, cloisters and cathedrals were robbed of precious artifacts, and many of the cathedral schools were closed, the only schools in Norway equipped to prepare students to pursue studies at the universities. Nor was anything done to maintain the cathedral chapters that had supported a number of students studying abroad. The thirty cloisters were dissolved, valuable books and letters were burned, and other valuables were wantonly destroyed, though no benefit could be derived by doing so. Hence, the Protestant Reformation as it first manifested itself in Norway was not a people's movement bringing new intellectual awakening or spiritual regeneration to the people but appeared as a destroyer of classical culture and education.

Catholic bishops were replaced with superintendents or Lutheran bishops who were to supervise the reforming of the church's doctrine. Catholic priests were often allowed to continue in their now Lutheran parishes, however, and new Lutheran ministers sent from Denmark were added. These pastors were often ill-treated and some were killed; "the inhabitants of the country were so displeased that they were filled with spite and hatred toward the Protestant clergymen and the whole ministry" (Gjerset 1915, 2:137). The church was reduced to the status of an administrative unit within the Dano-Norwegian monarchial state.

While those in political authority were devoting attention to securing their authority over the church and to the pecuniary benefits to be derived from the overthrow of the Catholic Church, little progress was being made by the reform movement. The new Lutheran bishops were unable to reach the masses of the people; in fact, most of the natives were scarcely aware that any significant changes had been made. People finally yielded more or less willing consent to the changes.

It may appear quite miraculous that against great odds of indifference and even hostility Lutheran thought on education would gradually become established in Norway, again not without state support, however. For Martin Luther the family was the highest form of earthly society. The family was the real school of character, not the cathedral schools or the monastery. From the time of the Reformation and for several centuries thereafter, there was a marked power shift from the church to the father in the family who was given freedom to be "lord and master in his own house" (Tønnessen 1982). Luther envisioned the father in the family as a priest in his own right, responsible for family worship and for the religious education of the young. He took great pains in writing the *Small Catechism* (1529), which he wrote for children and which he regarded as one of his most important works.

But Luther also thought that the ability to read was essential for a religiously informed public. Hence, beginning in the sixteenth century, strong emphasis was placed on literacy. The purpose was to educate children in the faith, but not exclusively for that purpose. As early as in 1524 Luther had published an open letter to the mayors and aldermen of all the cities in Germany in behalf of Christian schools. He did so not only because he thought people needed schools and the languages for the sake of Christianizing the people but also because society needed accomplished and well-trained men and women in order to maintain civil order and the proper regulation of the household.

The Reformation is said to have established the principle of universal education. In a sense that is true, for the preamble to the church ordinance of 1539 states that "the children must everywhere be so instructed, that the children of the peasants, as well as others, must obtain knowledge of that which not alone the peasants, but even the nobles and kings have hitherto not known" (*Danske Kirkeordiants* 1537). It was an exalted, visionary goal: it was very long in being realized. Actually the quality of instruction became worse for a time as Catholic priests and clerks were replaced by Lutherans who were not always as well educated as were priests from the old cathedral schools. However, with the immediate need to educate a clergy in the new creed, some Danish Latin schools were introduced into Norway (Skard 1980).

In 1552, Christian III decreed that a deacon should be appointed in each parish. The deacon should instruct the children in Lutheran doctrine, the pastor being responsible for instructing the adults. Bishop Palladius wrote in his *Visitats-bog*, "When he has rung the church bell for the first time on Sunday, then he shall strike the bell 15 or 16 times as a signal to the children. The young people shall come to church and seat themselves on the first benches, and the sextant [deacon] shall stand in the midst of them, and instruct them with pleasure and kindness according to the sextant's book published in Copenhagen, and he shall also teach them religious songs. He shall encourage the parents to send their children to the sextant, but if they will not come, they shall then be forced with the whip to do so." As an aid in the instruction of children in Christian doctrine, Bishop Palladius published a Norwegian translation of Luther's catechism in 1538, supplementing it with a second book.

Those first parish schools could probably be said to provide the first, but only the first, germ of a Norwegian public school system. The Reformation had established the principle of universal education, but it brought no marked improvement in general education because what was taught was only Christian doctrine through the medium of Luther's *Small Catechism* and the Bible.

Provision for a school tax was ratified by royal decree in 1578. But the peasants were often unwilling and perhaps even unable to pay the school tax, and it could not always be collected.

Though the condition of formal schooling was deplorable throughout the entire country during the first century of the Reformation, there was a growing demand for popular education in the seventeenth century as the few men of learning attempted to improve the religious and intellectual life of the people. Also, the rising reaction to orthodoxy and authoritarianism throughout Europe was having its effect on an intellectual level; the restiveness of the educated classes was stimulated by the free thought of the Enlightenment. It was supported by the growing bourgeois class that had its own agenda and was destined to put its mark on developments in Norway, first and foremost in urbanized and industrial areas.

To make a first, very small step to improve instruction, it was found necessary to increase the time spent in school from only on Sunday to Sunday plus one day. Thus in 1629 the clergy were instructed to see that the children of the parish were called together for an additional day. Coverage was still inadequate, for smaller churches hardly ever had their own deacon or clerk, and the teaching function was neglected. In sparsely settled areas the pastor might come only three or four times a year. He usually remained several days while he preached, taught, performed official duties and, if possible, secured some local man to read and teach the rudiments of religion to the young (Jensen 1928).

There was somewhat more to offer in the way of both schools and curricula in the cities, and school was in session more of the time. The Latin schools had the afternoons off on Wednesdays and Saturdays, and on those afternoons the teachers, who were also clerks for the churches, taught children who were not enrolled in the Latin schools. But the method of instruction showed no great improvement. It was extremely mechanical with almost endless repetition of letters and words and questions and answers.

Centralized control of the school and the curriculum was slow in coming to Norway. Elementary education had been looked on as a private matter with parents responsible for providing their children with the minimum education required. Only in cases where parents failed through lack of means, will, or ability were authorities required to intervene. From a legislative point of view, the state considered that it had a duty to teach, complemented by compulsory attendance, only where private responsibility failed. Private responsibility had accommodated itself nicely to a system with very sharp class distinctions, with parents in each social class supposedly seeing to the education of their children so that proper concern was given to the education of the citizens of each of the classes, according to the specific needs of the class (Dahl 1985). What that meant in effect was that a child whose parents were poor peasant or working class could expect to receive only minimal and mostly religious education.

In 1736, during the reign of the pietistic King Christian VI, when confirmation was made compulsory, a new situation for education was created in that no one was to be confirmed until he or she had been to school. But how could this requirement be universally met unless schools were available in all parts of the country? Opening schools was the answer.

Everywhere in Europe in the eighteenth and nineteenth centuries mass schooling became the common means of socializing children with Norway and Denmark leading the way in Scandinavia. Conservative elements in society were not convinced that the peasants needed formal education. August von Hartmansdorff led the conservative forces in the Swedish Riksdag, raising the question, "If peasant children are supposed to be in school . . . when will they learn to be peasants?" (as reported in Boli 1989:226).

By the famous Proviso of 1739 the Norwegian government established a system of rural public schools and attempted to enforce the compulsory attendance of all children. Recognizing the Proviso as the beginning of universal, compulsory education in Norway, the basic school (*grunnskolen*) celebrated its 250th anniversary in 1989. According to the Proviso, instruction was to be given six to seven hours daily, at least during three months of each year. The schoolbooks were to be Luther's Catechism, Pontoppidan's Explanation, the Bible, and the hymnbook. But more than that, reading, writing, and arithmetic were also to be emphasized. Teachers were to be appointed, and their authority over their pupils was legitimated by a provision borrowed from the Latin school, a provision justifying the use of the stick—a rattan cane (*span-*

skrøret) used on the fingers of pupils—to enforce discipline. According to Ariès (1962), by the sixteenth century corporal punishment had become the scholastic punishment par excellence in Europe.

Communities were encouraged to build schoolhouses. If no schoolhouse was provided or could be provided because of the state of the local economy, school was to be kept in private homes by itinerant teachers, the so-called ambulatory school (*omgangsskolen*). It was really the teacher who was ambulatory, of course. School was set up in the homes large enough to accommodate the teacher and pupils. The teacher, always a man as were nearly all teachers until the late 1800s, carried his teaching materials in a satchel and might stay at each farm long enough so that his board and lunch for the children equaled the amount of the school tax for that farm. School was held in the dayroom of the house along with many other activities that went on there. There could be small children on the floor playing, screaming, or crying. The baby in the family would be in a crib or cradle. The woman of the house would be cooking food, carding wool, or weaving; in the coldest weather men would also be inside performing various farm tasks that could be brought indoors. Mixed in with all the people there might be pigs routing about in the schoolroom as well. The rattan cane or birch whip helped the teacher keep discipline around the long table while all of that was going on.

School could begin as early as 9:00 A.M. with an hour off at noon and continue until four. During the noon break, besides eating a meal, the children played ball, threw snowballs, and skied or slid on the slopes (Jordheim 1984). Such schools imparted only a bare minimum of literacy and religious instruction. Bishops and pastors could bring pressure to bear on parents to send their children to school, if they chose to, since they could refuse to confirm a child who did not possess the required skills and knowledge.

Again this school was something imposed on the peasants from above; many of the peasants themselves were not convinced of the value of educational requirements and offered such resistance that the government had to substitute a new watered-down ordinance in 1741 making it optional for the parish to provide instruction for children.

Over the whole land among the peasantry the prevailing school pattern was that of the ambulatory school. The teachers in the ambulatory schools came mainly from the peasant or artisan class. Very often they combined school teaching with another occupation. What little preparation they had for teaching was ordinarily given them by the pastor or the clerk. Sometimes the teacher was merely examined in the catechism and the singing of hymns. If the teachers could write and do some arithmetic, they were above average in their preparation (Jensen 1928). Such a system of peasant ambulatory schools was common in a large part of the country until the last half of the 1800s (Dokka 1979).

It was common for children to begin ambulatory school at age seven or eight, depending on the distance a child would have to journey and the availability of such a school in one's area. According to the Proviso of 1739, children were required to attend at least until they were ten to twelve years old if they had learned to read well enough by that time, or until they knew enough religion to be accepted for confirmation. The church was still supreme in the appointment of teachers, the enforcement of school laws, the supervision of instruction, and the judgment of the quality of the results of the teaching effort.

Generally speaking, school was not held at times of the year when both adults and children had their hands full with essential activities such as planting, harvesting, herding, and fishing. A school might run for twenty weeks, but a school year of eight weeks was more common. Because of absences, the average amount of school time for an individual child was much shorter than that. The school term was always placed in the winter months. Absence wasn't only due to distance and weather; many neglected to come because they didn't have proper clothing and shoes for going a distance in winter, because of other duties that forced them to forego an education, or because parents saw little use in formal education.

It was common for both rural and city schools to have high absence in all years up to the end of the 1800s. In fact, absence from school tells much about the commitment to compulsory attendance. It was the school's largest problem. Authorities tried to impress the importance of attending; assessment of fines was legislated, but school authorities tried to avoid assessing fines because the poor were not able to pay, and fines were no threat to those with adequate means. In some rural communities, poor children had the best record of attendance of any because they got food and sometimes lodging in the home where the ambulatory school was in session (Jordheim 1984). Absence was highest in the lower grades and among girls. Work that girls commonly engaged in knew no season; for them there was no slack period in the winter. For boys absence was more often tied to crop and seasonal work.

Norwegian government reports on education issued in 1840 summarize conditions in rural Norway in the first hundred years after the adoption of the Proviso of 1739. There were some two hundred schools in the country districts enrolling 15,500 pupils. The bulk of the rest of the school-age population, about 160,000 pupils, received their instruction in ambulatory schools. According to government estimates, only about 35,000 pupils were taught how to write. There were more than 8,000 rural children who received no formal schooling at all, mostly because of poverty and sickness.

In the towns and cities the situation was different. There the common public school was characterized as a school primarily for the lower class and was under poor-relief administration. The common school was chiefly for training children of the lower classes in the knowledge, arts, and skills necessary for life in the social and religious group to which they belonged. Liberal learning was an elitist concept that applied only to the upper classes and for which they were willing to pay. The common or poor school had as a rule only one teacher for all the children in the district no matter how many there were. If there were many pupils, they were divided into two or three classes; but since there was only one teacher, the pupils in larger schools only had two or three days of school per week. The school term was somewhat longer than in the rural schools because the school year was less affected by seasonal work. Absences were also somewhat less frequent.

The schools for the poor in the cities were intended first and foremost to teach reading and religion. Pontoppidan's Explanation was the main book. Equipment was better than it was in the country in that there were more sitting places in the schoolrooms where children could learn to write and count. And in some schools the older children got to read books with not only religious content but also history and geography (Dokka 1979). Of the 12,000 pupils attending, an estimated 8,500 learned to write. For whatever reasons, around 3,600 town children did not go to any school. Only about 12 percent of Norway's population was urbanized at that time.

Urban parents with ability to pay did not enroll their children in the so-called poor schools but found alternate ways to educate their children. One possibility was a private school that went a little beyond the education required in the poor school, and in 1837 over 4,000 children were receiving private tutoring. It might also be possible to find a middle-class school (*Middelstandsskolen*), which was placed at a somewhat higher level but which also cost more. Here middle-class boys could receive an education in history, geography, and living foreign languages.

In a special place were the few remaining Latin schools. Latin schools were demanding: teachers were free to keep pupils under discipline by almost any means. There were limitations on how severe the corporal punishment could be, however.

In earlier times Latin schools had been open to some able-bodied boys from poor homes, but from the middle of the 1700s they became more and more schools only for the sons of government officials, civil servants, or others from the same social class. By the 1750s there were only four of them left in Norway (Barton 1986).

It could still be said at the middle of the nineteenth century that the rural schools were chiefly religious, that children learned in a mechanical way, and that the material taught was generally not suited to children. In farm society, work continued to be the main content in socialization; education and the school did not play a special role before the end of the 1800s. With an average of only eight to twelve weeks yearly of school attendance, children were able to take part in almost all the work that adults engaged in (Blom, I. 1984). Children's life in 1850–1900 was still a life of labor and integration into the adult occupational and social world. Only a small proportion of the population could afford to give its children the carefree leisure that we have come to associate with childhood.

As farming and schooling did not always accommodate easily, neither did factory work and school. One former child factory worker recalls the situation in a sawmill as follows: "We had school every day. We began in the saw mill at six in the morning and went to school at nine, and back again to work in the afternoon" (Bull 1984:77). Teachers complained that paid work took precedence over education, children did not get their lessons read, were tired in school, or were absent in order to work.

Even with the Proviso of 1739, the affairs of the school, especially the country school, remained in a rather chaotic condition because no national authority was in charge of standards, school term, or curriculum. Local option had left all to the discretion of the district school board and the parish pastor. Jensen (1928) refers to that period of nearly one hundred years of relative chaos as "The Great Interregnum." It was a period during which the recalcitrance of the peasants was pitted against both the clergy and the school. The fact that many of the clergy in positions of authority were Danish did not help matters. Their presence was often a point of contention.

Various religious and intellectual movements affected the thinking of churchmen and educators during the Interregnum. All over Europe there was a rising reaction to dominance of orthodoxy and authoritarianism, supported by the swiftly growing bourgeois class. In Norway the various movements can be roughly divided into a period of pietism from 1730 to 1770, a period of rationalism from 1770 to 1814, and a period of struggle between the ideals of philanthropists and a new pietism that made strong emotional demands and arose in Norway from 1814 to 1827. In Norway, after a brief period of Enlightenment intellectual radicalism, an impressive lay Lutheran pietistic revival movement emerged. It was a movement not imposed from the outside (as was Catholicism and State-Church Lutheranism) but led by one of their own, the peasant farmer's son and religious layman Hans Nielsen Hauge. It was the first popular social movement of national proportions in Norwegian history. The effects of the movement had social, political, and religious ramifications that caused alarm in the aristocratic and bourgeois classes and among clergy in the State Church. Haugeanism remained a strong spiritual tradition among much of the peasantry throughout the nineteenth century, and its influence still lives on today, not least in the

Christian People's Party (*Kristelig Folkeparti*), one of the major political parties in Norway. That the movement kept alive and further strengthened the resolve to teach Christianity in the elementary schools is without question. But since the schools were locally rather than nationally administered, the struggle between competing ideals and the strength of the various religious and intellectual movements showed variation in their effect upon the different rural and urban schools.

Some liberalization as well as some uniformity was brought into rural education in 1827 with a new law containing the modest requirement that writing and arithmetic, as well as Bible history, be made permanent subjects in every school. The law left the school under the control of secular and church officials but with one important proviso—it was now under the supervision of a national authority.

In 1848 more uniformity was brought into the educational system in the towns. From this date on the common school was not to be only for the poor, but every town was to have one common school (*allmueskolen*) for all children rich and poor, and schooling was required of all urban children between the ages of seven and confirmation.

One year after the unified common school for all urban children was prescribed in 1848, a school only for girls was opened in Kristiania (Oslo). The school and others like it that followed were based on Rousseau's assertions about the nature of children. Rousseau, as well as early Norwegian educators, had a quite different view of how girls and boys should be educated. Girls were to be brought up to be wives and mothers. It was a mother's duty to take care of children and bring them up, boys until they went to school and girls until they were married. In wealthy and cultured urban families, more affected by the Enlightenment than by Haugean pietism, it was believed that a good housewife should master more than just practical home and child care, however. Girls ought to learn foreign languages, especially German and French, a little history, a little geography, as well as a little Bible history. They should learn to read and write and do some arithmetic. But too much schooling could endanger their health; giving grades in school could encourage a boy to do better work, but it could make a girl vain (Blom, I. 1984). Girls were to possess womanly virtues such as obedience, industry, and courtesy, whereas boys were expected to show the trait of independence—and a certain amount of tomfoolery could be expected from them (Tønnessen 1982).

Educators warned against the dangers of theoretical education for girls. A school in Bergen, a whole-day school for both boys and girls, is a good example of this. Girls used the forenoon for handwork and the afternoon for reading, arithmetic, and writing. Boys used the whole day for theoretical subjects.

Major school reforms beginning in the latter half of the nineteenth century reflected a change in society. Instruction on the farm and within the family circle had sufficed for a simpler economic and communal life. In a life beginning to be industrialized and professionalized even on the farm, a new kind of education was necessary. Thus, the elementary school was basically changed from an institution organized for Christian indoctrination into a school of general preparation for civic life (Skard 1980). Material to be studied was extended into new subject areas. Books on religion had to take their place alongside readings from fiction, history, geography, and natural science. "The social-class school was on the way to democratization, the parent school was moving toward governmentalization, and the religious school towards secularization" (Dahl 1985:118).

The united school for all children was divided into a lower division (*folkeskolen*) and an upper division (*realskolen*). It was a seven-year school, and its conclusion was completely divorced from its relation to confirmation. Instruction was to be both comprehensive and practical. Writing and arithmetic got larger places in the curriculum, and pupils had their own textbooks in subjects such as history, geography, and natural science. The amount of time allotted for the required subjects in the seven years of school was: Norwegian, 70 hours; arithmetic, 42 hours; religion, 30 hours; observation and home geography (during the first three years), 18 hours; writing, 15 hours; nature study, 10 hours; singing, 9 hours; history, 8 hours; geography, 8 hours; drawing, 8 hours; manual art, 8 hours; physical culture, 8 hours. The course called Observation and Home Geography (*Heimbygdskunskap*) was especially impressive because of its sensitivity to the nature of the world and experiences of young children. This practical course involved a great deal of indoor and outdoor observation and activity. The goal was to accustom children to useful observation of surroundings and to obtain information through self-activity. It involved a great deal of practical gardening experience. In the early 1920s even half of the cities in Norway had school gardens, and the movement grew rapidly. The course has no direct parallel in American schools but is similar to the German *Heimatkunde* (Jensen 1928).

Quite commonly, the rural schools were so organized that the children attended every other day after the schools were divided into an upper and a lower division. The lower division met three days a week, and the upper division, the other three days. The teacher could then organize a schedule of homework so that the older children in particular would spend two or three hours reading lessons and preparing for the next day's classes on the days when they were at home (Jensen 1928). The school year continued to be modified somewhat to fit the needs of the local farm economy.

Even though the unified school in urban areas lost its characteristic as a school only for poor people, highly motivated, affluent families arranged for paid classes beyond the standard courses offered in the public school. So there still remained two classes of students at the elementary level, those with and those without an enriched curriculum.

The School Act of 1860 provided that an elementary school be established within walking distance for each pupil, hence bringing to an end the ambulatory school era in rural Norway. Gradually the rural school became a social institution in its own right and with its own building. It was now attached to the community and less attached to the person of the teacher and to farm homes with large enough rooms to accommodate an ambulatory school. Having schooling take place in a school building rather than in a home was more than a change of structure and setting. Norway was traditionally a *family society,* and protection of the family estate was a basic trait in tradition and legislation. The school's development had in large measure been seen in the light of that relationship (Jordheim 1984). Moving the pupils and the teacher out of the homes of parents and into a separate school building and having a unified school for the children of all social classes symbolically at least signaled a break in the family's close supervision over what was being taught.

Since Norway has a rugged terrain and is sparsely settled, the stipulation that elementary schools be provided within walking distance of every home was sometimes difficult to carry out. Pupils living more than two and one-half miles from the nearest school receive free transportation. Barth (1960) tells of a central Norwegian mountain community where children did not have a school within walking distance but instead received their education by attending a boarding school. They would stay at the boarding school for stretches of fourteen days. Similar arrangements were made in other thinly populated districts in northern Norway. Pupils who live too far from school to commute are given free living quarters in the area where the school is located. Even today there are some coastal communities with a one-room schoolhouse where children board in the community during the school week and return home to one of the numerous outlying North Sea islands and coastal neighborhoods over the weekends (Bjaaland 1988). On the island of Sula, with a population of approximately 300 persons, elementary school children attend school in a school building on the island; only the high school students must go to the mainland for their education.

Democratic school reforms that resulted in the common united school did not put an end to the strong desire for segregated education. In a sense, putting children with different backgrounds and from different social classes in the same classroom only intensified it. Many felt that not all children should be in the same school—not that pupils should be separated by social class but that the healthy and the able should not have their education impaired by the presence in the school of those not physically, intellectually, or morally suited to the activities in a normal classroom. It was part of social Darwinism and a eugenic movement that had some currency in England, Norway, and elsewhere at the time. The more insistent the demands for raising the level of activity and performance in the unified school to compensate for what was lost with the closing of most private schools, the stronger the felt need to separate those who could not compete or who were considered a bad influence on their classmates. There was another problem. The unified primary school designed to encompass all pupils was also to be a comprehensive school suitable for those seeking preparation that would lead to higher education as well as for those satisfied with a terminal degree. That meant quality pre-high school education had to be offered, and not all pupils had the talent for it.

As a result of those concerns, an elaborate plan was worked out (Dahl 1985). Children were to be divided into four groups based on their acceptability as pupils or according to the "degree of rejection they would be met with." Those to be eliminated from the unified primary school were divided into three groups. An A group was composed of those with mental and physical defects. Previously, they had merely been left behind year after year as their classmates progressed on toward graduation. Thus, they had not impeded the class.

The second group to be excluded from the regular primary school were the physically infectious—the group B children. These children were said to constitute a problem especially in Oslo where scab, itch, various hair diseases, as well as vermin, were said to flourish.

The largest problem was children in the C group, namely, those who were "morally infectious." They were children who were said to show such bad behavior that the other children were being exposed to very unhealthy influences. They were said to be "vicious or morally depraved" and to be the children of depraved parents. The children hampered teaching by their bad behavior. Their moral infectiousness tended to keep "better-class children" away from the public school. Not many were in favor of supporting the education of these children. Only children of parents "in need" were seen as deserving aid, which would have to come by way of poor relief.

By segregating B and C children, it was hoped that parents could protect their children against physical or moral infection. At first, no provision was made for the education of the rejected groups; parents were held responsible for whatever education they received. Eventually, reform schools (*skolehjemene*) were opened to take care of and educate the unfit and delinquent children. The number of schools for children and youth with such adjustment difficulties grew constantly until the 1940s, from ten schools at the turn of the century to about double that number. And the most retarded in group A were given educational opportunities in special institutions established by the state in a legislative act of 1881.

However, the system of separation was not rigorously enforced, and in practice there were never many children who were separated from the unified schools (Jordheim 1984). The eugenic features of school reform had begun to lose popular and professional support almost from the day the measures were first instituted.

Toward the end of the nineteenth century and the beginning of the twentieth there were signs of social and cultural ferment that would lead, among other things, to an increasingly democratic perspective on child rearing and on the educating of children, changes that in Norway would help to make the twentieth century the Century of the Child. The changes were in part an effect of a general humanistic perspective on child rearing that had its roots in Western Europe a century earlier but that had not until now had the cultural vigor in Norway that the religious teachings of the Church of Norway and the Hauge Movement had had. Now humanistic perspectives on children and children's education challenged entrenched Lutheran perspectives on child rearing and children's education.

In the struggle to change autocratic, bureaucratic, and dogmatic aspects of the Norwegian schools, radical changes were proposed, but in fact the schools changed only slowly and gradually (Grønseth 1975). Feeling saddled with a Lutheran upbringing and education that sought to achieve responsible, conforming behavior by stimulating feelings of fear, guilt, and shame, that inhibited and led to feelings of insecurity and inadequacy, some offered a competing perspective based on humanistic and psychological theories of personality that sought to free the human spirit from as many restraints as possible. "Free education" (*fri oppdragelse*) became the battle cry of its advocates. For the more extreme among them the goal was in effect to make children totally free, free to do as they wanted to do.

But free education was challenged by another new concept, a concept with greater prospects of general acceptance, namely, "caring education" (*omsorgspedagogikk*). That is, the school was not only to be less autocratic and more democratic as the free educationists proposed but also to be child-centered and less knowledge-transmittal-centered. Up to 1936 corporal punishment had been one of the tools available to school personnel in keeping order and asserting authority. The law was repealed in 1936. That was followed by a number of changes designed to direct attention to pupil needs and psychological development. Greater respect for the individual pupil contributed to changes that extended the prohibition against violent treatment of children not only to physical punishment but to violent handling in general, as discussed in an earlier chapter. Teaching methods became freer, discipline was maintained by less rigorous means, and the running of the schoolroom gradually became more democratic.

One of the unexpected results of the new perspective on children and on their education was the increased emphasis on girls' preparing themselves for traditional roles as wives and mothers. Knowledge gained from the field of child psychology was used as a basis for supporting the view that mothers were of irreplaceable importance during the formative years in a child's development and that girls should prepare themselves for that role. As a result, even as late as the school plan of 1939 there were differences in the course offerings for girls and boys; home economics was stressed for girls.

The School Act of 1969 finally extended compulsory school attendance from seven to nine years after years of experimentation with length of school year. The basic nine-year school (*grunnskolen*) is divided into two stages: a junior stage (*barneskolen*), comprising grades 1–6, and a youth stage (*ung-*

domsskolen), comprising grades 7–9. All eugenic features are gone; the basic school makes educational provisions for all children of compulsory school age, seven to sixteen. A very small number of private schools exist side by side with the public schools. According to the government's view, they are to be supplementary and not to compete with the public schools. Schools based on an alternative pedagogy are entitled to government grants.

Model Plans for the Basic School were adopted in 1974 and in 1987 (*The Norwegian Basic School*, Oslo: Basic School Council 1981, *Primary Education in Norway*. Project No. 8: Innovation in Primary Education, Strasbourg: Council for Cultural Cooperation 1988). As stated in the Model Plan of 1974:

> The purpose of the basic school is, in understanding of and collaboration with the home, to help give the pupils a Christian and moral upbringing, to develop their mental and physical abilities, and to give them a good general knowledge, so that they may become useful and self-reliant human beings both in their homes and in the community.
>
> The school shall further mental freedom and tolerance, and work for the creation of productive forms of cooperation between teachers and pupils and between school and home.

The Parliament decreed the fundamental purposes of the school, and the Ministry of Church and Education (note the combination of functions within this ministry) laid down the aims of the teaching through the Model Plan. And a number of courses and topics are obligatory, but at the pedagogic level the pupils are given a significant role. Teachers and the pupils together plan the program, select subject matter, discuss how the program is to be organized with its ways, means, and methods. They also discuss the teaching aids and the forms of evaluation to be used. Children are to feel that they belong and that they have a part to play in society, which includes taking responsibility for and having a say in what happens in school. Pupil participation is integrated throughout the whole of the curriculum.

Passing on of the cultural heritage of Christianity to the coming generation continues to be one of the school's important functions. All children whose parents are members of the State Church take courses on Christian knowledge as a part of their yearly curriculum. As an educational goal, the intent is that children shall be made acquainted with the major events in biblical and church history and with the Evangelical Lutheran confessions. Children of parents who do not belong to the Church of Norway (4 percent belong to other religious communities; 3 percent belong to no religious community) can be exempted from the subject, either wholly or partially, if the parents so wish. As far as possible these children are given instruction in another creed or philosophy of life. Over the years the time spent on religious instruction has been reduced from a period every day to two periods a week in the years prior to confirmation. As early as 1954, Castberg stated categorically that the teaching of Christian knowledge, which enjoyed a dominant position in the earliest elementary schools, had been relegated to a minor position. Nevertheless, religious conservatives, both in and out of government, have fought and continue to fight any reduction in the amount of time devoted to that part of children's education.

As primary education was made compulsory for all Norwegian children and as Norwegian society became more ideologically pluralistic, it is understandable that teaching Christianity in the basic school would be controversial. The church was gradually pushed into a pluralistic situation where secular views on life were joining in the struggle to define reality (Lindbekk 1975). If a primary function of the basic school is to socialize children, whose ideas and values is the school to affirm in a growingly complex and pluralistic society? Such a question has an urgency in Norway, still officially an Evangelical Lutheran society, that is difficult for one from a country without an official state religion to comprehend or appreciate.

The study plan gives advice to teachers on how important religious training is for their pupils as a basis for their future Christian faith and as a norm for guiding their adult lives. Christian knowledge is to be presented in such a way as to not lose seriousness and conviction but still leave room for criticism of fundamental values so that pupils develop powers of self-reliance and critical judgment. For Norwegian educational legislation to encourage tolerance and freedom of thought is something new in elementary education. If it is to be done well, it calls for great knowledge and sophistication regarding beliefs and values on the part of elementary school teachers. Other values the basic school is to inculcate in pupils are less controversial and ambivalent than are Christianity, tolerance, and freedom of thought—such nebulous values as truthfulness, honesty, justice, loyalty, and love of one's fellow human beings.

Despite apparent wide-scale indifference to the church on the part of adults today, there is a curious ambivalence in both Norwegian thought and practice regarding Christian indoctrination and freedom of thought. Most Norwegian families avail themselves of the church's rites of baptism and confirmation for their children. They also want their children to receive instruction in Christian knowledge. According to a Norwegian Opinion Institute poll (*Aftenposten,* 5 January 1984) 76 percent think children ought to receive religious instruction in school. Fifty-three percent also think that children ought to learn to pray evening prayers; 46 percent, that they ought to go to Sunday School as well; and 76 percent, that the Christian gospel should be presented to them on television.

Yet the teaching of religion in the public school continues and will continue to be hotly debated. In any session of the Parliament (*Storting*) there are apt to be proposals on education not only from the party or parties forming the government but also from the other political parties. Parties range in their views from the conservative proposals of the Christian People's Party to the liberal views of the Socialist Left Party. Recently two proposals were readied for introduction into Parliament that reflect this range of opinion—one supporting continuation of Christian values as a fundamental element in basic school education and another proposing to make the school confession-free and built on general ethical values, traditional humanistic thought, human equal rights, and democratic ideals (*Aftenposten*, 10 February 1987).

Religious education in the basic school, along with confirmation, probably has been the most significant contact that the Church of Norway has maintained with families. On the other hand, liberals have maintained that what the teaching of Christianity does to the compulsory school is a disaster, a tragedy. They maintain that the "sin-centered" character of some of the Christian teaching contributes to the development of strong feelings of guilt in children and that such a view of life contradicts the humanistic view prevalent in other aspects of national life—political, economic, recreational, and even familial (Flint 1960).

Today there are humanistic organizations in sixty countries, but Norway has the largest percentage of population who belong to the Human Ethical Society (*Aftenposten*, 4 August 1986). Humanistic rationalists generally prevailed in the intellectual debate in Norway, but they did not escape Norway's strong moral imperative that has created a respect for authority, whether the source of the authority is God, a set of moral standards, or society (Jonassen 1983). Norwegians have what Castberg (1954:38–39) called a "vague feeling that the Christian belief system is not only a set of religious dogmas, but an ethical philosophy which must guide modern people." That theme is current even today in lead editorials in *Aftenposten*,

Norway's largest circulation daily newspaper. No less than four editorials dealt with the subject in 1986–87 alone. In one editorial the editor viewed the Bible as relating to "valuable norms which through a long historical development have given our society identity" (*Aftenposten*, 20 September 1986:2). A second editorial urged a "stronger willingness to mediate the old gospel in a new way, in the language of our day, in the reality today's people live in. Then dechristianization can be stopped" (*Aftenposten*, 18 February 1987:2). In another editorial (*Aftenposten*, 7 December 1987:2) the editor admonished parents as to their responsibility in the upbringing of children, pointing out the importance of early training in Christianity in contributing to the loyalty to the faith in adolescence and adulthood. The school cannot alone be responsible for the proper upbringing of children, the editor asserted.

The Model Plan pays more attention to personality development than was ever true before. A reading of the Plan leaves one with the impression that the Norwegian basic school is very much a child-centered, over against a knowledge-centered, school. Not only is the school child-centered, but it is individual-centered. It is a perspective on children that is financially expensive and both physically and emotionally exhausting for teachers, for it treats each child as unique, each as having qualities that must be recognized or discovered and provided for through an enriched environment and curriculum in order that each child may reach its own unique, full potential. The Plan defines the objective as follows: Activities at school are to help the individual pupil to realize his or her potential, without relevance to what those abilities are, or whether they are great or small. All have the right to expect that the basic school will help them develop their personalities as fully as possible. Teachers are to consistently attempt to discover the gifts and aptitudes of each individual pupil.

Creative activities are given a great deal of scope as well, and practical and artistic abilities of the pupils are nurtured. Education is not to aim to make all children alike, but to make them feel they are as good as, but not better, than others. Hence, the school adjusts its teaching program to the individual abilities and needs of each child as far as is possible.

School authorities are persuaded that it is a good idea to keep members of a class together as a social unit throughout the basic school years. It is believed that working together in groups is important; it is said to foster a child's development as a social being. The ability to assert oneself in the company of others is seen as something every person must acquire. When the new system was first introduced, pupils at the youth stage were assigned to different branches in accordance with their plans for future education and choice of career. That was rejected in favor of a flexible arrangement including syllabi of varying degrees of difficulty in certain major subjects, such as Norwegian, mathematics, and English. This arrangement was also abandoned in favor of classes staying together for all subjects apart from classes that are optional.

No one fails: all class members are automatically promoted from year to year. There is no repeating of grades. At no stage and in no subject or activity is a child to be held back in learning and development or to be confronted with a pace of work or a degree of effort for which he or she is not capable. Pupils are separated from their class and given special education only after an assessment by experts indicates that it is absolutely necessary. An extensive pedagogical-psychological advisory service is organized within the school system. A small number of disabled children, estimated at 1 percent, attend special schools or specially designated classes.

Child-centeredness is especially apparent in the treatment children receive in the first three to four years of basic school. Organized activity centers around the teacher whose social function is to be at least as important for the child as is her teaching function; the beginning teacher, usually a woman, serves as a mother surrogate. A class has only one teacher, and commonly the same teacher stays with the class through the first three or even four years. In 1987–88 the average number of pupils per class in primary school was about eighteen and in lower secondary school about twenty-three. The relationship between pupils and teacher is likely to result in a transfer from parents to teacher of a measure of the child's need for protection and care. The teacher is expected to play this nurturant role, while gradually helping each child to see itself as independent, as one among several, each with equal rights (Lindbekk 1975). The nurturing role is demanding and can be emotionally exhausting for the teacher.

Hollos (1974) draws an impressive word picture of the transfer of the social-emotional function from mother to teacher as she describes her visit to one Norwegian elementary school in an isolated region of Norway where children's preschool contact with families other than their own is rare. The importance of the first school day was emphasized by the new clothes the child must wear, by his picture being taken, and by the overly considerate behavior of parents and siblings. The mother accompanied the child on his first day, partially to help him meet his new world. Mothers sat in back of the first-grade classroom while the children were told to take their individual seats. The result was a class full of "sobbing, crying, cringing, or deadly pale children and embarrassed mothers." The teacher in turn behaved very much like a mother. Relationship between these pupils, who had not previously attended a day nursery, developed very slowly, pupils taking refuge by hanging around the teacher and holding onto her hand or her skirt. Teachers tried to discourage that behavior but were often unsuccessful, especially with first-grade girls.

The teachers in first grade, and to some extent in second grade, try to make school as much like home as possible. There is little overt discipline, nor is there generally need for it. Teachers give as few direct orders as possible. The pupils appear to like their teachers and become quite relaxed about their schoolwork. Hollos reports that children did not worry much about doing homework, nor were they noticably embarrassed if they did not know the day's lesson. It is apparent that one role of the school teacher is to launch the young into Norwegian society as gently as possible. Experiments have been launched to look for ways to get a gentle transition from preschool to primary school as well.

A new emphasis in educational legislation highlights the importance of cooperation between school and home, school and community. The primary school is being decentralized, giving a high degree of responsibility for curriculum and syllabus to the local schools and school boards. There is genuine concern that parents shall have an influence on what happens in the school. Cooperation between home, school, and the local community aims to communicate to pupils that school is meaningful and that it relates to their past and present home and community experiences. For each basic school class two parents are selected to represent the parents in contacts with the class teacher.

By observation and activity out in the community, pupils learn at first hand how the community functions. Camp school (*leirskole*) is one more feature in the basic school curriculum that is intended to add to children's experiences in the world outside the schoolroom. Another purpose of camp is to further the spirit of comradeship and to ease growth into social beings. The goal is to have each pupil attend camp school for at least one week in the course of basic school education. Most camps are situated in the country—in the mountains, by the sea, in the woods, or on a farm—but in all cases in natural surroundings. At camp pupils deal with new, unfamiliar situations and solve problems in a natural setting. They are given a practical and theoretical introduction to such topics as ski instruction, mountain climbing, safety in the mountains, nature study and conservation, first aid, and care of animals. School camp should not be confused with summer camp. Some of the larger school systems have their own permanent facilities with teaching staff especially trained to offer programs of instruction appropriate to the natural setting.

There is a marked emphasis on the equality of the sexes in Norwegian schools today. All activities of the school are now based on equality. Books used in the schools are carefully scrutinized. They must not, for example, present a one-sided or discriminatory picture of the ways in which functions are divided between men and women in the home, at work, or in society in general. Schools have mixed classes in all subjects; both sexes receive the same instruction, the same allocation of periods in all compulsory subjects, and the same right to choose optional subjects.

Subjects in the basic school curriculum today include religion, Norwegian, mathematics, English, social studies, natural science, music, arts and crafts, physical education, and home economics. English begins in the fourth year, and there are proposals to begin in the third year. There are periods for optional subjects in the upper grades. The optional subjects include a second foreign language, music, art, office work, typing, fishing, seamanship, and agriculture. Periods are also set aside for pupils to participate in pupil and class councils. Pupils study certain other obligatory and nonobligatory topics. School council is an obligatory topic; others are traffic training, alcohol use, drug and tobacco use, environment, careers, family life, sex education, consumer education, nutrition, first aid, and dental health. Nonobligatory topics include drama, gardening, and plant care.

Pupils are evaluated on a regular basis, and that evaluation is shared with parents. One might wonder how pupils are evaluated or how they are graded in a system that gives so much latitude to teachers and pupils and pays so much attention to individual abilities and interests. At the lowest levels, up until the fourth year, it is thought to be natural to present the subject matter without dividing it into subjects. Little significance is placed on either division of the schoolwork into separate subjects or on grading, or in some situations even on dividing the pupils into classes, since it is felt that it is important that children from different age groups learn to work together. There are a number of very small schools in sparsely settled regions of Norway (there must be at least six pupils to maintain a school) in which pupils of different ages attend the same class, and there are schools in which up to twelve pupils of differing ages are all taught together as one class.

The evaluation that pupils receive deals with ability, talent, and potential for schoolwork, as well as with the effort they make. As pupils progress to higher classes, they and their parents must be informed of how they are developing generally and what progress they are making in particular subjects, based not only on the knowledge and skills acquired but also on how they tackle the subject, to what extent they are familiar with the appropriate teaching aids, and to what degree they are capable of solving problems in a rational manner. One reason why pupils are made part of a cooperative teaching-learning situation is to help develop good work methods and efficient learning techniques. There is a great deal of emphasis on pupils' learning how to learn rather than on being taught what they need to know. That approach to education is being challenged today; pressure is building to place more emphasis on content, on what children need to know. We shall return to the subject later in the chapter.

No grades are given during the first six years. At the youth stage, grades seven to nine, children are given grades for compulsory subjects twice a year. If the parents wish, their children can also be given marks in optional subjects.

The basic school's emphasis on helping children to believe in themselves and their potential and to work with and be tolerant of others reflects widely accepted values in contemporary Norwegian culture. In a recent survey, 1,105 Norwegian adults of different ages responded to a question inviting them to indicate which of twenty-two personality traits they rated most highly (*A-magasinet*, 18 February 1989). The question put to them was: "Here is a list of things which children can be encouraged to learn at home. Which of these do you regard as *especially* important in children's upbringing?" All age groups, fifteen to twenty-four, twenty-five to thirty-nine, and forty to fifty-nine, rated "Have faith in yourself, don't give up too easily," "Tolerance and respect for other persons," "Politeness/good manners," "Be orderly and conscientious in school and at work," and "Independent thinking" as most important. One choice was different for the over-sixty-years age group; they chose "Being thrifty, careful with money" instead of "Independent thinking" as one of their five preferred traits.

"Religious belief" received little support in the survey of favored traits despite the emphasis that is placed on the religious education of children. Those aged fifteen to twenty-four rated it the least preferred of the twenty-two traits; only those over sixty years old gave it a rating as high as thirteenth out of twenty-two traits.

Despite the current emphasis in Norway on developing self-esteem and asserting oneself, a need to suppress one's ego is deeply felt. It is a trait in Norwegian personality that has in part at least been attributed to the impact that early Christianity had on Norwegian values, instilling as it did a consciousness of guilt and shame, a morality that made modesty and self-abnegation central values (Jonassen 1983). That residual need to suppress one's ego is perhaps one reason why the novel by Aksel Sandemose, *A Fugitive Crosses His Tracks* (*En Fliktning Krysser Sit Spor*), has sustained its appeal in Norway and has appeared in a number of editions. The book was first published in 1933. It deals with a small town called Jante and the "law" (*Janteloven*) that governed the rearing of children, their relationships to adults, and the relationships between adults. The concept Jante law entered the Norwegian vocabulary and is a term used even today in describing Norwegian personality and the relationship between persons. Ask even young people in Norway if Janteloven means anything to them and they readily agree. According to Sandemose, the town of Jante kept its residents in check by means of the ten commandments of Jante Law. The ten commandments are as follows:

1. Thou shalt not believe thou *art* something.
2. Thou shalt not believe thou art as good as *we*.
3. Thou shalt not believe thou art more wise than *we*.
4. Thou shalt not fancy thyself better than *we*.
5. Thou shalt not believe thou knowest more than *we*.
6. Thou shalt not believe thou art greater than *we*.
7. Thou shalt not believe *thou* amountest to anything.
8. Thou shalt not laugh at *us*.
9. Thou shalt not believe that anyone is concerned with *thee*.
10. Thou shalt not believe thou canst teach *us* anything.
    (1936:77–78)

By means of the Jante law, people stamped out each other's chances of life, writes Sandemose. All struggled against it and writhed beneath it, but all heartlessly exercised it against all others. In Jante's school the teacher would be angry with the pupils for not asking questions, but the children soon learned that to ask a question in class could lead to unpredictable results. It might involve a topic that the teacher had decided was a dangerous topic, and what that topic might be was impossible to know beforehand. So one's question could lead to commendation or to a good sound thrashing. In fact, few topics could be discussed in Jante at all, and these only if brought up by the oldest in the family, haltingly, while others sat about "with downcast eyes taking inventory of their hatred." The fugitive asked: How may an individual hope to develop a soul in such an environment? How shall Jante ever be able to foster men other than slaves—with an occasional scorpion or murderer?

Pål Johnson, a Norwegian teacher, recently spent a year as an exchange professor at a college in the American Midwest and lived there with his young family. In reflecting on their year in an article in *Aftenposten* (19 November 1985:7), Johnson observed that one difference he sensed was an absence of Jante law in the midwestern community in which they lived. He saw it above all in attitudes toward child rearing. He felt more importance was placed on developing a child's belief in his own worth, and envy was less a folk sickness than at home in Norway. The conflicting values of self-abnegation and self-esteem both appear to be viable in Norwegian culture today.

There are changes taking place in Norwegian society today that are seen as negatively impacting on work in the basic school. Currently, problems are attributed to permissive upbringing; an increase in family breakups; the presence of narcotics; an increase in the tendency to use violence to solve problems; video violence; urbanization; and less commitment to traditional values (Guhnfeldt 1987, Hundeide 1988a, 1988b; Jonassen 1983; Nordlund et al. 1960). Children are characterized as restless, noisy, and lacking in motivation and in respect for authority. Teachers complain of having had pupils who hit, kick, bite, and knock them down and having had personal property and equipment damaged. There has been an increase in crime among young people. In one survey every seventh teacher reported having experienced either being hit or kicked (Guhnfeldt 1987), and in another survey among 250 basic school teachers, as many as 44 told of problem children who made their work difficult. The ombud for teachers reported in 1988 that 5,000 teachers had been so greatly afflicted by their pupils as to feel the need to take health leave.

The Norwegian sociologist Frønes (1988) alleges that most young people have no reason to complain about their childhood homes: they usually have rooms of their own and reasonable, liberal parents. However, school personnel are accusing parents and other community agencies of sending to the school children they themselves have not been able to control. There are calls for smaller classes, hence, a more favorable pupil-teacher ratio, or for two teachers for each class to handle the problems that are plaguing the teachers. Others blame the school, feeling that discipline in the school is too lax, that boundaries for acceptable behavior have not been properly articulated, and that the authority and the leadership of teachers have been compromised and need to be restored. The Norwegian teacher no longer has unquestioned authority as was true when the teacher had the right to physically punish children. In a system as democratic as the Norwegian basic school is today, authority has to be earned (Frønes 1989).

A large-sample survey (Raundalen and Raundalen 1979) designed to measure pupil satisfaction with school as judged by both the pupils and their parents showed that enthusiasm of children for school wanes over the years. Both children and parents reported that first graders had a high degree of satisfaction with school, but beyond sixth grade less than three-fourths of the pupils were satisfied. Children's answers showed much earlier dissatisfaction with school than their parents anticipated and greater overall dissatisfaction. Beginning in the fifth grade (eleven-year-olds), less than 80 percent of pupils indicated satisfaction, and the satisfaction rate dropped to 45 percent for eighth graders and 53 percent for ninth graders.

Children and their parents were also asked if school recess (*friminuttet*) was enjoyable. Many more pupils in the lower grades reported that they enjoyed recess than parents believed would. The average for pupils was nearly 90 percent, while parents' average was about 65 percent. At the youth level (seventh to ninth grade) the percentages were very much alike for parents and pupils; reported enjoyment of recess had fallen for both to about 40 percent.

The authors of the study saw no readily apparent explanation as to why young children reported much higher satisfaction with recess than their parents thought they would, suggesting that it might be that young children saw recess as a pleasant contrast to the more structured, disciplined regimen that they were having to become accustomed to in the classroom. Also, some parents were not aware that their children saw the environment in which they played in their home neighborhood as a tougher environment, for there they were sometimes exposed to bullying and teasing by other children while on the school ground they were reassured by the presence of adult supervisors. There is a high level of consciousness in Norway, as in Scandinavia generally, of the prevalence and deleterious effects of bullying and negative teasing in the lives of children.

The reported lack of satisfaction of many of the older pupils with what occurred during the school day—both in the classroom and on the playground—might well contribute to their alleged lack of motivation and to their restlessness, noisiness, and otherwise undisciplined behavior. Would student response to school be more favorable if there were more rules and regulations? That is a moot question. There are teachers in Norway who look enviously at their counterparts in England who operate within a system demanding stricter discipline.

The age at which children should begin attending school, the length of the school term, and the length of the school day are being debated at the present time. Norwegian pupils have fifteen to eighteen periods a week during the first three years in basic school, which increase to twenty-four to thirty periods in the higher grades, still a low number of periods of instruction when compared to other Western countries.

Another issue is the lack of universal availability of preschool institutions with educational content. Preschool education is voluntary and is provided by kindergartens (*barnehager*) or through in-school programs for six-year-olds (*førskole klasser*; Kurian 1988). At the present time only about half of the children six years of age are in attendance, some for whole days, others for only half days. A government proposal calls for the provision of 10,000 new places for each of the coming twenty years, since 380,000 places are needed and only 104,000 are available (*Aftenposten,* 7 March 1988). Since so few places are available, it means that of those starting first grade at age seven only about half have had any prior preschool or kindergarten experience. (For a discussion of the Norwegian kindergarten, see chapter 7.)

A related and perennially argued matter is whether or not children should be enrolled in the basic school earlier than age seven. Believing that the age should not be lowered, one study group recommended that instead all districts establish kindergartens for all six-year-olds for at least twelve hours per week (*Aftenposten,* 26 February 1985). There are many in Norway, including preschool consultants, who say that six-year-olds are not mature enough for the demands of a school situation—problems such as difficulties in getting six-year-olds to and from school, teaching methods used in teaching seven-year-olds that would be inappropriate for six-year-olds, teachers who would need to be especially trained to teach six-year-olds, content that would have to be more like that used in kindergarten than in first grade. On the other side are those who feel that the present system prolongs infancy and that children are ready for more demanding content than they now receive in kindergarten or preschool classes (Bjaaland 1988).

That educational policy is a topic of widespread debate is nothing new in Norway; educational policy is conspicuously politicized in Norway with the political parties including proposals on education in their party platforms. Basically, two groups have monopolized the debate: one argues for an obligatory curriculum, more discipline, and more basic knowledge, the reintroduction of grades in the lower grades and, overall, more result-oriented teaching (Telhaug 1989); the other is generally supportive of continuing the perspective set forth in the Model Plans of 1974 and 1987, arguing for pupil freedom, freedom for each teacher to develop instructional programs according to need, more cooperation and collaboration (rather than competition) among pupils. On one issue, however, there appears to be virtual universal agreement, that is, more discipline.

Part of what is at issue is whether children's psychological and social needs can be addressed properly, as the Model Plans attempt to do, while at the same time giving them the knowledge and skills that are necessary to keep Norway competitive in the world economy. Because of its limited natural resources, it is asserted that if Norway is to compete, it must do so in the educationally intensive fields related to the sciences (Dickson 1988). "Only by utilizing the population's intellectual resources can we succeed in a difficult international competition and thereby create advancement and growth in our nation" (Editorial, *Aftenposten,* 22 April 1989:2).

The recent Parliament Report no. 43 asserts that Norway's advancement becomes dependent in larger measure than ever before on how much is invested in gaining, using, and mediating knowledge. The whole report is directed toward the desire to create an educational system that will provide both greater competence and better knowledge. It calls for a greater depth

of understanding, a greater personal commitment, and a serious regard for responsible values. Norway sees itself in crisis
economically as a member of the world community. In the light
of this and a conservative tendency in the country, education in
the kindergarten, as well as the basic school, is subject to
critical analysis and review. Even the Labor government, which
has been supportive of the stipulations in the Model Plans,
proposed in its party program for 1989–1993 to lengthen the
school day for children in the first grades, to start school at age
six, and to add a tenth compulsory year of basic school. Forty-
eight municipalities have been engaged in a pilot project
comprising an educational program for six-year-olds. A decision on incorporating education for six-year-olds into the compulsory basic school will probably be made in the early 1990s.

Given Norway's current economic situation and recent
conservative tendency, it is tempting for politicians to see
children as a future economic and political resource. To what
extent can a society treat children as citizens entitled by right
to the freedom to fully realize the uniqueness of being a child,
and to what extent and at what age must they be trained and
educated to become competent, knowledgeable, dedicated,
economically productive adults? It is a debate that is not
peculiar to Norwegian society. According to the latest international professional educational literature, there was a shift in
thought on educational policy in the 1980s, a shift to "restorative education" (Telhaug 1990). It is an attempt to give new life
to some ideas and goals that have been on the defensive for a
long time, a time dominated by the popularity of democratic
and progressive educational policy. The dominant goals of
restorative education are expressed in such terms as standards,
competence, product, efficiency, excellence, and, before all,
diligence, self-sacrifice, hard work, and the competitive spirit.
Compared to the debate in such countries as China, England,
and the United States, these educational goals have played a

modest role in Norway and Sweden, however. During the past several decades, and somewhat belatedly in comparison to Sweden, Norway has been in the forefront of those societies focusing on children as children, rather than focusing on them as incomplete adults in the process of becoming competent, economically productive adults. There is strong, and for now, majority opposition to an extensive overhaul of the Norwegian child-centered basic school (Telhaug 1990). But some changes will take place in the 1990s, changes reflecting adult society's current perspectives on children and on what the goals of education should be for the good of children and society.

6

Children at Leisure

ONCE CHILDREN HAVE RECEIVED their primary rearing in the family, an inevitable process of disengagement from the family begins. It is a gradual process and one that is never complete. How rapidly it takes place, and how complete the disengagement, is markedly influenced by how isolated the family is from other families, how close-knit the family is, and how complex and differentiated the society has become. The isolation of the Flathill families described by Hollos (1974) is an example of how isolated some Norwegian families are.

The local environment and the resources and facilities it provides are of special significance for children, for it is in the local environment that children reside and spend most of their time. In many ways children have a more thorough acquaintance with what the local environment has to offer than do adults (Østberg 1979). Children's activity and culture take on the color of the neighborhood environment. If it is a stable neighborhood, child culture will be similar from generation to generation (Ørjasæter 1976). In neighborhoods that are stable and have primary occupations—farming, fishing, lumbering—child play will first and foremost imitate what adults do, since children and adults live and work in close proximity to one another.

For children play is the dominant reality (Åm 1984). It becomes more and more their own creation especially as they begin to play out of earshot and out of sight of their parents; and when out-of-doors Norwegian children have not been closely supervised, and many are not today, giving maximum opportunity to develop a culture of their own (Wike 1976b).

Children at Leisure

Throughout most of Norway's history, most children's play was reserved for short free periods or was a way of making work more tolerable by interlacing work and some elements of play (Tønnessen 1982). Though survival concerns are largely the responsibility of adults, children have had to help with the family's work. At a time when Norway was a rural farm economy, most play was imitative of farm life. Simple natural materials with little reworking were used as playthings; children's fantasy did the rest. Their play was populated with crudely constructed play barns and fields and toy domestic animals. Live animals have also been among the dearest playthings and playmates for rural children. Inside the house play was also imitative. Barth (1960) observed that when a mother was canning meatballs a daughter of eight was busy making small meatballs for the dog in her own little frying pan.

Work was thought to be not only necessary but good for children—no child was thought to have a self-evident right to food and shelter. Children were to be diligent and industrious, to contribute to the family larder, and to be content with little (Hagemann 1979). But children couldn't be diligently at work all the time, for the seasonal nature of most of the work in primary industries allowed, and climatic conditions often imposed, a good deal of leisure for both adults and children (Foote and Wilson 1970). Nordic parents' recognition of play as part of children's lives is evident in the asides in medical accounts dealing with children's accidents and injuries in medieval times (Krötzl 1989)—comments such as one about a boy who was chatting to another boy "in the way boys do" or about a girl who was playing and laughing "in the way that children do when they play together." Accounts of the circumstances surrounding accidents tell of a boy who was playing with other boys by a stream; a boy playing in a field with other boys; a boy playing with others of his own age beside an old barn; a four-year-old girl and her little brother playing near the edge of a

high riverbank from which she fell. In rural Norway the outdoors and outdoor occupations were rich sources both for participation and imitative play—hunting, fishing, rowing and
sailing boats, skiing, sliding, swimming, running, jumping in
the hay, climbing, riding horses, making flower crowns (Tønnessen 1982). Many of these activities lent themselves to competitive play as well.

Bats and balls as well as games with dice and boards were
known from Viking times. "They rolled or threw anything ring-
shaped or ball-shaped, including snowballs at their elders—
one twelfth-century Nobleman in Nidaros was believed to have
taken a whiz of the ax that killed him for the whiz of a boy's
snowball" (Foote and Wilson 1970:189).

As work became less demanding in children's lives, play
activity assumed greater importance. Organized leisure-time
opportunities also have steadily assumed greater importance.
In modern society organized activities in part replace work as
an arena for socialization (Aasen and Ingebrigtsen 1987).

Child Culture

As children move from near total supervision by parents to
more and more free association with peers, they move into a
community of children and enter, as well as help create, a
special social legacy of rules, regulations, and procedures that
constitute children's very own ways of dealing with the world
around them, with each other, and with adults. It is "a stable set
of activities or routines, artifacts, values, and concerns that
children produce and share" (Corsaro 1988:3). It is what has
been called child or peer culture (Østberg 1979). When together, children live a different life from that which they live in
association with adults. Their life together has qualities lacking
in adult society and vice versa. Child culture is not something

new; children have always had it, but adult awareness of it as a subject for research, social concern, and political action is new.

Child culture is more than just a system created by each generation of children to bring order out of chaos as they associate with each other (Enerstvedt 1984). Child culture has a content with its own life that is passed on from older to younger children as a traditional inheritance (Skard 1979). It is made up of games, riddles, jokes, songs, rhymes, as well as omens and magic ritual (Østberg 1979).

Elements of child culture spread from group to group, at times through years and over great distances. Blindman's buff is a game that has been found in different versions and is known from pictures to have existed from the Middle Ages. Hopscotch is probably only a hundred years old as played in Norway, but it is a game that has a long history and was known to have been played in antiquity. Liestøl (as reported by Tønnessen 1982) found child rhymes that have survived parallel to each other on Shetland and in Norway for at least eight hundred years. Østberg (1979) reports that children play the same games wherever one goes in Norway, with some minor adaptations in the various localities.

In a sense children's culture can be treated as any minority culture. Children's society is a society of equals; they possess common interests, common needs, and values that the central, or adult, society does not share and often does not recognize (Åm 1984). Through their culture, children express locked-in feelings and frustrations that are created by pressures and demands placed upon them by adults as well as by older children and youth. "The idea of childhood as the phase of idyllic innocence is one of the monumental myths of modern societies" (Das 1989:277). Songs, jokes, and rhymes center on topics that are problems for children, areas of life that adults are reluctant or unwilling to speak openly about, such as sexuality and death. Those problems come to the fore when children associate with one another.

Like many societies, Norway has not been a society in which people speak freely and openly about certain matters in the presence of children. Through forms provided by the child culture, repressed feelings find an outlet, a form of expression, understood by and acceptable to both the speaker and other children. Children's jokes, songs, and rhymes about sex, including erotic song games (Grambo 1984), arise out of the children's desire for openness and frankness and their consciousness of themes that are forbidden. Death is one of their play themes in which ghost stories are frequently used to frighten themselves and yet somehow to create distance between themselves and the taboo subject of death. Stories in very early times in Norway, stories that filled everyone's childhood, were tales of evildoers and evil deeds and how evildoers had to stalk the site of their sin forever, never being able to find rest. One such ghost story is about a girl who was sent to buy some liver for her mother. Grambo (1984) found that it is, in fact, an old internationally known story that later came to be a part of child culture in Norway. From a psychoanalytic perspective, when children find expression for what affects them, there is a release as they put into words and, so to speak, bring out into the light of day that which frustrates or frightens them.

Children present material in story form either as truth or as fantasy, very often with the wish to assert themselves. To urge or to desire the breaking of a taboo may also give impetus to the telling of the story. Stories dealing with death or warnings of death are commonly told by children from about five or six years of age (Grambo 1984). Cherished topics in children's stories, besides ghosts and death, are other subjects that are mysterious, unpleasant, or taboo. Besides stories, many children's riddles and witticisms also have an element of forbidden subjects.

Central themes in the jokes or witticisms of Norwegian children from around seven to eleven years of age are bragging and the anal area of the body. Østberg (1979) reports that around age twelve the earlier scatological material is repressed and real sex jokes and witticisms come through. As children near the teens, both sexes come forth with daring, outspoken, frank, or racy stories and gross jokes or witticisms.

Since taboo subjects are both forbidden and intriguing, it is understandable that children seek distance from adults through secret language and secret places in which to carry on some of their play. Doctor play is such an activity. The modesty of adults informs children that they should not investigate each other's bodies, at least not out in the open (Kjøndal 1984). Isolated places inaccessible to adults are sought for such play. Children's protest against what they do not like in adult society is generally voiced in mild and often humorous expressions; hence, their culture cannot properly be called a true protest or counterculture (Østberg 1979).

In Norway adults today usually say that girls and boys play the same games (Østberg 1979), but there are many important exceptions. Children in elementary school experience a stronger gender barrier in their play than do children at other ages. In the schoolyard girls and boys tend to each play their own games and with their own age group. Games that are gender-specific in Norway are jumping rope and playing with dolls, which are girls' games. Playing cowboys and Indians is a boy's game. Jumping rope was a late arrival as a game in Norway and was first played by both boys and girls (Enerstvedt 1984). Norwegian boys tend to have higher status on the playground than do girls, and if girls and boys do jump rope together, for instance, the aesthetic content preferred by girls tends to be replaced by the competition introduced by boys. Since Norwegian girls appear to accept the idea that males are the "natural" leaders, joint play takes on the characteristic of "boyish" play.

Song play gives girls an opportunity to sing of their feelings and thoughts around the subjects of love and boys. Several song games deal with love and marriage such as one with the title "Out Picking Flowers" (*Ut og plukke blomster;* Grambo 1984). It tells of a girl who is in love and a boy kisses her. He tells her to sit down on a stone and he will kiss her repeatedly. One of the girls chooses another with whom she dances while all sing the song. The one who is chosen next chooses one with whom to dance.

When not in school, boys and girls play together with less reference to gender and with greater age variation among the participants. Tiller (1983) found in Oslo that twice as many girls as boys preferred to play games that are gender neutral, such as tag and hide-and-seek.

Only a century ago, most children grew up in the country in Norway; today more live in urban than in rural areas. Children now play more indoors, in the space surrounding their home, in the driveway, in the street, or in playgrounds and schoolyards specifically designed to accommodate play. In many ways the residential areas of cities do not provide a very inspiring milieu for children; Norway is no exception.

Adult-Created Child Culture

The content of children's culture is not only that created by children. In fact, in modern times children's created culture has been supplemented and sometimes supplanted by content provided by adults. It is well at this time to expand our definition of children's culture to include these other elements.

There are at least four kinds of child culture. First, there is the culture that we have been discussing, namely, that spring-ing out of children's need to become engaged with peers and the world around them and which they pass on to other children. Second, there is orally transmitted tradition passed on from parents and grandparents to children in the form of stories, fables, legends, lullabies, and jingles. Third are children's created objects and displays, many of which are created while children are under the supervision and stimulation of day-care personnel and teachers. And last, are the children's books, toys, records, cassettes, tapes, and films, children's theater, programs on radio and TV, and organized sports, all created and largely supervised by adults and spread by way of technical means from the few to the many (Sætersdal and Ørjasæter 1981; Grambo 1984). It is the adult-created child culture that has come more and more to fill children's leisure time (Selmer-Olsen 1990).

Throughout several centuries it has been accepted in Norway that education through the school was society's responsibility. It is only in later years that responsibility for children's cultural life also has come to be seen as a public responsibility. Cultural politics is a distinct concept that developed in Western Europe in the 1950s. It represents a reaction against so-called refined culture, publicly supported and dominated by the middle class, which seldom reached out to the broader strata of the population. Reacting against it, and as a result of the impulse for radical change in the 1960s, the development and preservation of folk culture became an issue. In Norway, cultural politics of the late 1960s was broadened to include not only the preservation and fostering of adult folk culture but of child culture as well (Lyche 1976). The very concept *child culture,* when first introduced, was taken lightly and even treated with some ridicule (Eide 1975). But before long many were convinced that it was proper to include child cultural concerns as a matter for public debate and action. Hence, the concept child culture proved to be useful. Social consciousness was raised as to the importance not only of preserving child culture but also of providing valuable cultural offerings for children and giving them safe and stimulating environments in which to live and develop. A Nordic child culture conference was held in 1969 with other conferences to follow. In many respects Norway had anticipated the United Nations Year of the Child (1979) and was already moving forward with several initiatives.

It is now regarded as self-evident to many that social movements in modern society have endangered the lives of children—especially changes brought by urbanization and the marked environmental changes resulting as home and work have been separated for both fathers and mothers. The generations are largely separated from each other during most of the hours of the day.

Basically, children are in the way. Earlier on, it was thought that society had found a place for them in the school, a place where they could grow and develop until they would someday be useful members of society (Østberg 1979). In a society where adults have constantly less time and energy to devote to the lives of children and life in association with children, child culture is felt in Norway to no longer be self-evident, stable, and safe from destruction. It exists and thrives or fails to thrive on adult premises. Through their own self-interest and thoughtlessness as they devote themselves to careers and other adult interests, adults have damaged child culture (Sætersdal and Ørjasæter 1981). Child culture cannot thrive under adult malign intent; it may benefit from a degree of their benign neglect, however. That realization has led to the recognition that child culture is society's responsibility and hence the development of a politics of child culture. There is a growing sense in Norway that perhaps society should take children's needs for a culture of their own as seriously as they took children's need for schooling several hundred years ago (Ørjasæter 1976).

The concern about children and children's culture gave rise to a series of studies wherein the daily life of children was

taken as the central focus. Researchers went to children themselves (as well as to older persons for recollections about their
own childhood) to find out how children viewed their lives, what
they did, what their interests were, what they saw their needs to
be. The goal was to bring to consciousness the "special life form
that lives and blooms so closely around us" (Skard 1979).°

A child research perspective that focuses on the social life
of children rather than exclusively on children as the "property" of adults has a longer tradition in Norway than it does in
other countries (conversation with Per Olav Tiller, Child Research Center staff meeting, 6 February 1985). The greatest
emphasis on such research has come in the last two decades,
however. As consciousness was raised regarding children as
persons with their own culture and their own social life, what
has been discovered about that life and what conclusions have
been reached? This question is important, for, for the first time
in human history, societies are now able to create almost totally
planned and controlled environments if there are a strong
enough desire and the financial wherewithal. With urbanization and the many technological advances created—not always
with foresight and careful planning— various kinds of environments are possible. The children's playground is one small
example of an environment created for children. Children take
for granted the environments that are provided for them and
learn to live within such environments for good or ill. Nor are
they in a position to lobby for better environments. What
follows reflects current thinking in Norway about child culture
and children's play.

°   A list of the studies with a brief annotation about each is available in three
    publications of the Norwegian Center for Child Research (Norsk Senter for
    barneforskning). The first and third, *Barneforskning* (1982) and *Barneforskning i
    Norge* (1988), are available only in Norwegian. The second, *Child Research in
    Norway* (1987), is in English.

The recognition that primary play is first and foremost the children's way to become acquainted with themselves and with the world around them is crucial. Three conditions should be met if young children are to engage in primary play: first, there should be a safe milieu both within and outside the family dwelling; second, there should be varied activity possibilities that engage the children's creativity, and third, the play sites should be close to the places where the children live. More than that, the case of children's culture (along with the care for children) requires that children have room to be free from adult structuring; they need a child-child arena where their own culture can grow and flourish. In that sense they need to be apart from adults. But for a complete life they must also be included in the life of adults. Adults have the responsibility to explain and clarify themselves and their adult culture; children must see and learn clearly from adults who dare to share adult culture with them, for children will become adults (Selmer-Olsen 1990).

There are still many isolated, rural communities in Norway that are almost a paradise when it comes to meeting the needs of young children for both primary play and contact with adults. They are less ideal for children twelve to thirteen years of age who need more contact, organized activity, and companionship, however (Wike 1976a).

Secondary play, the play provided on playgrounds with permanent play equipment, is now recognized in Norway as no substitute, or a poor substitute, for primary play since it allows little room for children's initiative. Planned playgrounds are regarded today as having been designed according to a playground ideology that is obsolete. Play on such playgrounds results in children's becoming passive, making their peace with play as entertainment and a way to pass the time. Physical passivity, monotonous killing of time, or destructive protest activity may result (Kjøndal 1984).

In several studies, children have been asked to indicate where they play. Reflecting the fact that most Norwegian children now grow up in towns and cities, so many answer "in front of the garage" that it appears to be the most often used play area for Norwegian small children today (Raundalen 1976). For this reason, parents who "never bother to put the car in the garage" irk children. Children old enough to be permitted to leave the immediate premises of the home use the specially designated children's playgrounds (Tiller et al. 1983).

Today Norway, like other countries, has an abundance of toys and other playthings for children. Less is known about commercially produced toys from earlier times; purchased toys did not have great importance for Norwegian children's play (Tønnessen 1982). The classic children's toys appear first and foremost to have been balls, some dolls, and small animal figures made of wood, ceramic, or other materials. Some children's toys have been kept from earlier times. Most of them were likely regarded as too nice to be played with, for the things children played with on a daily basis wore out or were not regarded as worth keeping. Magnhild, a peasant woman born in 1910, tells the following about her father and the dolls he bought.

> I remember very well once (my father) had been to Svorkmo, and bought two dolls. They were dressed in national costumes. A boy and a girl. And they were so nice! And we got them when we got home. But we were not allowed to keep them and play with them, you know. They were put on a shelf. And there they have to stay. And so we were allowed to take them down and sit and look at them for an hour or so. You weren't supposed to make their costumes dirty or anything, you know. (Thorsen 1987:105-6)

Some of the dolls that have been kept were the style journals of the time and were not children's playthings at all.

The dolls kept from the sixteenth, seventeenth, and eighteenth centuries are adult dolls with small heads and long limbs. It was not until around 1800 that dolls began to have the proportions of children, and soon after baby dolls came on the market as well. Almost all were girl dolls (Tønnessen 1982).

Rocking horses were an early popular toy, and in the last half of the last century mechanical toys came on the market. About the same time the first educational toys were produced, blocks of wood with pictures and letters on them. At the turn of the century came the popular teddy bear.

The most recent study of Scandinavian children's leisure-time activity asked ten- to eleven-year-olds about their play equipment. Girls frequently mentioned dolls—Barbie dolls are very popular in Norway and were specifically mentioned. Some had one doll; some had many dolls with many pieces of clothing for them as well. Dolls played a part in their fantasy life as well, for instance, the romantic life of Barbie and her boyfriend, Ken. According to Berggreen (1987), Norwegian girls' fantasy world is one of romance and glamour—gilt-edged and rose-colored; the boys' fantasy world is Star Wars, steel gray and manly blue. (I recall only one Norwegian boy who mentioned having guns—guns that he had purchased a long time ago. The sale of guns of any kind is strictly proscribed in Norway.)

Battery-powered cars and games and felt pens with colored ink are important play equipment today. Sitting and drawing is something girls do together indoors. It is a popular activity also when one is alone. But the children have found that both felt pens and battery-powered toys and games have a tragically short life and hence are expensive to maintain. The felt pens dry out and become useless; the toys and games need new batteries. Comments about dried-out pens and worn-out batteries cover a good part of the impression Norwegian children have of that play equipment! Skis and skates are very popular play equipment for Norwegian children, both boys and girls. A marked change in Norway since the last generation is the extent to which girls have become involved in some of the active play previously the province of boys (Østberg 1979).

Reading, music, and TV and radio programs take up much of their indoor leisure time. Cassette and record players are popular, and children often have their own. One boy said that he listened to his cassette player all day, including when he studied. Mentioning him is not to suggest that he was atypical. Reading is a favorite activity (Berg 1985). When children are old enough to begin to read, a whole new world opens up to them (Blom, I. 1984). The Norwegian people as a whole are avid readers, reading both Norwegian and foreign authors. The four largest Norwegian publishers have about 170 door-to-door book salesmen, and more foreign books are sold in Norway than in any other European country. And they are serious readers; in 1975, of sixteen hundred titles not more than four or five were in the entertainment category (*Aftenposten*, 28 November 1975).

Children vary in their reading frequency from those who never read a book or only like to "look in books" to those who are real "bookworms." About 10 percent of Norwegian children are avid readers—reading several hundred children's books a year (Gjengset 1986). Parents are the most important influence when it comes to establishing book reading as a desirable activity for their children. Those who were often read to as children had a strong tendency to keep on reading books when they were older. In interviews with twenty-eight youth, fourteen said that their mothers often read to them when they were small, nine said mothers read to them now and then, four said never, and one didn't know. Only one said father was often the reader; ten said father read now and then; and seventeen said father never read to them.

In a study of fourth, fifth, and sixth graders in two communities, 89 percent said they read books in their free time. Children between the ages of nine and fourteen were the most avid

borrowers of library books, borrowing books both from the
school and public libraries. Those over fifteen years of age indicated that schoolwork and increased contact with comrades were
reasons why they spent less time reading books (Gjengset 1987).
There appears to be no basis for the belief that increased TV
offerings compete with book reading in Norway, for book reading
among children has remained fairly constant over the years.

It was in the 1920s that first attempts were made in Norway to
create books especially for children's leisure-time reading (Hagemann 1979). The earlier books showed a marked intent to
influence children's behavior in a way that pietism demanded.
There were moralistic examples of good behavior for obedient
children and books that warned disobedient children of the
consequences of their behavior. The stronghold that moralistic
religious convictions had on the first books published for children
was first loosened in the 1800s when Grundtvigian Christianity
broke through in the field of children's books (Tønnessen 1982).
Grundtvig was a Danish cleric, a writer, an educator, and a
practical man of action, widely known as founder of the folk high
school movement. Religious and moralistic issues have had only a
modest place in children's literature in Norway in this century.

Today's literature reflects the new recognition of children
as persons living an important life and culture of their own,
rather than pointing the way by which children can grow to be
responsible adults. In his book, *The Night Birds* (*Nattfuglene*),
contemporary author Tormod Haugen is credited with having
introduced this new trend in children's literature, a literature
of greater depth and greater psychological significance than
was characteristic of children's literature available earlier.
Because of the emphasis on the quality of children's books, the
present is recognized as an especially good time in the history
of Norwegian children's literature.

Norwegian children are not primarily readers of serious
literature, though in-depth interviews with school children,

parents, teachers, and librarians showed that they prefer serious books (Gjengset 1986). Gjengset asserts that it is not Norwegian children's fault that they read few good children's books but the fault of adults who abandon their children to comic books by not producing enough good children's books and by not making them readily available. The most prevalent leisure-time reading among Norwegian children today is the reading of comic books. Donald Duck is a favorite, as are Westerns and war comics (Ørjasæter 1976; Berg 1985). Such reading material is readily available. Children buy it and exchange it with friends. Also, adults in Norway often give children comic books as gifts, thus inadvertently influencing their choice of reading material. Ten- and twelve-year-olds were asked if they read the comics and, if so, how many comic books they read per week. Almost 90 percent read one or more comic books every week. Ten percent read five or six comic books per week. Their effect on children is a subject of debate as it has been in the United States.

Reading is the leisure-time choice that Norwegian children tend to turn to when they do not have other things to do. It is a winter and evening activity, and a favorite time to read is in bed at night before going to sleep (Gjengset 1986; Berggreen 1987). Other than comic books, the kinds of books ten- and twelve-year-olds were reading in the late 1970s follow:

Type of Books	Percent Reading
Detective	55.5
Tarzan, cowboy	27.2
Scandinavian children's books	18.4
Romance	10.0
Professional, technical books	10.0
Adult	1.9
Travel, nature	1.7

(Raundalen and Raundalen 1979:122)

Sex differences were marked. Besides detective books, boys had a high preference for Tarzan and cowboy books. Girls also read detective books, but what distinguished them was that they read three times as many Scandinavian children's books as did boys. Scandinavian children's books are widely regarded as quality children's literature.

Only four of one hundred families in Norway do not have TV. TV watching varies from a little to avid and frequent among children. (Kolloen 1985). Twelve-year-olds in the Oslo area, where several channels are available, watched about three hours a day in March 1987. In outlying areas where there are fewer things to watch, they watched about 1.5 hours a day (Frønes 1989). And they saw more on weekends. Satellite TV has established Saturday and Sunday forenoons as children's TV time. The amount of English-language entertainment available to Norwegian children has created a new relationship to the English language; it is no longer something foreign. The availability of English-language child TV means that if one wants to know what cartoon-series heroes are saying to each other, one must understand English. Boys watch more TV than do girls. Girls more often assert that they do not watch TV every day.

Ørjasæter (1976) found that children did not choose TV at the cost of other activities but watched TV when they did not have other things to do. Seventeen percent of ten- to twelve-year-olds reported that they liked the programs especially designed to appeal to children, while 26 percent said they didn't like such programs but preferred adult offerings instead. In general, sports programs, feature films, and detective stories were most popular. Cultural programs appealed the least. Parents sometimes ruled against certain programs either because they ran past the children's bedtime or because they "weren't exactly children's TV" (Berg 1985).

Radio drama was very popular with children; popular music was even more popular. Children also showed a preference for local material; that is, they indicated an interest in knowing more about the area in which they lived. Children were more positive about what they heard on radio than what was on TV. What they reported as not liking was similar for both radio and TV: daily news; politics; culture, especially serious music; and religion, such as morning devotions. Many mentioned that they did not like the stock market, fishing reports, and the news in Samish (Lapp). That suggests to Ørjasæter (1976) that there perhaps were many homes in which the radio was turned on in the morning and left on all day with no selection as to programs, no silence for thought, and no uninterrupted time when the family could listen and speak to each other.

Children were asked what they would like to have as TV and radio programs. First, they wanted to know more about how life is for children in other lands and in other places within their own country. Many wanted more programs about animals, birds, and nature in general. The answers prompted Ørjasæter to raise the question, Shouldn't the children's world, their problems, their environment, their daily life and their culture belong in the programming, commentary, and news reports?

Raundalen and Raundalen (1979) found the largest gender difference between boys and girls in preference for sports programs. Eleven percent of girls preferred such programs while 71 percent of boys did. Girls explained that the reasons for their low preference was that only boys' and men's sports were shown on TV. Neither boys nor girls preferred to listen to reports of sports events on radio, however.

An ongoing debate in Norway and in many other countries has dealt with the question as to whether or not children are adversely affected by what they watch on TV. Ørjasæter (1976) reported on a study made in northern Norway in 1967 that concluded that TV might affect children's hopes and dreams regarding their futures. Children no longer wanted to be teachers or nurses or to work at crafts or trades. Girls wanted instead to be pop singers and actors, and boys wanted to be flyers or sports heroes. After television came to that remote area, many wanted to move to the south or at least to a more populated area. To keep people in those remote rural areas by making life as agreeable as possible for them has been an ongoing goal of the Norwegian government. TV may have had the opposite effect on children, increasing their dissatisfaction with life in remote areas.

For the most part, Norwegian children's leisure-time activity is largely unorganized, or as they themselves say, "We don't do anything special" (Berg 1985). Much of their time is spent in playing games. In winter, snow play of various kinds is popular. In spring and summer, cycling is popular, causing worry to parents because of the automotive traffic. Marbles in spring continues to be a popular activity, especially for boys; so is playing cops and robbers. Jumping rope commands more of girls' attention (Andersen 1985). There are also birthday parties to attend and sleeping over at a friend's or grandparent's house that fill the weekly program.

Many families have a cabin where the family spends holidays together. Family vacation trips are popular. Norway is very much an outdoor-activities and sports-oriented society; there are families that "live and breath sports" (Berggreen 1987).

Ten or eleven years of age is a transition time in the lives of children as they move more and more from taking part in family activities to being with their friends. That is reflected in the study of leisure-time pursuits. Children of this age expressed a strong conviction that they themselves should choose activities based on their own interests. Norwegian parents are quite united in at least *saying* that they agree that children should have the right to choose their own leisure-time activities with as little family interference as possible. At the same time parents want their children to have as rich a leisure time as possible by taking advantage of the best that is available to them. That makes it difficult for parents to refrain from expressing their preferences. Also, through their daily association with their children, parents can hardly help conveying their own interest in certain activities. The research shows that, more than either parents or children realize, children of this age continue to be their parent's children (Berg 1985). That is, parents are a more important reference group for them than are their peers. If a child begins an activity and continues in it, it usually means that a parent, especially the father, is fully committed to the child's participation in that activity. Furthermore, when parents engage in the same activity as the children do, it also strengthens children's involvement. Mothers show a greater tendency to become involved when an activity involves religion or music, encouraging a daughter gifted in ballet, for example, or a son who plays an instrument (Berggreen 1987). An occasional Norwegian parent pays a son or daughter to engage in some activity that the parent strongly favors. A child sometimes engages in an activity that does not interest the parents, but such activity often has to be carried on without the parent's active support. Seldom does a child begin an activity on its own and persist in it without parental support (Berggreen 1987).

The parents' commitment to the child's choosing its own activities was especially tested when ten- to eleven-year-old children showed tendencies to move away from participating in family activities and began participating more and more with peers. Parents have expressed apprehension about some of the new possible involvement, such as mopeds, the gang at the local kiosk, and drugs. Having a child going to the discotheque also represents something new at this age: "He comes home red and warm and hoarse."

Out-of-home leisure-time activities also include occasions when children go to the movies; attend band and choir concerts; go to a museum, a circus, an amusement park, or an athletic contest. None of them fill free time to the same extent as does TV, radio, and listening to recorded music, however. Half of the children seldom or never go to the movies, and a like number do not go to the theater. Wike (1976a) judged participation of Norwegian children in theater and drama to be largely insignificant. There is a recognized need for more regional theater. Also, not many good children's films are available in Norway. There is an age restriction (twelve years of age) for many films regarded as not suitable for children. Finding ways to attend a movie for which one is not eligible by reason of age is part of the secret activity of children that they may be reluctant to discuss with adults. Viewing a violent video film, which only a very few Norwegian children had ever done, also comes under the category of secret activity, activity not discussed with adults (Berggreen 1987; Gjengset 1986).

The school is a centralized location for much of the organized leisure-time activities for children. A Norwegian school has a library, a gym, a football field, a place for concerts, and may have a theater where school drama is available. There are school bands and school and church choirs.

In Norway as well as throughout Scandinavia, both in the country and in towns and cities, sports are a dominant children's leisure-time activity, particularly team sports wherein children participate in groups with their friends (Berg 1985). The social side of sports is very important to them; it is important to children that several friends begin and continue an activity together. It isn't only those who are poor at a sport who choose to drop out. Good athletes will quit if a boy- or girlfriend is not good enough to continue playing on the team and has been eliminated by the coach (Berggreen 1987).

Fifty percent of all fourth graders in Norway take part in one or another form of organized sports. The number is even higher for sixth graders, especially for boys. Seventeen percent of girls and 8 percent of boys are active in more than three kinds of organized activity. On the other hand, 32 percent of boys and 14 percent of girls ten to twelve years of age are not in any form of organized activity.

Outside of sports, no type of organized leisure-time activity stands out as dominant other than music. There has been a marked change especially in girls' participation in both organized sports and organized musical activity in Norway within one generation. If one goes back to the parent generation, one finds that today's mothers were largely excluded from two dominant activities during their childhood, school music and football; football was purely a boy's and man's activity as was the school band. If a girl did take part in a musical organization, it was as a member of a choir (Berggreen 1987). The single nationally most popular children's choral group in Norway today is *Sølvguttene,* which is a boys' choir.

As with sports, children prefer music as a group activity. When a child does play an instrument without its being part of an organized activity, it usually means that there is strong involvement and encouragement from a parent (Berggreen 1987). For example, Simen, a fourth-grade boy who is in many activities, sometimes complains about having to play the violin—there are boring pieces, there are difficult notes, one has to be so precise. He says he plays because "his mother likes it" (Berggreen 1987).

Though sports and music are major leisure-time activities for Norwegian children, they are not without some frustration, especially where adults are involved in the activity. The children like to play, and they like to play together with their friends. But they complain that that is not enough to satisfy adults; adults want to see their sons and daughters reach their highest possible level of competence and efficiency in an activity. In other words, adults want to professionalize children's leisure-time activity (Berg 1985). That means practice and selectivity—selecting the children who can contribute to the highest level of performance of the organization, for instance. Adult supervisors emphasize practice. There is band practice, choir practice, football practice, handball practice, ski practice, swimming practice, piano practice, violin practice, as well as the conditioning required for competitive activity. Many Norwegian children expressed their dissatisfaction at having to practice at the insistence of a parent, a coach, or an activity leader. Practice often requires their being alone, and that makes it tedious and boring.

Even more discipline is required of a child who is in several activities. Lene Cecilie has ski practice on Mondays and Thursdays and handball on Tuesday (Berggreen 1987). Vegard plays the cornet and the bass and is learning to play the guitar: music is his strongest current hobby. He is also involved in sports and outdoor life; jujitsu is his sport. He jogged everyday until he sustained an injury. He reads mysteries, is in a church youth club, and is taking confirmation instruction. He also spends some time with friends. He has a small TV set of his own and a small cassette player, but with his priorities there isn't much time for such things or for going to movies (*UKE-Adressa*, 13 April 1985).

It is common to hear Norwegian parents say that they don't like a child of theirs to begin an activity and then drop out. On the other hand, it is parents who sometimes encourage their child to drop out of an activity. Camilla comes from a religious family. She is in Scouts and in Juniors at church. She also went out for handball. The latter required the parents to be up by 7:00 on Saturday mornings in order to drive her to practice.

There were also matches played during the dinner hour on Sundays. For those reasons, Camilla was influenced to drop handball but to continue in Scouts and Juniors.

A distinctive type of adult-initiated organization for children appeared in Norway around the middle of the last century—an organization intended to pass on to children, and to inculcate in them, a world of ideas and ideals subscribed to by their parents (Ropeid 1984). The result was a spate of organizations that in effect are a link in the socialization process of children—a process guided, even controlled, by adults. In other words, indoctrination rather than children's free choice has been the watchword of the organizations. The last two centuries have been a period of great interest in ideas in Norway, and parents have become eager that their children be led to embrace the "right" ideas.

It is convenient to divide the organizations and their activities into three types, based on the ideas espoused and the resulting content of the programs. The first is sports activity, which Ropeid (1984) designates as hobby activity (*hobbyaktivitet*). One of the results of adult control in organizations set up to foster and support sports activity is the professionalization of sports, a development that children may see as good in many ways but also as a development with disadvantages as we have pointed out earlier.

The second kind of organization is that with specific Christian ideals, content, and purpose. In Norway the first Sunday School was organized in 1844; subsequently, the idea spread in cities and rural areas (Ropeid 1984). In 1889 the Norwegian Sunday School Federation (*Norske Søndagsskole forbund*) was established to help organize the Sunday School activities of the Norwegian State Church. In 1898 the Norwegian Sunday School Union (*Norsk Søndagsskoleunion*) was formed, representing Sunday School work in the Baptist, Methodist, other free churches, and the Missionary Federation (*Misjonsforbundet*). Sunday Schools of the Salvation Army (*Frelsesarmeen*) and the Evangelical-Lutheran Free Church (*Den evangelisk-lutherske frikyrkja*) are not a part of either the Federation or the Union. The objective of the Sunday Schools today is as it was in 1844, namely, to assemble children and to tell them about Jesus. Different ideas have appeared from time to time as to the best way of accomplishing that goal, and the perspectives of sacramental Christianity and conversion Christianity differ somewhat in their emphasis.

The Sunday School is not a vital, inclusive organization for children in all Norwegian communities. In group interviews in public schools in two communities in 1985, one on the island of Sula and the other in Trondheim, all of a class of ten- and eleven-year-olds on the island and none of a class in Trondheim said they attended Sunday School.

Christian churches and religious organizations that maintain Sunday School programs are likely to carry on intensive children's activity in other organized ways as well. A survey from 1951 showed that a good 18 percent of all Norwegian mission organizations were children's organizations, and it isn't much different today (Ropeid 1984). A fifth of all the primarily Christian organizations in Norway are children's organizations. As much as 40 percent of them belong to the Norwegian Lutheran Mission Society (*Norsk Luthersk Misjonssamband*).

Religious work with the young is usually divided into groups by age: children, pre-teens, and teenagers. The activity is often more practical than ideological, unlike that of some of the secular children's organizations in Norway. Church youth often spend their time making things that will later be sold at a church bazaar, the proceeds 187 of which are designated for good works at home or on the mission field, often activity that will benefit children. There has always been much singing in the religious children's organizations, and recently a number of choirs have been formed. Scouting has also been incorporated within the church's child and youth work. Girls take part in more of the children's religious activities than do boys (Raundalen and Raundalen 1979).

Communities that have a religious meetinghouse (*bedehus*) are better equipped to carry on an organized, indoor child and youth program than are communities with only a church nave. The meetinghouses normally have a large meeting room, and some have kitchens as well. In some communities the religious meetinghouse is used strictly for religious meetings. Other meetinghouses have become much more like community centers with a great variety of cultural, recreational, health, and even money-making (for good causes) activities. In many rural communities the religious meetinghouse is the only large meeting center in the community, and those who control access to it can control much of the group activity that goes on in the community.

Preparing children for confirmation at age fourteen or fifteen years of age is by far the church's largest youth work (Wagle 1985). Nearly 60,000 children are confirmed each year or 85–90 percent of those in that age bracket. In some districts all children are confirmed, but there are urban congregations today wherein no more than half are confirmed.

A widely held understanding of confirmation in earlier times was that the confirmand was to confirm the baptismal promise, the promise made by parents and sponsors while the child was in his or her infancy. That is, baptism was not fully valid until the young affirmed it at the time of confirmation. That view of confirmation had its roots in pietism and is tenacious despite the fact that as early as 1912 the confirmation rite was defined as a benediction or a blessing ceremony. A personal relationship to Jesus Christ is not prerequisite to taking part in confirmation today. God's promise in baptism is seen as valid with or without subsequent affirmation.

The aim of the church's confirmation instruction is to give knowledge and to show that religion has relevance to life. The church expects more of prospective confirmands than it did in earlier times, not in the form of more knowledge, but in increased participation during the preparation period. Confirmation preparation time in most places has been extended from three to four months to eight months or so. In that course of time about forty-five meetings are held. Along with classroom instruction there are religious services, weekend trips, service projects, and perhaps camping. An alternative system of preparing for confirmation has been added. Rather than weekly meetings for about half a year, a district may offer eight days of camping. The camping alternative got a boost in 1988 when the now crown prince, Haakon Magnus, chose to prepare for confirmation through a camping experience. His confirmation was a prominent royal event, with a bishop conducting the service and relatives, visiting royalty, ambassadors, government officials, and others in attendance. The event and the accompanying receptions and dinners received extensive media coverage.

Confirmation is so important an event in Norway that young people and their parents may want confirmation even though they have no interest in or attachment to the church. To accommodate that interest, a group of parents in 1951 instituted a program of civil confirmation (*Stockholm Dagens Nyheter*, 22 May 1988). A few years later the Human Ethics Federation (*Humane Etiske Forbundet*) became involved. Thirty-five hundred (between 5 and 10 percent) youth of confirmation age chose civil confirmation in 1988. The ceremony is held in the city hall or in some other secular setting and is much like the church ceremony—with music, a procession, speaking, and the receiving of diplomas. The ceremony comes at the end of a long line of meetings wherein the youth discuss ethics, lifestyles, human equality, the United Nations Declaration of

Human Rights, legal rights, and world religions. The goal is to inform and educate but not to indoctrinate.

A third set of organizations is built around a societal ideal (*samfunnsidé*). We will discuss three of these — Scouts, *Fram-fylkingen*, and 4-H. Not much has to be said about Scouting and 4-H activities since these organizations are also found in the English-speaking world.

The Boy Scout movement was founded in 1908 by Robert Baden-Powell, a British general whose aim was to enliven the church cadet corps with elements of army life. He ended up producing a much more inclusive activities program (MacLeod 1987). Scouting soon spread to other countries including Norway. Its progress was most marked in cities and in the middle class in Norway. It did not reach rural areas or the laboring class. The probable reasons were the cost involved as well as the ideology of scouting. The scouting movement sprang out of a liberal and tolerant cultural optimism and had Christian roots. Its ideology did not suit the militant labor movement during its early years (Ropeid 1984), though the basic activities of scouting are not so foreign to those of worker-sponsored organizations in Norway.

The labor movement of the early 1900s determined that labor should organize groups specifically to meet the needs of the children of laborers. The intent was clearly ideological. The reasoning was as follows: The middle class had its plans and intense activity to bring up children to be faithful defenders of the capitalistic system, and the church had organized activity to inculcate in its children the beliefs and precepts of Christianity. Therefore, the labor movement needed children's organizations to promote its ideals and to serve as a home for the children of laborers so that they would have something to go to other than Sunday School, Scouts, and the other middle-class organizations. They attempted to accomplish the task by forming a number of socialistic children's groups. By 1922–23 there were fifty-one such groups with six thousand members. Most groups held their meetings on Sunday between the hours of eleven and one, a traditional time for church services in Norway. Through short talks, stories, and songs, they sought to awaken labor-movement ideals in the children. But the movement didn't make the progress that had been hoped for. There was a steadily growing dissatisfaction with the Sunday meetings, which interfered with Sunday tours in the woods and countryside, for instance.

The discovery of similar developments in Austria and Germany revived the flagging spirit of the movement, however, and at the Labor Party's meeting in 1933 the organization called *Framfylkingen* was begun. The name of the organization is Norwegian, but the goals and organizational patterns are similar to those of youth organizations in Germany, Austria, and Sweden. Many of the early goals of the labor movement, goals dealing with wages and working conditions, for instance, were eventually realized, and neither the labor movement nor its youth movement is as conscientious as it was before World War II. There is more emphasis today on protecting and carrying forward goals that have already been won (Ropeid 1984).

Framfylkingen's idealistic goals today are to develop personality and feelings of solidarity, responsibility, and tolerance and to awaken children's interest in cultural values, social relationships, and international friendship. Three terms that are frequently used are cooperation, comradeship, and democracy, the end being the full realization of democratic ideals in social life. The organization emphasizes teamwork and places great emphasis on life in the out-of-doors. *Framfylkingen* has not emphasized practical tasks, such as preparing packets to send to the mission field, as have the Christian organizations. The emphasis instead has been on a variety of courses — music, leadership, language, art, and hobbies.

The first groups organized specifically for the children of Norwegian farmers were established in 1926 (Ropeid 1984), and the various local groups were organized into an association in 1936. The name of the organization was officially changed to Norwegian 4-H in 1956. In the ten years after World War II the 4-H movement was gradually built up as an organization comparable to the Scouting movement, but with its roots in agriculture. An organization designed to awaken, stimulate, and sustain an interest in agriculture, homemaking, and nature seemed almost imperative, for research had shown that 25 percent of farm boys wanted to be farmers when they were seven years old, but by the time they were fourteen years old, only 2 percent wanted to be farmers. There is no doubt that the 4-H movement hoped to reduce the migration from rural areas by creating secure, contented rural youth, thereby diminishing the prestige and the appeal of urban life. The goals of 4-H were to awaken interest in a healthy and harmonious rural life through club work and to give children training in the care of soil, woods, plants, and animals and in the proper and aesthetic ways of preparing food and textiles. The movement has had a strong growth, which is testimony to its appeal to rural children. Today 4-H has also spread to towns and cities in Norway, showing that a children's organization that concentrates on nature, the care of animals and plants, and the production of food and textiles meets an interest of urban children as well.

In sum, it can be said that the idealistic children's organizations started by adults in the hope of implanting high ideals in the next generation, combined with large amounts of play and outdoor activity, continue to be popular with children in Norway. Ever more units are being formed with a comparable growth in the number of dedicated adults (most of whom volunteer their services) willing to support and administer the programs. Yet despite the large number of organized activities available to children in Norway, nearly one in every five children ten and twelve years of age did not belong to any organization, club, or team at the beginning of the 1980s. Girls took part in a more varied spectrum of the organized cultural offerings than did boys. They more often had music education of various kinds and took part in more religious activities.

There is a current uneasiness over the health of children's culture and children's play and leisure-time possibilities in Norway and throughout Scandinavia. What is positive about children's lives is often drowned out by frightening accounts in the media of children who do not play enough, are neglected, mistreated, overly exposed to commercial TV and violent video, and suffer mental stress. As Berggreen (1987:202) states it, "A willingness to find misery is strong, and likewise a willingness to find one or a limited number of scapegoats such as video or TV—which contribute to passivity—or coaches and ambitious parents who create pressure to achieve."

Such concerns are not limited to the Scandinavian countries, of course. In a position paper on play for the Association for Childhood Education International, the authors (Isenberg and Quisenberry 1988) assert that children are growing up in a rapidly changing world characterized by pressure to succeed in all areas, that they have less time and opportunity to play than did children of previous generations, and that research has shown play to be crucial in their healthy development and must be defended by all adults. That is a message that teachers and other adults are hearing in Norway today. The methods by which play transmits culture to children are being compared to what is done to transmit culture in the elementary school, often in a way that disparages the school: the theoretical and passive learning that goes on in the school is contrasted with the active, participant, instant learning that takes place in children's groups. In children's culture, teaching is directed to the moment, to the occasion, while the school teaches about the future. It is the folk culture's educational principle that is said to be practiced in child culture—learning through observation, imitation, participation (Enerstvedt 1984). Hence, it is argued that the techniques of learning used in child's play are more effective transmitters of culture—child or adult culture—than are the techniques used in school. "Despite the fact that they have been through six years of daily influence with the goal of learning, not a few leave school with impoverished knowledge in a school subject. At the same time they have learned many games, songs, rhymes and jokes that would fill a large book" (Østberg 1979:86). Introducing children to adult culture is what the school does, and this is absolutely essential, but it is asserted that without incorporating the techniques of play it is very difficult to transmit anything to children in a way that is either meaningful or useful to them. It is argued that children view what they learn in school as having little connection with their daily lives.

Nevertheless, the pupils who are successful in school are very often the same ones who are active in child culture and leisure-time activities; the tragedy is that the opposite is not true (Wike 1976a). There are attempts today to plan schoolroom environments in which children learn concepts by the use of play materials and activities. Traditionalists in Norway are not convinced that a curriculum that incorporates play techniques strengthens and supports children's intellectual development and preparation for later social responsibility.

Norwegian children may not play any less today than they did in earlier times, according to Østberg (1979), but with the reorganization of the basic school (*grunnskolen*) into an elementary school (*barneskolen*) and a youth school (*ungdomsskolen*), children tend to stop child play at earlier ages than they used to. A generation or two ago child play in Norway continued until fourteen or fifteen years of age. Children now continue child play only through sixth grade or until around age twelve or thirteen. Childhood experts do not see the change as a positive development. Parents, especially among the better-educated classes, appear to approve of their children's moving out of childhood at this early age; the move is not accidental (Østberg 1979).

When children move from total parental care and supervision into child culture, they are on their way to becoming independent individuals among equals. When they leave elementary school and begin youth school, they make a similar jump, this time from child culture into teen culture. Play may be dominant in children's lives for fewer years than formerly, but there is nothing to indicate that Norwegian children are playing less or are dropping out of adult-approved leisure-time activities as some have feared; the opposite is true (Berg 1985).

But what of the children themselves? Are they enjoying their childhood? Are they satisfied with the play possibilities and leisure-time activities available to them? Variations on these questions have been addressed to children in several major studies (Raundalen 1976; Raundalen and Raundaulen 1979; Tiller et al. 1983; Tiller 1984; Berg 1985; and Berggreen 1987).

In the Raundalen and Raundalen study, four thousand pupils from the first to the sixth, and in some cases the ninth, grade from three regions within Norway were asked if they were satisfied in their relationships and with the environment and resources available in their communities. In some cases their parents were also interviewed. In the Tiller studies, two hundred eight-year-olds and about the same number of mothers were interviewed, and in the 1985 pilot study, one hundred fifty fourth graders (ten–eleven years old) and their parents from Norway and the other Scandinavian countries were interviewed.

In general, younger children appear to be more beset by problems in their social lives—being excluded by others and being pestered or intimidated—than are older children, whereas older children experience greater dissatisfaction with what the communities have to offer. That is, more of them are bored with the possibilities. There are children in all grades who report that they are sometimes or often pestered by their peers. (Peer molestation and violence is taken very seriously in Norway, and measures are taken to deal with it.) In no class, in the first six grades, did less than 28 percent mention being teased. The percentage was highest in the fourth grade (53 percent).[*]

Finding that a child sometimes ends up being totally left out by other children without the other children appearing to notice or to feel badly about it was disturbing. Many children go through a shorter or longer period when they feel left out before they find a secure group in which they are included. That is reflected in the finding that 50 percent of first graders but only 7 percent of ninth graders mentioned being excluded by their peers sometimes or often.

Also very unpleasant for a child were those cases in which a child felt that he or she was being bullied (*mobbet*) by one or more children. Unlike teasing, which appears to be an integral part of child culture and to be commonly carried on in the open and even in the presence of adults, Norwegians and other Scandinavians find this kind of invasion of personal space difficult to regard as having any place in child culture. It is what Gullestad (1990) refers to as the reverse or wrong side of

---

[*] The type of teasing complained about is no doubt unkind pestering. Teasing is a typical way of regulating association between children. Sometimes it is used to point out a weakness or something that is thought to be ludicrous or different in another. A large part of it is scornful, making a fool of another because of some apparent stupidity demonstrated in school or elsewhere. The teaser may combine the teasing with boasting about his or her own greater ability. On the other hand, teasing can be good-natured and friendly. Children tease each other as a way of inviting contact with one another or as a way of showing that one belongs and that one "rates." Teasing is often a prelude to, or an indication of inclusion, and being included is one of the most pleasant experiences of childhood, whereas being excluded is one of the most painful. The form used in teasing is often humor—the intent dictates whether the one being teased feels humiliated or honored by the attention.

children's own culture. It is offensive, hidden, usually not carried on in the presence of adults and commonly kept from adults, even by the child who is being persecuted (Østberg 1979). Pestering (*plage*) meant a number of things and varied in its severity—being frightened with something, being hit, being threatened with a beating, being beaten, being intimidated into doing something one does not want to do, or not being permitted to do something one wants to do. By far the largest number of children who reported being pestered (54 percent) were first graders; 48 percent reported that it happens on the way to school or on the school grounds. The percentages reported decrease in each grade to only 7 percent in the sixth grade. Boys account for about 60 percent of the pestering and girls about 40 percent. Girls hit, pulled hair, and kicked, but not as much or as hard as did boys. There is some evidence that pestering small children is something older children do when they feel they have nothing else to do.

Forty-two percent of first graders mention being frightened or threatened, and 34 percent mention being intimidated into doing something they do not want to do. A large percentage of first graders (49 percent) and only 8 percent of sixth graders mention not daring to go outside. Big boys and naughty girls are mentioned as reasons. There are also certain older persons or other things in the environment that younger children in particular find threatening.

Raundalen and Raundalen (1979) report that a very large percentage of children eight to fifteen years of age are bored with the neighborhoods they live in, as many as 42 percent among the fourteen-year-olds. Children who are least likely to report being bored with the opportunities in their communities are the ten- to twelve-year-olds, under 20 percent. There is a risk that children who are bored with the available activities, especially the older children, will find activities to engage in that are dangerous and destructive to themselves and to others (Kjøndal 1984), including pestering younger children, stealing, and destroying property. There has been a growing concern over an increase in deviant criminal behavior especially among older children and youth in Norway since the fifties.

During the last few decades much attention has been given to peer violence in Scandinavia, violence in the form of pestering and bullying that goes on between children out of view of adults. The phenomenon has been extensively studied in an effort to determine the incidence, causes, and prevention (Juul, forthcoming). The first European conference on bullying was held in Norway in 1987.

Measures that have been recommended in a program of control or prevention include: school children's reading and discussing literature on the subject with the opportunity to clarify and strengthen positive values; pupils' expressing their thoughts and feelings through essays and other written work that they read to each other; pupils' writing plays on the subject and doing role playing; students' assuming responsibility for others by being companions, usually of younger children who have problems; parents' and teachers' active involvement; adults' developing clear rules against bullying with enforcement of sanctions against rule violators. There is evidence that these and other endeavors have had positive results, but there is also concern that bullying continues at unacceptable levels.

In an attempt to determine what children see as an ideal environment in which to live, Raundalen (1976) asked 508 ten- to twelve-year-olds from twenty different schools what kind of environment they would like for their children in the future. They mentioned mainly that it would be good if children could live in smaller places, could have many things to engage in— including hobbies, belonging to clubs, having contact with animals—and would encounter little or no traffic in their play areas. In a similar vein, they were asked for concrete things that they would change in their own communities. They had a flood of suggestions reflecting perceived inadequacies in one or more of the communities. They wished for safe, well-equipped play areas; bicycle paths; places to ski, toboggan, and play tennis, golf, badminton, handball, volleyball, football; a swimming pool; rooms and facilities for hobbies, Scouts, clubs; more organizations and clubs; courses in drawing and carpentry; contact with animals, including a riding school; work places; a movie house and cheaper tickets. Norway is a very mountainous country; some children indicated that they would like lower mountains in their region!

Another question Raundalen asked was what children wanted from adults. Over the whole country the wish was for parents who would spend more time with them—play with them, help them to do things, go on trips with them. Very few wanted parents to buy them things—new skis, new bicycles, and such. Raundalen concluded, "They want more of us" (Raundalen 1976:22).

In the Raundalen studies, children were encouraged to focus on inadequacies in their neighborhood and what they wanted. The result was something of a litany of dissatisfaction, as one might expect. The 1985 pilot study (Berg 1985; Berggreen 1987), on the other hand, was designed to give an overview of the cultural engagement of average ten- to eleven-year-olds and how satisfied they were. In that study the children expressed themselves as generally well satisfied with their present lot in life. They engaged in the activities that were available to them and seldom expressed the wish for something else. Most appeared to enjoy themselves—"It was fun to do exactly what they were doing." They felt loved by their parents and took for granted that they belonged in one or another activity with family or friends. They were ardent in their leisure-time activities, whether organized or spontaneous and incidental. They were "unspecified," open to most opportunities; strongly desirous of experimenting; willing to try most things; going from one thing to another; and displaying enormous energy. They sought experience, understanding, adventure, and mastery. What they liked to do most was that which they were most developed in and that which was most creative. Through it all the social factor was decisive for their happiness and well-being; that is, they liked being together with other children and doing things in common with friends. They were concerned with the here and now; it was exceptional that a child had thought ahead and planned realistically for the future. These ten- and eleven-year-olds appeared to be well-adjusted children. Childhood for them was something very different from the media image of "video violence, parental neglect, and boutique thievery." Neither their culture nor their lives appeared dominated by the offerings of commercialized industry as many adults feared (Ørjasæter 1976). They were also relatively free from the clothing industry's emphasis on clothing styles, especially the boys. It varied from area to area, however, varying from city girls who were the most clothes conscious to country boys who paid the least attention to what they wore.

Publication of the results of the pilot study was something of a media event. The results published in 1985 gave the mass media the impression that no problems were found, that there were only well-adjusted children in Scandinavia. To find such positive results after all the gloom and doom that had appeared in the media was newsworthy. Researchers who made the study reacted to the press reports; they were not cocksure about their optimistic findings. After all, it was an overview; they had not probed deeply; besides, children this age have their secret lives; that which is unacceptable to adults, taboo-laden, or painful is not readily expressed when children are being interviewed by adults. Their fear of war falls in this category as does their love life; only a small amount of teasing by parents appeared to be enough to rule parents out as confidants in their love life. Sexuality as a whole was not a theme touched on in this study. These caveats notwithstanding, the positive response of ten- and eleven-year-olds to child life in the 1980s was reassuring.

The Norwegian Culture Council (*Kulturrådet*) recently launched a new program focused on investing in child culture, still considered something of a stepchild in Norway (Kjørholt 1990). A long list of projects for children are under way, and more are planned. The goal of the program, called Try It Yourself (*Prøv Selv*), is to stimulate the imagination and creativity of children and to give increased visibility and appreciation to child culture by supporting projects proposed by children. The program has been successful in attracting some children who have not previously been active in organized child activity. Ten percent of the participants said they had never or seldom been active in such activities before. In one community a group of children received support for the cleaning of a fishing lake with the aim of improving the quality of the fish stock. In a child center for refugees in Trondheim, the children opened a cafe. The cafe has become a social gathering place and a permanent enterprise operated as an elective subject in school. Another conspicuous project is cabin building, especially among boys. A cabin gives them a place to be, a place to have club meetings. A bicycle workshop is another project with a practical outcome. One of the main goals of Try It Yourself is to stimulate activity in the arts, and that too has been successful. There are projects in theater, film, music, dance, and literature. Art schools for children and youth in the municipalities is another program supported by the Culture Council. Growing public recognition of the importance of preserving and enhancing the many facets of children's culture should bode well for the future social and cultural life of children in Norway.

7

Children and Child Advocacy

NORWAY WAS A *family state* for many centuries, and interference by an emerging welfare state in the affairs of the family and the lives of children came about only gradually and was grudgingly received (Seip 1988).

Norwegian parents continue to be legally responsible for their children, and they are expected to provide the care and attention children need. When children become a public concern, it is out of what is referred to as "in the best interest of the child" or out of concern for the long-range well-being of society.

Public concern can take the form of (1) financial and other support to the family in the best interest of the child; (2) removal of the child from the home, sometimes for the good of the child and sometimes for the protection of others in society; (3) advocacy on behalf of children viewed as persons entitled to rights and freedoms of their own; and (4) funding of research on child development, children's culture, children's needs, and children's rights. All of these have been part of the public concern for children at various times and in various ways in Norway.

There is evidence of legislation from as early as the 1200s dealing with public concern for the care of children. Laws prohibiting the exposure of unwanted infants date from about that time. Magnus Lagbøter's Law dealing with the care of illegitimate children—in this case, the children of mistresses and concubines—is also an early example. The law specified that the mother was to be responsible for the child until age three and the father until age seven. In early times children were regarded as dependent only until about the age of eight. Also, the earliest homes for fatherless children did not take in children over the age of eight. The first so-called children's asylum was established in 1838. The asylums were primarily intended for children in the age range from infancy to age seven (Borchorst 1988). After the age of eight, children were thought to be old enough to work and to take care of themselves. In other words, by age eight childhood had ended and children had entered a kind of young adulthood. It was not until 1821 that fathers were held responsible for contributing to the care of their offspring between the ages of eight and fifteen. From that date on, the age of fifteen came to be the accepted dividing line between childhood and adulthood in Norway. Actually, the ritual of confirmation, introduced in 1739, became the recognized rite of passage from childhood to adulthood rather than a precise chronological age (Tønnessen 1982). An age group of persons falling between childhood and adulthood, known as adolescents or teens today, was not recognized until later.

Throughout the 1800s and the beginning of the 1900s a network of laws was enacted that reflected a growing public sense of responsibility and obligation to serve the needs of children. A significant motive was to foster greater similarity in the conditions of life for all children, between legitimate and illegitimate, between the poor and those with greater means. There were efforts to regulate child labor (which we discussed earlier); to expand and systematize public concern for the care of children; and to compensate for a lack of resources by giving support, in cash or in kind, to families for their own support and to provide healthful conditions for their children (Seip 1988). Norway was not the leader in those efforts, but Norway did enact the first law in the Western world establishing a national child-welfare system. The act was drafted in 1892, passed in 1896, and put into effect in 1900, the first year of the so-called Century of the Child (Dahl 1985). The law designated classes of children who were to be supervised by a newly created social entity, the welfare board. Covered were children who had committed immoral or punishable acts; those who were persistent school truants; those neglected by their parents—through moral laxity, for instance; those who could be expected to be spiritually deprived and potentially guilty—that is, children who would likely drift into a career of crime. The welfare board had the power not only to warn and admonish children and their parents but also to take the radical actions of depriving parents of their parental rights, revoking parental authority, removing the child from the home, and placing the child in some form of foster care. The first objective of such drastic action was to get the child out of an unhealthy environment. A second objective was to see that the child received upbringing "in a trustworthy and honest family," in a residential children's home, a compulsory residential school, or, as the last resort, in a reform school (Seip 1984). A child did not have to commit a crime in order for the child-welfare board to take charge of placement. New institutions were created by the welfare act for different categories of problem children in addition to the residential institutions for the care of children established much earlier. In the eyes of the law children were not being punished by being taken out of the home; instead, they were being protected and educated to be law-abiding, thereby sparing them and society the burden of having to punish them through imprisonment later in life.

Clearly, properly bringing up the child to become a responsible adult took precedence over the child's feelings and perspective on what was needed in order to have a rewarding childhood. Though the goal of public interference was not to punish the child, punishment for wrong behavior was seen as a necessary element in disciplined upbringing (Seip 1984). The ideal regimen for children in public care required the severity necessary for good discipline plus kindness on the part of the staff. For example, it was believed that boys in residential homes or reformatories were to be treated kindly, yet their treatment should promote good morals — "a healthy life, a cold bed and hard mattress, and frequent inspections beneath the bed covers to prevent sexual phantasies or worse," and frank discussion of boys' problems (Seip 1988:338).

The number of children cared for by the welfare boards increased rapidly, increasing by two and one-half times in the first five years that the 1892 act was in effect. Besides cases that the board itself investigated, cases were referred to the board by the police (the largest number), the school boards (the second largest number), as well as by poor-relief boards and health commissions (Dahl 1985).

The welfare board would summon children and their parents to appear. In almost two-thirds of the cases, the board only admonished or warned the children and their parents or asked the parents or the school to properly chastise the children judged to be recalcitrant. In the other one-third of the cases, the children were placed in a foster home or in one of the residential institutions.

That system of public child care had barely gotten into operation before an exposé threatened its very existence. It was in 1908, only eight years after the child-welfare law went into effect, that a novel, *Under Loven* (Beneath the law), on life in the residential schools was anonymously published by a former teacher and housemaster at Bastø, the state's model residential school for boys. The author made serious charges concerning conditions in this and other children's institutions. An investigative committee was quickly convened. Staff, employees, and the boys themselves were interviewed. The results were shocking, pointing out grossly unsanitary conditions and mistreatment of boys committed to the homes. The committee reported such things as wet and half-rotten mattresses; tattered and wet blankets, especially on the beds of bed wetters; stinking urine pots in the sleeping quarters. Boys told of supervisors who hit them with sticks, which they always had with them when at work, and employees complained of miserably inadequate resources due to budgetary constraints.

The press had a field day with the report, characterizing the residential homes and schools as child prisons or institutions of torture. Children were reported as preferring a short sentence in prison rather than risking an indeterminate sentence in a compulsory residential facility (Dahl 1985). As a result of the scandal, the character of the population in the residential schools changed. Other resources were used in dealing with neglected and incorrigible children; hence, there was a marked decline in their numbers in compulsory residential facilities and a proportionate increase in children with a criminal status—boys primarily because of theft and girls because of immoral behavior.

There were calls for thoroughgoing reform of the welfare system. In many ways the situation out in the field was alarming. There were not enough compulsory residential schools, the reformatories were on the verge of bankruptcy, inspection continued to reveal cases of serious mismanagement of institutions, and children were even placed in old-age homes or were being moved from better-run to cheaper foster homes to save money. Most shocking were the cases in which children were being put up for auction by local authorities, though the practice had been explicitly forbidden for decades (Seip 1988).

In 1922 diverse groups interested in the welfare of children organized into an umbrella organization to coordinate and regularize the efforts at child welfare being carried out by government agencies, the church, and the private sector. Funds were lacking for support of the effort, and because of the poor economic conditions, Parliament was unwilling to provide financial support. But there were some bright signs. In the capital city of Oslo an office for child care was organized in 1918 headed by a physician appointed as child-care inspector. The Oslo program was directed toward hygiene; the inspector had no thought of an extensive care system for all children. It was the weak and the poor who were to profit (Seip 1988). Each child was inspected once a year and, if it was deemed necessary, was given medical treatment. Undernourished children were treated in so-called vacation camps, and some "open-air" schools were created. A special scientifically composed school meal, which came to be called the "Oslo breakfast," was introduced in 1925.° Subsequent to the introduction of the system in Oslo, and in collaboration with one of the large voluntary organizations, school medical inspection was promoted in the whole country by 1924 and with rather successful results.

The emphasis on hygiene as a major component in the public concern for child care embraced more than physical health. It also included eugenics, or concern for the "hygiene of the race" and ridding the race of weak elements. In other words, eugenics became a dominant theme in child care as had been true for a time in elementary education. It was customary to categorize children as abnormal, morally defective, or inferior due to handicaps or illness. Categorizing was not new to Norway, but concern about the hygiene of the race strengthened interest in medical inspection to classify children more objectively and scientifically. Developments in psychology, especially developmental psychology and intelligence testing, reinforced the interest in more rigorous classifying and segregating.

° It is alleged that the Swedes magnanimously gave that name to the meal that they had introduced earlier.

The introduction of psychology into the child-care program was much broader, and more positive, than just the classifying of children. To paraphrase Ingvald Carlsen, a clergyman known as the grand old man of Norwegian child-care work, in the period from 1920 to 1936 there had been much talk about nutrition, normal weight and normal growth, law reform, and symptoms of illness, but now the understanding of spiritual needs was deepened by psychology. They now understood, he said, that the child "does not live by vitamins alone but by love from God and man" (Seip 1988:339). Carlsen declared that the era of materialism in child welfare work was over and the time of the psychologist had arrived.

The introduction of developmental psychological principles ushered in a period, which still prevails, in which two goals in child care are dominant—individualized treatment for each child in care along with adequate material support. From the point of view of the best interest of each child, it would appear to be a most significant improvement in the techniques employed in the public care of children.

Child welfare reform in Norway was unduly delayed by the invasion of Norway by Nazi Germany on April 9, 1940, and the subsequent five years of war devastation and occupation. By the time social reform was prioritized again after World War II, public responsibility was extended by the state into fields that had formerly been dominated by private organizations. It ushered in a more rational-scientific, less moralistic, approach. The word *omsorg* (care) became the key word in service to children with needs. The concept was directed more toward solving personal and psychological problems and less toward what the private organizations had regarded as proper upbringing. The rational approach to diagnosis and treatment of children and their problems characterized the revised Child Welfare Law passed in 1953. Parents' rights and the rights of professionals were both stressed; the rights of the child remained mostly unspoken, however. The role of professionals in child welfare was greatly extended to include pediatricians, psychologists, psychiatrists, and social workers. When speaking about child care in Norway today, the historian Seip (1988:342) says with only thinly veiled irony, "If professional people make the world a more caring world, there ought not to be any problems."

Child care today has shifted from an emphasis on differentiating and segregating children to the combining and integrating of all types of children into the community (Dahl 1985). Hence, the trend has been to reduce the number of children in care outside their homes. At the present time, care of small children outside the home is usually due to parental neglect or abuse; whereas for older children and youth, their own behavioral problems—conflicts with home or school, alcohol or drug abuse, criminality—are the factors involved in their detention (Grinde 1988). In the 1980s the problems of child abuse and neglect have gotten renewed attention. The public discussion still centers on the best interest of the child.

The changes that have occurred in child welfare in Norway in recent years include an increase in the number of children involved in welfare decisions; more children in open care, that is, involved in preventive programs; and fewer children in care away from home. Of the children who are removed from their homes, most are placed in foster homes, while some are placed in institutions or treatment units. In 1970, 67 percent of welfare decisions for new cases resulted in children's placement in care away from home and 33 percent in so-called preventive programs, whereas in 1985, 82 percent were placed in preventive care and only 16 percent in care away from home. Comparatively speaking, the number of children in care in Norway is very low compared to other countries, including the other Nordic countries.

When and how to intervene with compulsory care is a very sensitive question in Norway today, and threatened families have help of a lawyer, free of charge, if they wish to lodge a complaint against the welfare system or if a case goes to court. When interrupting or terminating parental rights, welfare agencies do so for different reasons than did the welfare boards at the turn of the century when children were taken into custody in order to segregate them from "good" children on whom they might have a bad influence or to provide a "proper" upbringing. Today a welfare agency is more likely to intervene if there is thought to be acute danger for the child or if a prognostic evaluation determines that physical or psychological development of the child may be in jeopardy if the child remains in his parental home. But, generally speaking, weight is given to supporting parent-child relations and to general support of families; hence, the effect of adjustment problems and deviancy must be quite serious before welfare agencies intervene. There has also been growing reluctance to return a child to its parental home if there is doubt about the parents' ability to care for the child and if the child has become stabilized with emotional ties in a foster home. In extreme cases, child-welfare legislation continues to allow termination of parental rights of one or both parents. That may be done even for a newborn to insure a future through adoption (Grinde 1988).

In 1984 Norway had 4.8 children per thousand in care compared to 7.8 in Finland, 8.0 in Sweden, and 15.8 in Denmark (Grinde 1988). Does that mean that there are fewer or less serious problems in Norway than in the other Nordic countries? It could, since Norway scores lower on several indicators of family problems, such as divorce and alcoholism, and there are many small communities with close family ties and social networks that reduce the apparent severity of the problems and hence the number of families at risk. Norway has many small communities often geographically isolated by fjords and mountains or in sparsely populated areas; there are more children in care in large cities than in small communities in all countries.

Nowhere is public commitment to child day-care centers more extensive than in the Nordic countries (Wolfe 1989). Norway is something of an exception, however, in that Norwegian mothers who work are more likely than other Scandinavian mothers to work only part-time and to use day care only part-time or to have a relative watch their children while they are at work.

In the 1960s and 1970s, while Sweden and Denmark were integrating women into the labor force, Norway was implicitly at least supporting a family model of mother as homemaker–father as breadwinner (Borchorst 1988). In Norwegian politics the concept of mothers as both earners and care-givers has had only a modest impact. There has not been the partnership between working mothers and the welfare state that is true in the other Nordic countries (Leira 1988). The structures and policies in both politics and the work world that discriminate against women are by and large still intact in Norway (Holter 1984). Despite those limitations, the number of mothers of small children in the work force continues to grow—and in spite of the low availability of child-care facilities. The rate of female participation in the labor force is about 65 percent for women with children and 55 percent for women with pre-school-age children. Those are high percentages when compared to a number of other Western countries but low when compared to Sweden where 85 percent of women with children work and 80 percent of women with preschool-age children work.

Despite the popularity of the child-care centers and the demand for them, the supply has never kept pace with the demand. Norway is not unique in that regard, for no country offers enough services to meet the needs, especially day centers for infants and toddlers (Kamerman and Kahn 1989). Norway has lagged behind its Nordic neighbors in providing child-care services and, in some ways, behind most European countries. Both Sweden and Denmark make much greater public investment in child care.

Norway was the latest of the Nordic countries in developing a national child day-care policy (Borchorst 1988). In 1975 Norway passed the Kindergarten Act (*Loven Barnehagen*), which integrated two systems providing out-of-home daytime activities for children under school age. One of the systems dealt with social relief measures; the other provided educational activities for children. The integrated system called for all daytime-activity institutions to focus on social education, emphasizing children's development, learning, and upbringing, along with care and supervision. At present there is one unified system composed of various types of daytime facilities that are governed by the provisions of the Kindergarten Act.°

A few daytime centers were established in Norway by the late 1800s; the first known center was founded at Trondheim in 1870. Some of the daytime centers were built on the principles of the German educator Friedrich Froebel. Froebel had established the first children's nursery or kindergarten at Blankenburg, Germany, in 1837. Some Norwegian women teachers took kindergarten training at the Froebel school and brought his ideas back to Norway; subsequently, Froebel's educational ideas spread throughout the land (Kvalheim 1980). That Froebel was greatly influenced by Rousseau is clearly evident in his

---

° Referring to all of the facilities as kindergartens, as they do in Norway, is confusing since they serve a wide range of children from infants through six-year-olds. Terms such as nursery school, infant school, and day-care center, along with kindergarten, are commonly used in various countries to cover such preschool facilities.

educational laws. Self-activity was the means by which a child was to develop. Great emphasis was placed on playing, singing, and practical training both indoors and out-of-doors. The goal of Froebel's system was to stimulate children spiritually and intellectually. Self-activity with guidance was the means by which development would take place. Self-activity was impossible under restraint. Nor did children need to be punished if properly motivated because they love to do right more than to be destructive (Froebel 1902). Restrictions, coercion, and the domination of the teacher were removed from the list of Froebel's disciplinary agencies. Froebel was confident that if the teacher was made a friend rather than a domineering autocrat discipline would settle itself in a natural way. The teacher's duty was to supply the desired conditions. Those ideas, plus Froebel's belief that women were the proper educators of children, were radical ideas for Norway where nearly all teachers were men at that time and strict discipline was regarded as an integral element in good education. The influence of principles such as those that guided activity in the Froebel kindergarten is very apparent in the way both daytime centers and elementary schools are run in Norway today, however.

The first child-activity centers of the Froebel type in Norway came about not because working mothers needed help with the care of their young children while they were at work but as a supplement to home care in families wherein the mother was a full-time homemaker (Bjørklund 1988). In other words, the first mothers who utilized daytime centers were not mothers who out of necessity or by choice were employed outside the home. Centers were usually started on the private initiative of one woman in the community and were designed to receive children below school age for a few hours a day. In the 1950s Norway's Housewife Association (*Norges Husmorforbund*) took the lead in seeing that day care provided educational activities for preschool children and not primarily physical care (Andenæs and Haavind 1987). That educational perspective continued to characterize developments in day care in Norway.

The Kindergarten Act defines a daytime center (kindergarten) as an educationally oriented facility for children under school age that shall ensure children an ample opportunity for development and activity. Emphasis is placed on learning through play, work, and social contact with children and adults. The authorities have not established any specific curriculum for the daytime centers; they are not part of the formal education system. It might be said that the Norwegian kindergarten has taken the considerate and, to an extent, protective mother as its ideal rather than the "achievement-demanding" school (Kjørholt et al. 1990). In fact, it is arguable that the ideology of the primary school, especially the lower grades, has been more affected by kindergarten ideology than has the kindergarten been affected by the ideology of the school. The tradition of development through play in a social context is emphasized. Norway has a kindergarten tradition that has defended the young child against the demands not only of the school but also of the family, the church, and the political arena with its concern for the nation's need to begin early the training of a highly skilled work force in order to compete in international trade. In other words, society's need did not play a special role in the formation of goals and programs in the kindergarten (Kjørholt et al. 1990).

Those sweeping assertions about the inviolability of the kindergarten were challenged and compromised in amendments to the Kindergarten Act in 1981 and 1983, however. After 1983 the kindergarten was required to work in close cooperation with the children's families. The child was still ensured opportunity for development and activity, but now it had to be in agreement and cooperation with the parents. The Norwegian kindergarten continues to be independent of the school but not of the home and the family.

Following the 1983 amendment, greater emphasis was placed on a more structured approach to the day center's program of activities. The personnel in each center is required to draw up a plan for the educational work, both for short periods of time and for the entire year. In turn, the plan is to be discussed with the parents.

An amendment to the Kindergarten Act introduced two years earlier proved to be more controversial, however, for it introduced a stipulation that daytime centers shall be founded on basic Christian values. It was passed at the strong urging of the Christian People's Party (*Kristelig Folkeparti*). Norway is the only country in Europe with that objective in public daytime centers. It is evidence also of the closer connection between state and church in Norway than in the other Scandinavian countries. Religious songs, table prayers, and celebrations of religious holidays had their place in day centers before 1981. But now if the majority of parents want it, local government-run day centers must provide the same content as church centers have previously provided. If there is conflict over the philosophy of life being promulgated, the sponsor of the center has the last word.

The indications of the right of parents and the local community to influence the program of the centers is consistent with the current strong central tendency in Norway in a direction of decentralization and more local control of activities in both kindergartens and elementary schools. In each municipality there is a daytime center or kindergarten committee that is responsible for the administration of the day centers, both public and private. Public institutions, business enterprises, private organizations, and others may run centers under the supervision of the municipality. About 40 percent of the centers are established by private organizations, including mothers' groups and parents' cooperatives (Bjørklund 1988).

Day centers for very young children are not numerous in Norway, compared to Sweden and Denmark; hence, mothers who need help with child care often have to develop their own solutions. They almost always start with private arrangements if they hope to have regular supervision of their child from as early as one to two years of age (Andenæs and Haavind 1987). Nearly one-fourth of the children are taken care of by relatives or close acquaintances without charge. Of other private arrangements, the day mother (*dagmamma*), who takes care of a limited number of young children in her home, is central. There are regulations governing such care as well. For instance, she may take in no more than four children at a time including her own children of preschool age. A preschool teacher acts as educational advisor for up to thirty children.

Day centers are open during different periods of the day. Full-time centers are open nine or ten hours daily five or six days a week; part-time centers, four to six hours five days a week; and short-time day centers, three to four hours two or three days a week. There are also day centers run on an ambulatory basis in order to cover the need in more neighborhoods. In these the professional staff of preschool teachers rotate between centers in two or three different places in the municipality. On the other hand, large centers have a principal, and the children are divided into sections comprising children over or under the age of three, with each section having a teacher. Both the principal and the section leaders are qualified preschool teachers (*førskolelærer*) or have equivalent qualifications in order to ensure a high educational level. After completion of upper secondary school, the preschool teachers follow a three-year course of training in the preschool teacher division of one of the colleges of education. The duration of the training is the same as for primary school teachers, though the curriculum is somewhat different. Preschool teachers constitute about one-third of all employees in the day centers;

assistants and trainees are employed in positions for which there is no special requirement regarding educational preparation.

One of the provisions in the Kindergarten Act of 1975 was that an educational-psychological advisory service organized within the school system be extended to apply to children of preschool age as well. In large municipalities the service is organized through one or more centers where a team consisting of a teacher or a special teacher, a psychologist, a doctor, and a graduate social worker provide advice aimed at creating a good environment, preventing behavior difficulties among pupils, and promoting cooperation within that environment. The service may also give advice in individual cases.

Each preschool teacher may have fourteen to eighteen children over the age of three in a full-time center and seven to nine children if the children are under the age of three. The number of children per staff member may vary with the quality and suitability of the premises and with whether there are handicapped children requiring extra care, for example. The vast majority of employees in day centers are women; only about 3 percent are men.

Today, as a generation ago, the great demand for child placement outside the home comes not from mothers who must of necessity work outside the home, though many of them appreciate the service, but from middle-class mothers with a high level of education who demand that such service be made available for their children. It is the children of these mothers who most often populate the day centers in Norway (Gulbrandsen and Tønnessen 1988).

From 1960 to the present there has been increased emphasis on providing child daytime facilities, yet even today Norway has the lowest percentage (less than 30 percent) of preschool children in nursery schools and kindergartens in Europe (Flekkøy 1989). The total number of children with a place in a publicly approved care arrangement in 1986 was 7.7 percent for those from birth to two years old and 46.4 percent for those three to six years old. The comparable percentages for Denmark were 43.4 percent and 62.5 percent. In quantitative terms Norway has the least offerings at all ages and especially for the youngest children (Leira 1988). In a recent study, Kjørholt and others (1990) compared educational offerings for young children in England, France, Japan, and the United States and found that nearly all five- and six-year-olds had places in either kindergarten or school. By contrast only 64 percent of Norwegian six-year-olds had a place in kindergarten in 1987, and none were in elementary school unless in a special experimental program.

Besides day centers there are supervised outdoor playgrounds (*Barnepark*) that provide short-time outdoor activity for young children. They are primarily intended for children who would otherwise have few opportunities for outdoor play in the company of other children. The supervised playgrounds are required to have at their disposal a warming room, a toilet, a wind shelter, and a lockable storage space for portable play equipment. There should be access to a telephone as well. Children normally play at such playgrounds for no more than three hours in winter (they come equipped to stand the snow and cold) and four hours during the remainder of the year. The number of children per adult at a playground is not to exceed fifteen.

The felt need for day centers can be expected to be especially acute in a country such as Norway where most children still do not begin school until they are seven years old and even after that age are apt to go to school for only two to three hours per day during the first two or three years (though an earlier starting age and a longer school day for the lower grades is expected to be phased in during the 1990s). Resistance to providing more daytime centers and to putting young children through the rigors of formal education in the elementary school reflects a traditional Norwegian reluctance to permit any children's institution to take over the roles of the home, the mother, and the children's play group as the principal socializers of infants and young children. Norwegian society continues to be organized in large part as if mothers were at home and could care for the children in the preschool and young school ages, whereas in fact more Norwegian women work outside the home than do women in the United States, France, or England. Given the reluctance of Norwegians to recognize that women have moved to the work force and that an adequate number of daytime centers are not available, Kjørholt and others (1990) question Norway's reputation as a child-friendly land in which to grow up.

The same question might be raised concerning school-age children of working parents who need supervision before or after school. Norway has the poorest coverage of any Nordic country, there being only six thousand places in leisure-time centers (*fritidshjem*), while there is need for an estimated eighty thousand or more places (Mjaavatn 1988). The problem is compounded by the fact that seven- to ten-year-olds in Norway go to school fewer hours than in the other Nordic countries and therefore require more out-of-school supervision.

There has been "raging controversy" (Wærness 1984) in Norway, among both experts and lay people, concerning whether or not placements of infant and preschool children in out-of-home daytime settings is detrimental to the development of children, especially in those cases in which young children are in a center all day, from 7:30 in the morning until 4:30 in the afternoon. There is increased belief in Norway in what is called *community care*, people caring for each other, as being both cheaper and morally preferable to public care. This signals a growing ambivalence regarding increasing professionalization of child care and the weakening of family and informal networks of concerned people. At the same time all the political parties agree that all families who desire day care for their children should have it (Andenæs and Haavind 1987).

There is no question but that public day care, as opposed to family care of children, creates a new kind of living space for children and hence a new kind of childhood (Dencik 1989). When parents decide to place a child in a day center, the child enters into a dual-socialization situation; children who spend part of the day at home and part of the day in day care alternate between two socializing sociotypes, the family and the day center. It creates the kind of childhood that in Norway has been called "woman friendly," for to the extent that children are taken care of outside the home during their daytime waking hours mothers are free to hold jobs outside the home or to pursue other interests.

Whether public day care is also "child friendly" is arguable despite the fact that day centers are custom-designed to be child friendly, emphasizing as they do a safe place to be active under the supervision of a staff of professionals. A number of studies have been made of day centers in Scandinavia, and in 1985 an ongoing comprehensive study was launched with a interdisciplinary research team and branches in all the Nordic countries—Denmark, Finland, Iceland, Norway, and Sweden (Dencik 1989). The project is coordinated by the Danish child researcher Lars Dencik. Within the project the socialization configuration of select groups of young children is investigated and compared. The everyday life of these unexceptional young children is mapped, and how the children cope with the conditions confronting them on a day-to-day basis is examined. Many of the children are in day centers. In the first round separate books were published on young children's material, social, and cultural living conditions in the different Nordic countries. (For Norway, see Andenæs and Haavind 1987.)

What kinds of socializers of children are professional day center workers? According to Dencik (1989), they are friendly enough to the children but keep a distance between themselves and the children; they are instruments for the implementing of correct rules of behavior. Dencik suggests that perhaps the disguised function of the public center is to "civilize" children at a tender age, thereby facilitating the course of social development. Children are compelled by the bureaucratic nature of things to adapt to abstract rules of time structuring and social organization. According to Dencik, there is an increased tendency for the child to be trapped inside a shell of "existential solitude" because he or she comes and goes between different social arenas and because of a single-minded preoccupation with an instrumental form of communication in the day center. On the other hand, there is a strengthened incitement to develop the capacity to communicate effectively, and communicative competence and development of a general social vitality are highly prized in modern society (Frønes 1989).

Critics of public day care in Scandinavia point out that the impersonal and fragmented character of public service means that professionals tend to lose the very qualities of personal commitment that transform a service into care. In private life, peoples' interactions are governed to a large extent by emotional relations, and in dealing with parents, a child exhibits a whole range of emotions showing the desire to be held, cuddled, and generally shown love and affection, as well as showing frustration and aggression. Perhaps none of that is visible while the child is at the day center. Early on they must learn to control their feelings and exercise restraint in all kinds of situations. It is as though a child's "childishness" and regression are forbidden in public day centers (Dencik 1989). In public life, such as that involving contact between any professional and client, it is dispassionate behavior that is uppermost while the affective aspects of the interaction are kept in check. Hence, the interaction becomes instrumental. It is difficult for day-center staff to combine a professional attitude toward their work with personal attachment they might feel toward a child. Personal attachment to a client has its price. It may mean showing partiality to one child, working for more hours than one is being paid for, or otherwise doing something that is contrary to the rules of a unionized profession. It can be characterized as "the compassion trap" that plagues the conscientious professional care giver (Wærness 1984). Dencik (1989) reports an astonishingly small display of emotion in the everyday life of the public day-nursery dayroom.

Most of the day-center workers in Scandinavia are young women under thirty years of age, and professionalization by its very nature contributes to the "defeminization" of the care-giving occupation; that is, the occupational role requires fewer of the qualities that have traditionally been ascribed to women (Wærness 1984). Many day-center workers are not only young but also are unionized, and they insist on their rights, such as periodic vacations, routine coffee breaks, and regular working hours (Wolfe 1989).

In Norwegian culture there is a strong tradition that children should have the opportunity to play with their peers without adult intrusion. Thus, there is a strong suspicion that children who spend long periods each day in a daytime center may be denied that important type of unsupervised play. In her book on the role of the staff in children's play in day centers, Åm (1984) recognizes that children play in order to play, not to realize goals, and that they seek secret places in which to play, whereas staff may value guided activity that they feel is more meaningful for children's development. In observing interaction in Norwegian day centers, both Berentzen (1980) and Kvalheim (1980) met with children's desire for a secret place in which to play. Berentzen reports that in some situations the girls in the day center didn't like him to be present when they played "hospital" and also when they played in the dollhouse. Kvalheim reports that in a few cases she was sent out of the room by a group of boys when they had secret things to do.

Åm (1984) reflects on the ambivalence of the responsible day-center worker and how easily one can get into a control mode. She suggests that steering play content in a "correct" way can develop into an attack on children's integrity and personal freedom. Yet if conscientious staff are not systematic in working to stimulate and to lay the groundwork for play, they fear that play might be governed by chance or accidental circumstances. Åm is an example of a conscientious day-center professional. She has goals for the children's play — goals that she hopes will have larger social consequences. For instance, she feels that children should get the experience of play and interaction with peers of both sexes. Why? Because children must be given incentives that can create a counterbalance to the "stagnant or congealed" attitudes toward gender roles that exist in society. Staff should work to "correct the imbalance" in the attention given to boys and girls in Norwegian society. She also asserts that the staff should pay attention to whom the children play with because children should not only play with peers of both sexes but also with older and younger children; children age three to seven attend the same day centers in Norway.

Friendships between children should be respected, but there are open and closed friendships. In a closed friendship, partners may stick together and possibly close others out of their play. According to Åm that tendency should be counteracted. Another of the great challenges in the day-care center is children who stand outside the play activity; the goal of the center is that children with special problems shall be integrated. The staff ought also to contribute to a general stimulation of children's fantasy. Children also must interact with adults in and outside the day-care center who are committed to meaningful work. And so the dilemma builds as workers attempt to respect children's freedom to play and yet feel the importance of realizing goals.

After looking at the pros and cons of day care being expressed in Norway and in the other Scandinavian countries today, Wolfe (1989) concludes that if there is a consensus among the experts as to what child care does to and for children, it is that public day care can help build a child's healthy feeling of autonomy, but only if care is limited to about twenty hours a week. Less than that, and children become withdrawn. More than that, and they tend to become aggressive (Wolfe 1989). Apparently many parents in Norway agree in principle with that conclusion since so many mothers who work outside the home work only part-time.

To help insure that children get a good start early in life, the Scandinavian countries have instituted the most adequate maternity leave provisions in all of Europe. A comprehensive leave policy covers lost income, job protection, seniority, and pension when a parent must be absent from work because of the needs of a child. Sweden's parental-leave system, in which leave can be divided between the parents, allows the longest leave time. A parent may be gone from work for up to 450 days (sixty-four weeks), 360 days at 90 percent of salary, and 90 days at a lower rate of compensation. Norway permits twenty-eight weeks of leave with up to 100 percent of salary. Most European countries, other than the Scandinavian states, have leaves ranging from twelve weeks to eighteen weeks with compensation ranging from 50 to 100 percent of salary. The United States, by comparison, makes no provision for paid maternity leaves.

When the welfare state was first developed in Scandinavia in the 1930s, a great deal of attention was given to the importance of providing financial aid to families to equalize the economic burden of those who had children and those who did not, for it was assumed by social theorists that women would be staying at home and caring for their children. The family allowance is a policy strategy devised to alleviate the financial burden of rearing children. Family allowances have the effect of redistributing income from households with no children to those with children. Norway has such an income-transfer system in the form of a family allowance that covers all families with children, as have all European countries. In Norway the legislation was passed in 1946. Neither Norway nor any other country comes close to fully compensating for the economic costs of rearing children through family allowances, however (Kamerman and Kahn 1989).

Despite Norway's general affluence, there is concern with poverty in Norway today. There is no child poverty that compares with child poverty in the United States, nor are there ghettos; but families with young children are relatively poorer today than they were in recent decades, both those with one parent and those with two parents (Frønes 1989). It is parents with small children who work the longest hours and have the most debt. It is paradoxical that the group that child advocates and politicians assert ought to work fewer hours because they have children are those who work the most hours in the very years when their children need them most.

A mother working full-time with a young child in day care for a full day is not a reality for most families in Norway today and will not be for the foreseeable future. Though an increasing number of women are remaining in occupations during periods when their children are below school age, they continue to work primarily part-time. Most Norwegian women take a short-term view of paid work because of their anticipated roles as wives and mothers (Hoel 1984). Norwegian mothers of small children continue to let regard for the child decide the amount of work outside the home (Andenæs and Haavind 1987). With the birth of the first child, the mother commonly stays at home. After a year or two, most mothers take part-time work, followed later on by full-time work. Andenæs and Haavind (1987) found Norwegian mothers to be creative in planning leisure-time activities for their children; they create time to be with their children by pushing housework to the evening hours after the children have gone to bed. Yet many feel that they do not do enough with their children (Andenæs 1984).

The traditional family wherein the husband goes out to work and the wife stays at home accounted for only about 10 percent of all households at the start of the 1980s. Yet even with the increased number of divorces and single-parent families, Norwegian families continue to show a great deal of stability. Most adults choose to marry, though it often happens after a couple's first child is born. Only 2 percent of small children's parents live without a marriage license, and only one of ten mothers of small children is single. Eighty percent of today's small children live with mother and father until they are eighteen years of age, the average age for children's leaving home having increased in recent years (Flekkøy 1989). Yet the fear that many children will experience when their parents separate continues to be mentioned when the question of the quality of children's social relationships is raised (Andenæs and Haavind 1987).

Another fear that is constantly raised is that many Norwegian children are growing up without siblings. Recent research findings take exception: since more Norwegian women are having children, and at least two children, eight of ten Norwegian children sooner or later have a sibling. That does leave two of ten without siblings, however, and many children have no more than one sibling.

Many parents today see the neighborhood in which they live as too dangerous and unsafe a place for children to be out playing without supervision. The large number of children's accidents partially confirms their fears, but accidents are not something new. What is new is that the neighborhood has become an environment largely devoid of adults during the day when both parents are at work outside the home. An environment devoid of adults who are out and about in the neighborhood contributes to weak social control. The voice that called out "Stop doing that!" was a signal that there was a world with limits and rules that would hinder bullies from terrorizing other children in the neighborhood. Another factor that has weakened neighborhoods is the lack of daytime centers. Many neighborhoods do not have centers for preschool children that make it easy for them to meet and associate with other children and their parents. Children who fail to get places in a day center miss many of their playmates who disappear each morning to go to their center some distance away; there are not many peers remaining to play with. A consequence of this dwindling of interaction in the local neighborhood is that parents are tempted to let their preschool children take part only in more controlled and limited activities where they feel that their children are safe (Frønes 1989). For those who get in, the daytime center provides a safe, secure place to play. On the other hand, it also cuts children off from adults and normal adult activity other than that of the center staff, creating a day-center culture with its own rules, values, and norms. Not all parents or all students of day-care life are sanguine about such a total separation of children from what they believe should ideally be the normal give-and-take of everyday life (Holen 1984; Sundin 1984). In its recent *Family Report*, the Norwegian Housewife Association indicated that 70 percent of Norwegian women think that the home can take better care of children than can an institution (Kjørholt et al. 1990), further evidence as to why mothers in Norway work only part-time outside the home.

In recent years child advocates in Norway and in other Western countries have become concerned about developments that are said to infantilize children because of the imbalance of power relationships. In the course of the gradual development of the modern and postmodern urban industrial-service society, children were increasingly pushed out of the public system of decision making and production; the school became more and more dominant in their lives (Berggreen 1986). Going to school was the approved child behavior; it was a disgrace, in fact it became illegal, not to go to school. Child labor came to be frowned upon and was regarded as a mark of poverty within the child's family. Life in the school isolated children from full social participation and cultural understanding. Adults hold power and *ascribe* dependency, irresponsibility, and the need of protective services for powerless children (Berggreen 1988). In his book *Hvis skolen ikke fantes* (If the school did not exist; 1971), Nils Christie asks what would have been done with children and youth if the school had not existed, since cities are not built for children, automobiles are not built for children, machines don't need them, and adults don't need them. We have not equipped ourselves to have children around us all the time; children's long vacations from school become a burden. Young children have become almost completely and unavoidably dependent on those who have power over them; it is a dependency that can be and has been artificially prolonged into later childhood and adolescence in urban-industrial societies (O'Neill 1988).

As we have seen in earlier chapters, Norwegian children were not always infantilized. A 1621 law obligated parents to provide useful occupations for their children; if they did not do so, public officials could take over the responsibility and see that the children were usefully employed (Flekkøy 1989). No one is proposing a return to that type of integration of children into the work force; it is widely held in Norway today that children cannot and should not be treated as adults or with the single goal of bringing them to adulthood as quickly as possible. Children are seen as having unique value *as children* (Kaul 1983). Childhood is seen as an important stage in life in its own right. There is substantial evidence from cross-cultural studies that children have ability to observe and interpret society, ability that is beyond the imagination of most adults today. Child advocates in Norway believe that respect for children and their needs should determine the development of society to a far greater degree than is the case, believing as they do that all children who have the opportunity to develop their potential fully, to be independent, and to be socially responsible will be a social asset.

As articulated by Flekkøy, the first child ombud for Norway, the goals of public responsibility should be to maintain and protect those aspects of society that are valuable for children and to protect the growing generation from the negative consequences of social development and change. Also, public intervention and planning are necessary to compensate for lost values that are beyond the means of individual families to repair or provide substitutes for (Flekkøy 1989).

Public policy issues that affect children do not generally attract substantial and sustained public interest in any country. Specific incidents, such as a case of child abuse or a missing child, will capture brief, even spectacular, public attention, but there is little continuing awareness of how children are affected by public policy decisions (Cahill 1986). What child advocates see as ideal for children is a concerned and informed citizenry engaged in educating and influencing elected officials and all other public and private decision makers as to the policy concerns, needs, and interests of children; children constitute the largest disfranchised segment of a democratic society. The concept of a child as a person with rights as well as needs is relatively new (see Model V, Children as Citizens, in chapter 1). Children easily become victims; if they had rights, redress would be possible.

One way to deal with the issue of child advocacy is to institutionalize it as has been done in Norway. There are only four countries with an agent or representative (ombud) for children; three of them are Nordic countries. And of the four countries with a representative for children, only in Norway is the position a national, public position created by an act of Parliament. The idea of a national, public representative for children was talked about in Norway as early as 1968; the first proposal was not made until 1977. The idea received additional impetus when the United Nations declared an International Year of the Child in 1979. When Parliament first took up the matter there was political opposition. The parties on the right were united in their belief that children's interests should be strengthened, but not through the establishment of a child representative. The Christian People's Party (*Kristelig Folkeparti*) wanted to strengthen the family; other nonsocialists wanted to strengthen child welfare. But in 1981 the Labor Party (*Arbeiderpartiet*), the Socialistic Left Party (*Socialistisk Venstreparti*), and the Left (*Venstre*) constituted a majority and favored the idea of an ombud (Andenæs and Haavind 1987).

Hence, in 1981 the Parliament passed the Commissioner for Children Act that established the first, and until now the only, national ombud or advocate for children (*barneombudet*) in the world. Målfrid Grude Flekkøy, a psychologist, was chosen to be the first Ombud for Children for a four-year term. Her term of office was renewed for four additional years. The present ombud is a physician, Trond Viggo Torgersen.

The ombud is an independent spokesman for children, a national defender, and a public-conscience arouser. The Office of Ombud for Children is independent of all other institutions, and regardless of any political or other considerations, the ombud has the right and the obligation to criticize any administrative level, group, organization, or person who disregards the interests of children. The office, with the ombud and a small staff, is free to handle any case in any way considered efficient. The ombud's instruments are information and persuasion. His or her duty is to further children's interests over against the public and the private sectors and to be attentive to the improvement of children's living conditions. Oftentimes the ombud is the only person analyzing a proposed measure's consequences for children; many times the institution or office proposing a change is unaware that the matters it deals with have any consequences for children. The ombud sees that legal provisions for the care of children's interests are fulfilled; proposes initiatives that can strengthen children's legal security; puts forth proposals to solve or prevent conflict between children and society; and sees that the public and private sectors have adequate information on children's rights and initiatives (*Barneombudet: Årsmelding for 1983*).

Anyone can contact the ombud by writing or calling. The office phone number is listed in every telephone book in Norway. At present a toll-free number is being set up so that children can phone in messages about what they think is important. Once a week on television the ombud plans to talk to them about those topics. Each year the office receives about two thousand complaints, as many as 20 percent of them directly from children.

A four-year-old girl called the Office of Ombud for Children to express regret that she could not get a job! The ombud made some inquiries in the girl's neighborhood and found an old woman who needed some companionship and occasional help. The ombud suggested that they contact each other, and the girl got a job. That is not a typical case, of course. A majority of the issues that come to the attention of the ombud are problems experienced by children because of separation or divorce of parents, child custody conflicts, child-parent visitation rights, and daily care. Many of the cases are outside the jurisdiction of the child ombud, but information regarding the law and the helping agencies is given. When a child calls or writes, he or she is often acting on behalf of a group of children, for instance, a whole class of pupils calling about some matter in the school. Teachers' organizations report cases of pupil violence against teachers; the child ombud hears instead complaints from pupils about their teachers.

There are some definite restrictions on what the ombud can do for children, however. In a sense, the ombud has no authority to act, only the right to speak. The ombud does not have the power or right to make decisions on behalf of children; that is left to parents, legislators, and the courts at the local and national level. The Office of Ombud can give the child or the parents advice on where they can receive help but cannot on its own initiative intercede in conflicts between individual children and their parents or in conflicts between parents (Flekkøy 1989). The limitation on the ombud's authority was necessary to allay the fears of those who worried over what child advocacy would mean to the privacy of the family and to parental authority, since there were opponents, not only legislative, who felt that the establishment of an Office of Ombud for Children was both inappropriate and unnecessary.

It is arguable that the position of Ombud for Children was established not because Norway was doing so well in meeting the needs and interests of children but because of a widespread feeling that Norway should be doing much better. We have already mentioned Norway's limited parental leave policy, comparatively high neonatal mortality rate, high rate of child accidents and accidental deaths, and the shortage of day-care and leisure-time facilities.

Improving the economy for families is a central political goal in Norway, through more substantial income transfers, for instance. The ombud promotes a more generous leave policy for working parents of young children than is in effect today—a policy to cover birth and sickness of a child, as well as time off when a child begins school for the first time, as is the policy in neighboring Sweden. The ombud has also promoted the idea of parental leaves from work to coincide with times when the children are on vacation from school (*Barneombudet: Årsmelding for 1985*).

Many of the problems highlighted by the ombud are common to most modern urban industrial nations and are, therefore, not peculiar to Norway. The ombud, for example, stresses that family responsibilities are much more difficult today than in earlier times: children do not have contact with adults while they are at work, and many parents have long commuting distance to and from work; a number of children are only children, and very few have more than one or two siblings; a number of children are from broken homes, and more single parents have the responsibility of raising children than was true earlier.

A record that Norwegian child advocates have not been proud of is the daily average of fourteen- and fifteen-year-olds in prison; it has been higher in Norway than in most European countries. It is not because of a higher crime rate but because children fourteen and fifteen years of age could until recently be imprisoned for criminal offenses. By raising the age to fifteen years, the law has now been changed to conform with that of the other Nordic countries, but it is still a low age when compared to the United Nations Convention on the Rights of Children, which generally bars incarceration before the age of maturity.

A major goal of the child ombud is to empower children by increasing their rights under the law, arguing that so long as children's rights are not clearly secured, other interest groups, such as business organizations and automobile associations, realize their demands before the needs of children are met. The ombud and other child advocates argue that children need to have personal and direct rights under the law, as subjects of the law, not objects. For example, children have only indirect rights to health care in Norway. That is, parents have the right to take a child to a well-baby clinic for checkups, inoculations, and so on. But nothing is done if a child is not brought to the clinic by its parents after a public nurse has recommended it. The child ombud asks, Would it not be more reasonable for the right to health care to be the right of the child, not the right of the parent (Flekkøy 1989)? Another example of children's powerlessness is in the school where the School Act and the Labor Act regulate employment conditions for teachers and other personnel. For instance, work may be stopped if the temperature rises above a permissible level or if some threat to an employee's health or life occurs. But, argues the child ombud, twenty-five pupils have no similar rights, so that if the teacher enjoys a hothouse climate, the pupils must suffer and endure. In one case, a pupil was defined as being a threat to the health of the teacher. Work was stopped until the pupil was removed and expelled from school. Knowing how difficult it is to get rid of a teacher who well may be a threat to a number of pupils, the ombud asks if a similar procedure should not be available to the pupils. At the instigation by the ombud, legislation was passed prohibiting teachers from having pupils expelled on such grounds. Now the problems with troublesome children have to be approached with the aim of solving them and helping the children, not by getting rid of the child and thereby the problem (Flekkøy 1989).

The ombud argues that children should have the right to a fully satisfying work relationship at school and the right to special help if they have special need. They should also have the right to a place in a day center when they are of preschool age, the right to have their parents at home when they are small, the right to safe places to play, the right to safe housing, and the right to safe and adequate routes to and from school.

A number of the issues brought up by children or their advocates have to do with the adequacy and safety of the environment. It has been proposed that children and youth should participate in solving environmental problems in institutions with which they have something to do; otherwise, the problem may be settled in such a way as to satisfy the needs and interests of adults—for example, places where adults can conveniently park their automobiles taking precedence over places where children can play. Children should have input in planning housing areas, schools, playgrounds and other play areas, streets, and pedestrian and cycling paths. The ombud points out that youths' pessimism about the future would be reduced if they discovered that they can influence the environment around them—home, neighborhood, school—giving them a feeling of being useful and as counting for something.

It is apparent from the above that there is no lack of initiatives that could be taken on behalf of children. The child ombud and other child advocates are ceaselessly at work on the issues. What is needed are favorable adult attitudes and the allocation of necessary funds.

In 1981 *Norges Almenvitenskapelige Forskningsråd* (Norwegian Research Council for Science and the Humanities [NAVF]) established a working group to make proposals for strengthening child research. The working group proposed that an interdisciplinary center be established. At the same time a catalog of Norwegian research proceedings in the field was prepared to assist in planning the center's activities. The working group's proposal for a center was accepted and an interdisciplinary research center (*NAVF's Senter for Barneforskning*) was provisionally established for a five-year period beginning in 1982. At the end of the five years the center was given permanent status as the *Norsk Senter for Barneforskning* (Norwegian Center for Child Research). Its interdisciplinary nature, its public status, and its national responsibility make the Norwegian Center for Child Research unique among child-research institutes in the Western world. Its statutes state its aim to be to elicit new knowledge and insight relevant to children's environment and the way the environment influences children's development. That aim clearly recognizes that a child's development always happens in a social context and can only be understood from that perspective. From that viewpoint research on children must be a study of the child's social milieu (Tiller 1983). The center coordinates existing research, funds research, engages in research, and arranges research seminars and lectures. Another important task of the center is to disseminate research findings to researchers, practitioners, and planners by maintaining an up-to-date catalog of research completed or in process throughout the nation, as well as to generally disseminate information about children in cooperation with other groups and organizations.

Child research in Norway has a political as well as a fact-finding mission. Child research is seen as interdisciplinary partly because it gives priority to children's political motives. It is argued that children need researchers who can research on their behalf; the researcher's goal must be to fully identify with children (Kaul 1983). An engaged common investment is seen as necessary to cancel out children's invisibility in society, as well as in social research. Child research projects must answer the question, Has the completed research given the child visibility in a way that advances the understandings of a child's human worth?

A political agenda is not peculiar only to child research in Norway, nor is it peculiar only for child researchers to advance an interdisciplinary perspective. Social research in Norway has had a history of being broadly critical of the social situation, and it is often associated with studies of groups that the welfare state has either forgotten about or has not reached (Løchen 1982). In other words, it has not been a neutral or value-free science but a potential agent of change.

Child researchers find that there are so many well-meaning defenders of children that getting to the children to get information from them is very difficult. Hence, except for the childhood experiences recalled by adults, with all the limitations of recalled data (Hodne, B. 1984), most of what we know about children is secondhand—from teachers, social workers, health personnel, parents, and above all mothers. Norwegian researchers see that secondhand knowledge as valuable knowledge but also as very inadequate. Tiller (1984) challenges researchers to put in focus the responsibility of protecting children's freedom of expression in such a way as to get knowledge directly from children. The child's guardian has a right to know what the research is about, but the child has the right to open expression without control or censorship. Child protection is necessary to provide safety and security for children, but child protection can also, inadvertently perhaps, contribute to steadily making children more invisible, to a further infantilizing of them, hence contributing to their powerlessness and working against their emancipation.

Empowering the child to have self-understanding or self-awareness is on the way to becoming a central theme in child research in Norway. Child-awareness is seen as an important motivating force, representing even for preschool children the most important source of motivation for behavior, for relationships to others, and for relationships to the social milieu (Hyrve and Lillemyr 1987).

Child advocacy, child research, and legislation and litigation on behalf of children are all important, but in the eyes of children's rights advocates in Norway they are not a cure-all in the effort to give children status in society. Child law was made a subject in the jurisprudence faculty at Oslo in 1978, that is, children's law seen from a child's perspective, children as subjects of the law, not as objects of the law (Smith 1984). The Norwegian Children's Act adopted in 1981 went into effect in

1982. According to provisions of the act, all children insofar as possible shall be on an equal footing whether their parents are married or not. Parents who are married share responsibility; parents who are separated or divorced may agree to share responsibility or may agree that it shall rest with only one of them. Parents are duty-bound to support children in accordance with their financial circumstances, each according to his or her ability. Contributions may be required to meet particular expenses, for instance, in connection with confirmation. Contributions continue until the child is eighteen years old, or longer if the child decides to continue in school. The child has the right to be with both parents even if they live apart and whether or not they are married to each other. If those with parental responsibility are minors themselves or if no one has parental responsibility, the authorities appoint a guardian (Steenberg 1984). Children over the age of twelve must always be allowed to give their opinion before agreements are entered into or decisions made concerning parental responsibility, permanent residence, and the right of access to both parents. We have already discussed a later addition to the law that required that no child of any age be exposed to physical punishment or other violent treatment by his parents or by others.

Norwegian legislation covering the rights and freedom of children, while improving over the years, is still weak as compared to legislation protecting the rights and freedom of adults. Determining what rights and freedoms are appropriate for children in a complex, impersonal urban-industrial society, such as Norway has become, is not a simple matter. It is a matter of balancing the child's rights of citizenship with (1) the child's special need for care and protection, (2) the state's interest in insuring that those needs be met, and (3) the perquisites of parental authority. A Danish sociologist has proposed that the age of voting rights be lowered so that children as young as six years of age be allowed to vote. Many ideas for increasing children's rights and privileges have seemed intemperate when first proposed, and that no doubt is one. The subject is open to discussion. Norway, like the other Nordic countries, is giving more attention to children's issues than are most societies today.

Norway has a tradition as a child-friendly country; it is a society with humanistic values that sets high goals for the lives of all its citizens, including its children (Kjørholt 1990; Andenæs and Haavind 1987). Well-fed, healthy, and happy children are taken for granted (Frønes 1989). Children who grow up in Norway are arguably some of the most fortunate in the world. In his study of the strengths and weaknesses of the world's cultures, the anthropologist Naroll (1983) gave Norway his highest rating. The Scandinavian nations are seen as models of the good society as evidenced by a number of studies made over the years, studies that have included the other European countries as well as the United States. In analyzing the level of satisfaction with the quality of life in thirteen European countries, Listhaug (1990) found that on satisfaction with one's life as a whole all five Nordic countries recorded higher average values than any other country. The high levels of satisfaction were strengthened even more when various aspects of the work domain were analyzed.

Norway is in substantial compliance with stipulations of the Convention on the Rights of Children recently adopted by the United Nations, yet discussion of Norwegian children's policy would, at a number of points, benefit by further reference to the Convention (we draw on a seminal article on Norwegian children's policy by Melton 1989). Besides offering children social programs fulfilling the rights to health, education, nutrition, housing, and family care, Norway offers legal protection from abuse and neglect. The provision of the Convention stating that children shall be heard by their parents before decisions are made about their lives is covered in Norway's Children's Act of 1981, although probably not at the level or at as young an age as the Convention requires. The Norwegian Parliament could empower the child ombud—in a manner analogous to Norway's other specialized ombuds, all of whom have authority to guard against violation of certain statutes—by giving the Office of Child Ombud express authority to bring Norway into full compliance with the Convention. The Convention's core value, respect for the dignity of children as persons, has been a goal of Norwegian child advocates for some time and could continue to be used to remind politicians and others of the desirability of bringing Norway into full compliance.

Western societies, and not least welfare states such as Norway, have a history of promoting social action intended to ensure social order and the common good. Much of that action, while providing benefits, does of course impinge on the rights and freedoms of individuals, including those of children. Laws such as those on child labor, curfew, compulsory education, vagrancy, to name a few, are laws that were allegedly enacted with the best interests of children in mind but that children had no voice in creating, interpreting, or enforcing. The danger of infringing on freedoms and rights of children is great in a welfare state asserting humanitarian principles. Focusing on the dignity of children is an overarching construct that helps prevent protection of children from becoming oppression of children.

References
Index

References

Aasen, Petter, and Jan Erik Ingebrigtsen. "Socialisering til og i idrett." *Barn*, no. 2(1987):69–92.

Andenæs, Agnes. "Hverdagsliv I Småbarnsfamilien." In *Barns oppvekstmiljø*, edited by Einar M. Skaalvik, 75–94. Oslo: Aschehoug/ Tanum-Norli, 1984.

Andenæs, Agnes, and Hanne Haavind. *Små barns livsvilkår i Norge*. Oslo: Universitetsforlaget, 1987.

Andersen, Bjørn G. "Barns vår leker lever fortsatt." *UKE-Adressa*, 25 May 1985, 8.

Ariès, Philippe. *Centuries of Childhood: A Social History of Family Life*. New York: Vintage Books, 1962. Translated by Robert Baldick.

Awes, Leif H. *The Pioneer Pastor: Highlights from the Life of Rev. Elias Aas*. Minneapolis: Free Church Press, n.d.

Barth, Fredrik. "Family Life in a Central Norwegian Mountain Community." In *Norway's Families: Trends, Problems, Programs*, edited by Thomas D. Eliot and Arthur Hillman, 81–107. Philadelphia: University of Pennsylvania, 1960.

Barton, H. Arnold. *Scandinavia in the Revolutionary Era, 1760–1815*. Minneapolis: University of Minnesota Press, 1986.

Beales, Ross W., Jr. "In Search of the Historical Child: Miniature Adulthood and Youth in Colonial New England." *American Quarterly* 27(1975):379–98.

Benedictow, Ole J. "Breast-feeding and Sexual Abstinence in Early Medieval Europe and the Importance of Protein-Calorie Malnutrition." *Scandinavian Journal of History* 15(1988):167–206.

———. "The Milky Way in History: Breast-feeding, Antagonism Between the Sexes and Infant Mortality in Medieval Norway." *Scandinavian Journal of History* 10(1985):19–53.

Berentzen, Sigurd. *Kjønnskontrasten i Barns Lek: Analyse Av Forholdet Mellom Begrepsdannelse og Samhandling i En Barnehage*.

References

Universitet i Bergen: Sosialantropologisk Institutt Skriftserie, Occasional Paper no. 3(1980).

Berg, Anne-Jorunn. "Barnekultur i de nordiske land: En evaluering av tilbud og engasjement." Noen foreløpige resultater fra et nordisk forskningsprojekt av Anne-Jorunn Berg et al., NAVF Senter for barneforskning, Trondheim, 1985. *Barn og Kultur i Norden,* no. 4 (November 1985):1–8.

Berge, Ase. "Barneulukker I Heim Og Naermiljø." Oslo: Forbruker-Og Administrasjonsdepartementet, Handlingsutvalget Mot Barneulykker, 1983.

Berggreen, Brit. *Etter skoletid.* University of Trondheim: NAVF Senter for barneforskning, 1987.

———. "Infantilisering av barn." *Barn,* no. 3(1986):28–48.

———. "Infantilization of Children as an Historical Process." In *Growing into a Modern World,* vol. 2, edited by Karin Ekberg and Per Egil Mjaavatn, 829–42. Proceedings of an International Interdisciplinary Conference on the Life and Development of Children in Modern Society, Trondheim, Norway, 10–13 June 1987. Trondheim: Norwegian Center for Child Research, 1988.

Bjaaland, Pat. "The Norwegian Education System." *The Norseman* 28(1988):8–9.

Bjørklund, Tor. "Barnetilsyn: Introduksjon." *Tidsskrift for samfunnsforskning* 29(1988):501–4.

Block, Jeanne, and Bjørn Christiansen. "A Test of Hendin's Hypotheses Relating Suicide in Scandinavia to Child Rearing Orientations." *Scandinavian Journal of Psychology* 7(1966):267–86.

Blom, Ida. "Barneoppdragelse." In *Barn av sin tid,* edited by Bjarne Hodne and Sølvi Sogner, 37–48. Oslo: Universitetsforlaget, 1984.

Blom, Ådel G. "Sangtradisjon." In *Barn av sin tid,* edited by Bjarne Hodne and Sølvi Sogner, 154–67. Oslo: Universitetsforlaget, 1984.

Boli, John. *New Citizens for a New Society: The Institutional Origins of Mass Schooling in Sweden.* Oxford: Pergamon Press, 1989.

Boocock, Sarane. "The Life Space of Children." In *Building for Women,* edited by Suzanne Keller, 93–116. Lexington, Mass.: Lexington Books, 1981.

Borchorst, Anette. "Institut for Statskundskab." *Tidsskrift for samfunnsforskning* 29(1988):523–38.

Bull, Edvard. "Barn i industriarbeid." In *Barn av sin tid,* edited by

References

Bjarne Hodne and Sølvi Sogner, 77–86. Oslo: Universitetsforlaget, 1984.

Cahill, Brian F. "Training Volunteers as Child Advocates." *Child Welfare* 65(1986):545–53.

Castberg, Frede. *The Norwegian Way of Life*. Melbourne, Australia: William Heinemann, 1954.

Christie, Nils. *Hvis skolen ikke fantes*. Oslo: Universitetsforlaget, 1971.

Clover, Carol J. "The Politics of Scarcity: Notes on the Sex Ratio in Early Scandinavia." *Scandinavian Studies* 60(1988):147–88.

Cohen, Yehudi A. "Ends and Means in Political Control: State Organization and the Punishment of Adultery, Incest, and Violation of Celibacy." *American Anthropologist* 71(1969):658–87.

Corsaro, William A. "Routines in the Peer Culture of American and Italian Nursery School Children." *Sociology of Education* 61(1988): 1–14.

Dahl, Tove Stang. *Child Welfare and Social Defense*. Oslo: Norwegian University Press, 1985. Translated from the Norwegian *Barnevern og samfunnsvern*.

———. "Women's Right to Money." In *Patriarchy in a Welfare Society*, edited by Harriet Holter, 46–67. Oslo: Universitetsforlaget, 1984.

Das, Veena. "Voices of Children." *Daedalus* 118(1989):263–294.

Demos, John. "Developmental Perspectives on the History of Childhood." *The Journal of Interdisciplinary History* 2(1971):315–27.

Dencik, Lars. "Growing Up in the Post-Modern Age: On the Child's Situation in the Modern Family, and on the Position of the Family in the Modern Welfare State." *Acta Sociologica* 32(1989):155–80.

Denzin, Norman K. "The Significant Others of Young Children: Notes Toward a Phenomenology of Childhood." In *The Social Life of Children in a Changing Society*, edited by Kathryn M. Borman, 29–46. Hillsdale, N.J.: Lawrence Erlbaum Associates, 1982.

Dickson, David. "Norway: Boosting R & D for a Post-Oil Economy." *Science* 240(1988):1140–41.

Dokka, Hans-Jorgen. "Barn i skolen." *Forskningsnytt* 4(1979):32–41.

Dyrvik, Ståle. "Barnet i familien og slektskrimsen." *Forskningsnytt*, no. 4(1979):8–13.

———. "Barns oppvekstår som emne for historisk forskning." NAVF's Konferanserapport: Barn og Kultur i humanistisk forskning, 1980.

References

Eide, Ingrid. "Åpningstale." *Barn og Kultur* (1976):7–9. Report from a conference arranged in 1975 for Norsk Kulturråd.

Eliot, Thomas D., and Arthur Hillman, eds. *Norway's Families: Trends, Problems, Programs*. Philadelphia: University of Pennsylvania, 1960.

Enerstvedt, Åse. "Norske Barneleiker." *Barnekulturens Ytringsformer: Seminarrapport*, no. 1:70–80, Trondheim: Senter for barneforskning, 1984.

Fingerhut, Lois A., Joel C. Kleinman, Michael H. Malloy, and Jacob J. Feldman. "Injury Fatalities Among Young Children." *Public Health Reports* 103(1988):399–405.

Flekkøy, Målfrid Grude. "Child Advocacy in Norway: The Ombudsman." *Child Welfare* 68(1989):113–22.

Flint, John T. "The Church in Relation to Family Life." In *Norway's Families*, edited by Thomas D. Eliot and Arthur Hillman, 387–406. Philadelphia: University of Pennsylvania Press, 1960.

Fløystad, Ingeborg. "Vi laerte tidlig å arbeide! Barnearbeid i Norge i de siste 200 år." *Forskningsnytt* 4(1979):20–31.

Foote, Peter G., and David M. Wilson. *The Viking Achievement*. New York: Krager, 1970.

Froebel, Friedrich. *Education by Development*. New York: D. Appleton, 1902.

Frykman, Jonas, and Orvar Löfgren. *Culture Builders: A Historical Anthropology of Middle-Class Life*. New Brunswick: Rutgers University, 1987. Translation of Den kultiverade manniskan, 1979.

Frønes, Ivar. *Den norske barndommen*. Oslo: J. W. Cappelens Forlag, 1989.

———. "Youth in Norway and Images of the U.S." *Scandinavian Review* 76(1988):143–151.

Gjengset, Gunnar H. "Barn, Ungdom og Bok-lesing." *Barn* no. 1(1987):9–48.

———. *Barns Lesevaner: Em prosjektrapport*. Trondheim: Senter for barneforskning, Rapport no. 9(1986).

Gjerset, Knut. *History of the Norwegian People*, vol. 2. New York: MacMillan, 1915.

Grambo, Ronald. "Barnekultur." In *Barn av sin tid*, edited by Bjarne Hodne and Sølvi Sogner, 169–77. Oslo: Universitetsforlaget, 1984.

Grinde, Turid Vogt. "Child Welfare in the Nordic Countries." In *Growing into a Modern World*, vol. 3, edited by Karin Ekberg and

References

Per Egil Mjaavatn, 281–94. Proceedings of an International Interdisciplinary Conference on the Life and Development of Children in Modern Society, Trondheim, Norway, 10–13 June 1987. Trondheim: Norwegian Child Research Center, 1988.

Grønseth, Erik. "Familie, slektskap og ekteskap." In *Det Norske Samfunn*, edited by Natalie R. Ramsøy and Mariken Vaa, 39–94. Oslo: Universitetsforlaget, 1975.

Guhnfeldt, Cato. "Når eleven slår laereren." *Oslo Aftenposten*, 10 January 1987, 29.

Gulbrandsen, Lars, and Catherine U. Tønnessen. "Barnehageutbyggingens fordelingsmessige virkninger." *Tidsskrift for samfunnsforskning* 29(1988):539–54.

Gulbrandsen, Liv M., and Per Miljeteig-Olssen. "Barns Sosiale Nettverk." *Tidsskrift for samfunnsforskning*, no. 5-6(1979):416–34.

Gullestad, Marianne. "'Barnas egen Kultur'—finnes den?" *Barn* no. 4(1990):7–27.

———. "Children's Care for Children." In *Growing into a Modern World*, vol. 3, edited by Karin Ekberg and Per Egil Mjaavatn, 1205–17. Proceedings of an International Interdisciplinary Conference on the Life and Development of Children in Modern Society, Trondheim, Norway, 10–13 June 1987. Trondheim: Norwegian Center for Child Research, 1988.

———. *Kitchen-Table Society.* Oslo: Universitetsforlaget, 1984.

———. "Omsorg og Subkultur." *Tidsskrift For samfunnsforskning* Bd. 24(1983):203–220.

Haavind, Hanne. "Analyse av Sosialisering i Småbarnsfamilier." *Tidsskrift for samfunnsforskning*, no. 5–6(1979):447–72.

Hagemann, Sonja. "Barnelitteraturen Som Speil." *Forskningsnytt* 4(1979): 42–49.

Hambro, Cato. "Skoleungdommens Syn på Oppdragelsen: En Undersøkelse blant Skoleungdom i Oslo i Alderen 12–18 År." Thesis, Pedagogisk Forsknings institutt, University of Oslo, 1951.

Hansen, Kare. "Farlige fritidsparker?" *Oslo Aftenposten*, 18 June 1987.

Haugen, Tormod. *The Night Birds.* New York: Delacorte, 1982. Translated from the Norwegian by Sheila La Farge.

Heffermehl, Inge-lise. "Fyrstelig klegg mot omde makter." *A-Magasinet*, 6 October 1990, 24–27.

References

Hendin, Herbert. *Suicide and Scandinavia.* New York: Grune and Startton, 1964.

Higginbotham, Ann R. "'Sin of the Age': Infanticide and Illegitimacy in Victorian London." *Victoria Studies* 32(1989):319–37.

Hobbes, Thomas. *Leviathan.* 1651.

Hodne, Bjarne. "Barndomsminner." In *Barn av sin tid,* edited by Bjarne Hodne and Sølvi Sogner, 51–62. Oslo: Universitetsforlaget, 1984.

Hodne, Bjarne, and Sølvi Sogner, eds. *Barn av sin tid.* Oslo: Universitetsforlaget, 1984.

Hodne, Ørnulv. "Spedbarnet i Norsk folkekultur." In *Barn av sin tid,* edited by Bjarne Hodne and Sølvi Sogner. Oslo: Universitetsforlaget, 1984.

Hoel, Marit. "The Female Working Class." In *Patriarchy in a Welfare Society,* edited by Harriet Holter, 106–18. Oslo: Universitetsforlaget, 1984.

Holen, Astrid. "Barns Sangaktivitet i 1½-3-års-grupper i Barnehagen-presentasjon av et prosjekt." *Barnekulturens Ytringsformer: Seminarrapport,* no. 1:132–6. Trondheim: Senter for barneforskning, 1984.

Hollekim, Gisle. "'Kvinner tilbake til hjemmet.'" *Oslo Aftenposten,* 18 October 1986, 14.

Hollos, Marida. *Growing Up in Flathill: Social Environment and Cognitive Development.* Oslo: Universitetsforlaget, 1974.

Holter, Harriet, ed. *Patriarchy in a Welfare Society.* Oslo: Universitetsforlaget, 1984.

Hudson, W. H. *Far Away and Long Ago: A History of My Early Life.* New York: Dutton, 1918.

Hundeide, Karsten. "Contrasting Lifeworlds: Slum Children and Oslo Middleclass Children's World Views." In *Growing into a Modern World,* vol. 2, edited by Karin Ekberg and Per Egil Mjaavatn, 646–58. Proceedings of an International Interdisciplinary Conference on the Life and Development of Children in Modern Society, Trondheim, Norway, 10–13 June 1987. Trondheim: Norwegian Center for Child Research, 1988a.

———. "Lydighet og selvstendighet: Kulturell mangfoldighet i oppdragelsesog sosialiseringsmål," *Barn,* no. 4(1988b):46–63.

Hyrve, Geir, and Ole F. Lillemyr. "Barns selvoppfatning i lys av sosialisering og kulturformidling." *Barn,* no. 1(1987):68–91.

Ingnes, Eli K. "Seksuelt misbruk av barn." *Barn,* no. 2(1984):53–54.

References

Isenberg, Joan, and Nancy L. Quisenberry. "Play: A Necessity for All Children." *Childhood Education: Infancy Through Early Adolescence* 64(1988):138–45.

Jensen, Arne Sigurd. *The Rural Schools of Norway.* Boston: Stratford Company, 1928.

Jonassen, Christen T. *Value Systems and Personality in a Western Civilization: Norwegians in Europe and America.* Columbus: Ohio State University, 1983.

Jordheim, Knut. "Skolensrolle." *In Barn av sin tid,* edited by Bjarne Hodne and Sølvi Sogner, 89–101: Oslo: Universitetsforlaget, 1984.

Juul, Kristen D. "Mobbing in the Schools. Scandinavian Initiatives in the Prevention and Reduction of Group Violence Among Children." *International Journal of Special Education.* Forthcoming.

Kamerman, Sheila B., and Alfred J. Kahn. "The Possibilities for Child and Family Policy: A Cross-National Perspective." *Proceedings, The Academy of Political Science* 37(1989):84–98.

Karras, Ruth Mazo. "Concubinage and Slavery in the Viking Age." *Scandinavian Studies* 62(1990):141–162.

Kaul, Dagny. "Barneforskningens Tverrfaglige Komponent." *Barn,* no. 3(1983):40–47.

———. "Barnerett-En Menneskerett?" *Barnekulturens Ytringsformer: Seminarrapport,* no. 1:9–26. Trondheim: Senter for barneforskning, 1984.

Kjøndal, Jorunn. "Alternativ til Lekeplassideologien." *Barn,* no. 3 (1984):9–44.

Kjørholt, Anne Trine. "'Vi slutter aldri.'" PRØV SELV-prosjektet, Del II. *Barn,* no. 1(1990):44–58.

Kjørholt, Anne Trine, Tora Korsvold, and Alfred Oftedal Telhaug. *Pedagogisk Tilbud til 4-7-åringer i internasjonalt perspektiv: En studie av England, Frankrike, Japan og USA.* Trondheim: Norsk senter for barneforskning, Rapport no. 18(1990).

Knitzer, Jane. "Children's Rights in the Family and Society: Dilemmas and Realities." *American Journal of Orthopsychiatry* 52(1982): 481–495.

Kolloen, Ingar S. "Våre liv i TV-stolen." *Oslo Aftenposten,* 21 May 1985:7.

Kristiansen, Jan Erik. "Familien i endring: Et demografisk perspektiv." In *Familien i endring,* edited by Jan Erik Kristiansen and Tone Schou Wetlesen, 17–45. Oslo: J. W. Cappelens, 1986.

References

Krötzl, Christian. "Parent-Child Relations in Medieval Scandinavia According to Scandinavian Miracle Collections." *Scandinavian Journal of History* 14(1989):21–37.

Kurian, George Thomas, ed. *World Education Encyclopedia*, vol. 2. New York: Facts on File Publications, 1988.

Kurth-Schai, Ruthanne. "The Roles of Youth in Society: A Reconceptualization." *The Educational Forum* 52(1988):113–132.

Kvalheim, Ingeborg L. *Barns lærning av sosiale roller.* Oslo: Universitetsforlaget, 1980.

Kvidelund, Reimund, and Henning K. Sehmsdorf, eds. *Scandinavian Folk Belief and Legend.* Minneapolis: University of Minnesota Press, 1988.

Leira, Arnlaug. "Barndom i velferdsstaten." *Tidsskrift for samfunnsforskning* 29(1988):505–22.

Lereim, Inggard, and Ylva Sahlim. "Barnulykker," *Barns Fysiske Miljø Seminarrapport*, no. 2:38–58. Trondheim: Senter for barneforskning, 1984.

Lerstang, Tor. "Barns Miljø i Spreddt Bygde Områder." *Barn*, no. 2(1983): 29–48.

Liliequist, Jonas. "Peasants Against Nature: Crossing the Boundaries Between Man and Animal in 17th- and 18th-Century Sweden." *Journal of the History of Sexuality* 1(1991):393–423.

Lindbekk, Tore. "Utdannelse." In *Det norske samfunn*, edited by Natalie R. Ramsøy and Mariken Vaa, 214–65. Oslo: Gyldendal, 1975.

Listhaug, Ola. "Macrovalues: The Nordic Countries Compared." *Acta Sociologica* 33(1990):219–34.

Lund, Johan. "Barneulykker: Registreringssystem som basis for forebygging. *Barn*, no. 3(1985):11–18.

Lyche, Ingeborg. "Forord." *Barn og Kultur,* (1976): 5–6. Report from a conference arranged in 1975 for Norsk Kulturråd.

Løchen, Yngvar. "Norwegian Sociology: Social Rebellion and/or Professional Participation?" *Acta Sociologica* 25(1982):359–65.

MacLeod, David I. "Act Your Age: Boyhood, Adolescence, and the Rise of the Boy Scouts of America." In *Growing Up in America,* edited by Harvey J. Grauff, 397–413. Detroit: Wayne State University Press, 1987.

Mead, Margaret, and Martha Wolfenstein. *Childhood in Contemporary Cultures.* Chicago: University of Chicago Press, 1955.

References

Melton, Gary B. "Respect for Dignity: Blueprint for Children's Law in the Welfare State." *Barn*, no. 4(1989):73–95.

Mjaavatn, Per Egil. "Aktuelt nå." *Barn*, no. 4(1988):6–7.

Naroll, Raoul. *The Moral Order: An Introduction to the Human Situation.* Beverly Hills, Calif.: Sage, 1983.

Nordland, Eva, and others. "Child Management: Trends in Urban Middle Classes." In *Norway's Families: Trends, Problems, Programs,* edited by Thomas D. Eliot and Arthur Hilman, 191–221. Philadelphia: University of Pennsylvania, 1960.

"A Norwegian Anthropologist Talks About: *Typisk Norsk—The Norwegian Way of Being.*" *News of Norway,* November 1990, 57, 71.

O'Neill, Onora. "Children's Rights and Children's Lives." *Ethics* 90(1988):445–63.

Pollock, Linda A. *Forgotten Children: Parent-Child Relations From 1500–1900.* Cambridge: Cambridge University Press, 1983.

Ramsøy, Natalie R., and Mariken Vaa. *Det norske samfunn.* Oslo: Gyldendal, 1975.

Raundalen, Magne. "Kulturen i barnas dagligliv. Barnas plass i samfunnspolitikken. Retningsgivende problemstillinger." *Barn og Kultur,* (1976): 14–23. Report from a conference arranged in 1975 for Norsk Kulturråd.

Raundalen, Tora Synøve, and Magne Raundalen. *Er du på vår side!* Oslo: Universitetsforlaget, 1979.

Rauschenbusch, Walter. "The Rights of the Child in the Community." *Religious Education* 10(1915):219–25.

Rodnick, David. *The Norwegians: A Study in National Culture.* Washington, D.C.: Public Affairs Press, 1955.

Rogoff, Barbara, Martha Julia Sellers, Sergio Pirrotta, Nathan Fox, and Seldon H. White. "Age of Assignment of Roles and Responsibilities to Children: A Cross-Cultural Survey." In *Rethinking Childhood,* edited by Arlene Skolnick, 249–68. Boston: Little, Brown, 1976.

Ropeid, Andreas. "Organiserte aktivitetar for barn." In *Barn av sin tid,* edited by Bjarne Hodne and Sølvi Sogner, 103–12. Oslo: Universitetsforlaget, 1984.

Ross, Catherine J. "Of Children and Liberty: An Historian's View." *American Journal of Orthopsychiatry* 52(July 1982):470–79.

Rousseau, Jean-Jacques. *Emile.* New York: Basic Books, 1979. Originally published in French, 1762.

References

Sandemose, Aksel. *A Fugitive Crosses His Tracks.* New York: Knopf, 1936. Originally published as *En Flyktning Krysser Sit Spor,* 1933.

Sandvik, Gudmund. "Rettsstillinga for barn i gamle dagar." *Forskningsnytt* 4(1979):50–54.

Sather, Kathryn. "Sixteenth and Seventeenth Century Child-Rearing: A Matter of Discipline." *Journal of Social History* 23(1989): 735–43.

Saunders, Edward. "Neonaticides Following 'Secret' Pregnancies: Seven Case Reports." *Public Health Reports* 104(1989):368–72.

Schjelderup, H. K. *Nevrose og opdragelse.* Oslo: J. W. Cappelens, 1937.

Schrumpf, Ellen. "Var gamle dager gode for barn? Barns uppvekstvilkår i historisk perspectiv." *Barn,* no. 1(1988):8–36.

Seip, Anne-Lise. "Samfunnets ansvar." In *Barn av sin tid,* edited by Bjarne Hodne and Sølvi Sogner, 123–37. Oslo: Universitetsforlaget, 1984.

———. "Who Cares? Children, Family and Social Policy in Twentieth-Century Norway." *Scandinavian Journal of History* 12(1988): 331–43.

Selmer-Olsen, Ivr. "'BOKSENGÅR!'—om barns egen kultur, og om barnekulturens vilkår og funksjon." Trondheim, Norway: Norsk kulturråd og Norsk senter for barneforskning, 1990.

Skard, Aase Gruda. "Forord." In Berit Østberg, *Barnas egen kultur,* 7–9. Oslo: Cappelen, 1979.

Skard, Sigmund. *Classical Tradition in Norway.* Oslo: Universitetsforlaget, 1980.

Slettan, Dagfinn. "Barnearbeid i jordbruket." In *Barn av sin tid,* edited by Bjarne Hodne and Sølvi Sogner, 65–75. Oslo: Universitetsforlaget, 1984.

Smith, Lucy. "Barnerett." *Barn,* no. 1(1984):48–52.

Solberg, Anne. "The Working Life of Children." In *Growing Into a Modern World,* vol. 2, edited by Karin Ekberg and Per Egil Mjaavatn, 1069–77. Proceedings of an International Interdisciplinary Conference on the Life and Development of Children in Modern Society, Trondheim, Norway, 10–13 June 1987. Trondheim: Norwegian Center for Child Research, 1988.

Solberg, Anne, and Guri Mette Vestby. "Children Tasks in the Home and the Local Community." *Child Research in Norway,* 57. Trondheim: Norwegian Center for Child Research, 1987.

References

Steenberg, Knut R. "Children and Parents." *Norway Information,* June 1984, 1–8.

Stephenson, John C. "Family Life in an Industrial Community." In *Norway's Families: Trends, Problems, Programs,* edited by Thomas D. Eliot and Arthur Hillman, 108–129. Philadelphia: University of Pennsylvania, 1960.

Strand, Arvid. "Barn og trafikkulykker: Hva forteller forskningen oss?" *Tidsskrift for samfunnsforskning,* no. 5–6(1979):573–98.

Sundal, Alfred. *Mor og Barn.* Oslo: Fabritius and Sons, 1950.

Sundin, Bertil. "Estetisk Sosialisering." *Barnekulturens Ytringsformer: Seminarrapport,* no. 1:114–36. Trondheim: Senter for barneforskning, 1984.

Sundt, Eilert. *Om renligheds-stellet i Norge Verker i utvalg 9.* Oslo: Gyldendal Norska forlag, 1975. Originally published in 1869.

Svalastoga, Kaare. "The Family in Scandinavia." *Marriage and Family Living* 16(1954):374–80.

Sætersdal, Barbro, and Tordis Ørjasæter. *Barn kultur kreativitet.* Oslo: Universitetsforlaget, 1981.

Telhaug, Alfred Oftedal. "Gjenreisning av eldre idealer i oppdragelse og undervisning? En analyse av internasjonale tendenser i 1980–årenes utdanningspolitiske tenkning." *Barn* 2(1990):32–50.

———. "Utdanningspolitiske dilemma fram mot år 2039." *Barn,* no. 1–2(1989): 40–58.

Thorsen, Liv Emma. "Farmer Women and Intimacy." *Ethnologia Scandinavica,* (1987):97–109.

———. "Jentesosialisering og mentalitetsendringer." *Barn,* no. 4 (1986a):8–26.

———. "Love Me Tender, Love Me Sweet?" *Dugnad* 2/3, vol. 11(1986b):3–15.

———. "Work and Gender: The Sexual Division of Labour and Farmers' Attitudes to Labour in Central Norway, 1920–1980." *Ethnologia Europaea* XVI(1986c):137–48.

Tiller, Per Olav. "Barns Medvirkning i Forskning om Barns Levekår." *Barn,* no. 2(1983):49–59.

———. "Kulturelle variasjoner i persepsjon av foreldre." *Nordisk Psykologi,* no. 102(1960):192–98.

———. "Underveis—Rapport fra en reise i barns sosiale landskap." *Barn,* no. 2(1984):59–66.

Tiller, Per Olav, in cooperation with Lars Grue, Per Miljeteig-Olssen,

References

Liv Mette Gulbrandsen, Tove Bastiansen, Jan Vidar Haukeland, and Ivar Frønes. *Å vokse opp i Norge*. Oslo: Universitetsforlaget, 1983.

Troels-Lund, Troels Frederik. *Dagligt liv i Norden i ded 16de aarhundred*. Copenhagen: C. A. Reitzel, 1880–1901.

Tønnessen, Liv Keri. *Slik levde småbarna før*. Oslo: Universitetsforlaget, 1982.

Undset, Sigrid. *Saga of Saints*. New York: Books of Libraries Press, 1968. Translated by E. C. Ramsden.

Waal, Nic. "Er 'Normale' Mennasker Normale?" *Oslo Dagbladet*, 5 October 1953.

Wagle, Fin. "Kirkens største ungdomsarbeide." *Oslo Aftenposten*, 11 May 1985, 2.

Werner, Emmy E. "Children of the Garden Island." *Scientific American* 260(1989):106–11.

Whiting, Beatrice Blyth, and Carolyn Pope Edwards. *Children of Different Worlds: The Formation of Social Behavior*. Cambridge, Mass.: Harvard University Press, 1988.

Wike, Johs. "Kulturpolitiske problemstillinger." *Barn og Kultur* (1976a):42–48. Report from a conference arranged for Norsk Kulturråd.

———. "Oppsummering." *Barn og Kultur* (1976b):170–2. Report from a conference arranged for Norsk Kulturråd.

Winsnes, A. H. *Sigrid Undset: A Study in Christian Realism*. New York: Sheed and Ward, 1953.

Wolfe, Alan. "The Day-care Dilemma: A Scandinavian Perspective." *The Public Interest*, no. 95(1989):14–23.

Worsfold, Victor L. "A Philosophical Justification for Children's Rights." *Harvard Educational Review* 44(1974):142–57.

Wærness, Cari. "Caring for Women's Work in the Welfare State." In *Patriarchy in a Welfare Society*, edited by Harriet Holter, 67–87. Oslo: Universitetsforlaget, 1984.

Zelizer, Vivian A. *Pricing the Priceless Child: The Changing Social Value of Children*. New York: Basic Books, 1985.

Ørjasæter, Tordis. "Barn og kulter." *Barn og Kultur*, (1976):25–41. Report from a conference arranged in 1975 for Norsk Kulturråd.

Østberg, Berit. *Barnas egen kultur*. Oslo: J. W. Cappelens Forlag, 1979.

Åm, Eli. *Lek i barnehagen—de voksnes rølle*. Oslo: Universitetsforlaget, 1984.

Index

Note: Norwegian letters Æ, Ø, and Å are alphabetized after the letter Z.

Index

64; and child uncertainty, 75; and
direction of change, 75; emotionally involved, 58, 64; focused
on feelings and freedom, 69–70;
indulgence vs. stern discipline,
71–72; nonemotional, 61; parental ambivalence and, 74–75;
peasant, 48; professionalized,
68–69, 74; putting out, 38–39;
and ruling control, 70, 74–75;
traditional, 35–36; in working
class, 70
Childhood: birth of the concept,
79; defined, 1–2; history of, 12–
13; normative perspectives on, 2;
power of in society, 12–14
Child labor laws, 94–95; enforcement of, 94
Child ombud. *See* Ombud for
Children
Child-related concerns, current:
children without siblings, 209;
infantilization, 211–12; neighborhood change, 209–10; poverty of
parents with young children,
208; school dominance, 211
Children: in bourgeois families, 50–
51; and grandparents, 56, 63;
latchkey, 55; in one-parent families, 57; in peasant society, 4–5;
in rural, pre-industrial society, 4–
5; in Viking times, 41–42; in
worker's families, 49–50
Children and work: in agriculture,
89; beginning age, 4, 79–80, 93;
changing perspectives on, 99–
100; as child watchers (*pas-
sepiker*), 97–98; in "children's industries," 89–90; and children's
reaction to, 91–92; decrease in,
87, 90–91; in early times, 4; end
of, 94; as herders, 81–83; as hired
farm laborers, 80; at home, 95–

97, 98–99; and remuneration, 83;
as socialization, 88–89; and strikes,
92; on tasks for others, 97–98
Children, in law: as becoming, 5, 8;
as being, 8; definition of, 1; as
objects of law, 12; as subjects of
law, 12
Children, in society: and active personal network, 39, 77–78; best environment for, 14–15; in community, 39–41, 77–78; and family as
reference group, 78; and social life
4–5, 15, 50; in social network, 39
Children, models of: as becoming
adults, 5–8, 14; as citizens, 8–12,
15; as evil, 5; as participants in
socioeconomic life, 4–5, 14; as
private property, 2–4, 26, 51
Children's allowance, 95–96
Children's homes: for boys, 186,
187; corporal punishment in,
188–89; for parentless children,
30; and school segregation, 123–
25; today, 192
Children's rights, 10, 12 and the
United National Convention on
the Rights of Children, 222–23
Children's satisfaction with social
life, 178–81, 182–83; and mistreatment by peers, 178–80; and
suggested changes, 181; and ways
of dealing with bullying, 181
Child sexual abuse, 75–77; National
Center for Prevention of Sexual
Abuse of Children, 76–77; treatment of, 77
Christian Church: and abortion, 30,
33; and neonaticide and infanticide, 27, 28–29; and perspective on children, 65–66
Christian IV and baptism, 17–18
Christian V's Norwegian Law of
1687, 30, 66

Index

Index

Index

Index

Index

Index

Floyd M. Martinson, Ph.D. in sociology and anthropology from the University of Minnesota, is research professor of sociology at Gustavus Adolphus College. He is the author of four books, two book-length monographs, and numerous articles and chapters on adolescent relationships, marriage, family, child sexuality, and other topics. In 1988 he received the Alfred C. Kinsey Award "in recognition of his contributions to the study of sexuality and the family and for his pioneering research into child sexuality." His current research is on the social life of children and on aspects of social life in Scandinavia. He is writing a book on the sexual life of children.